Our Mothers' Daughters

Judith Arcana

SHAMELESS HUSSY PRESS   BERKELEY

This book is for my mother

Ida Rosenfield

Distributed by
THE CROSSING PRESS
Trumansburg, New York 14886

Copyright © 1979 by Judith Pildes Arcana

Published in 1979 in the United States of America
by SHAMELESS HUSSY PRESS

Box 3092
Berkeley, California 94703

ISBN 0-915288-38-9

Printed and bound in the United States of America

Acknowledgments/Credits

Grateful acknowledgment is made to the following for permission to reprint previously published copyright material.

Anchor/Doubleday: for excerpts from *Through the Flower: My Life as a Woman Artist*, by Judy Chicago. © 1975.

Common Woman Press: for an excerpt from *Talk Among the Womenfolk*, by Susan Saxe.© by Susan Saxe.

E. P. Dutton: for an excerpt from *Woman Hating*, by Andrea Dworkin. © 1974 by Andrea Dworkin.

Farrar, Straus & Giroux, Inc.: for an excerpt from "Betrothed," from *The Blue Estuaries*, by Louise Bogan. © 1954, 1978 by Louise Bogan.

Feminist Press: for excerpts from *Voices*, a play by Susan Griffin. © 1972 by Susan Griffin. Reprinted by permission of the author.

Harcourt Brace Jovanovich, Inc.: for excerpts from *A Biography of Virginia Woolf*, by Quentin Bell. © 1972. Also for excerpts from *A Writer's Diary*, by Virginia Woolf. © 1954.

Harper & Row, Inc.: for an excerpt from the poem "Daddy," from *Ariel*, by Sylvia Plath. © 1961, 1962, 1963, 1964, 1965 by Ted Hughes.

Harper Torchbooks: for an excerpt from *Memoirs of a Dutiful Daughter*, by Simone de Beauvoir. © 1958.

Janet Heller for her poem, "Sacrament."

Houghton Mifflin Company: for an excerpt from *All My Pretty Ones*, by Anne Sexton. © 1961, 1962 by Anne Sexton. Reprinted by permission of the publisher.

Alfred A. Knopf, Inc.: for an excerpt from *Kinflicks*, by Lisa Alther, © 1975 by Lisa Alther; for an excerpt from the poem "Salome," by Leonora Speyer, from *The World Split Open: Four Centuries of Women Poets in England and America, 1552–1950*, edited by Louise Bernikow, © 1931 by Leonora Speyer; and for an excerpt from *Menstruation and Menopause, The Physiology and Psychology, The Myth and Reality*, by Paula Weideger, © 1975, 1977 by Paula Weideger.

London House: for an excerpt from the poem "Miss Rosie," from *Good Times*, by Lucille Clifton. © 1969 by Lucille Clifton. Reprinted by permission of the publisher.

Audre Lord for a poem from *From a Land Where Other People Live*, Broadside Press. © 1973 by Audre Lord.

Monica McCall of International Creative Management: for excerpts from *Breaking Open*, by Muriel Rukeyser. © 1973, 1978 by Muriel Rukeyser.

The New York Times Magazine: for excerpts from an article, "Patty Today," by Lacey Fosburgh. © 1977.

W. W. Norton & Company, Inc.: for excerpts from *Of Woman Born*, by Adrienne Rich. © 1976 by Adrienne Rich.

Panjandrum Press: for an excerpt from Heidi Gitterman's "Poem for My Father," from *This is Women's Work*. © 1972 by Heidi Gitterman.

Pathfinder Press: for excerpts from *Woman's Evolution*, by Evelyn Reed. © 1975 by Evelyn Reed.

Primavera: for Shelley Simon's poem "Meals with Mother," from volume I of *Primavera*. © 1975 by Shelley Simon.

Rusoff Books: for excerpts from *Mothers and Daughters*, by Nor Hall. © 1976.

Schlesinger Library, Radcliffe College: for excerpts from *The Autobiography of Charlotte Perkins Gilman*, by Charlotte Perkins Gilman. © 1963.

Shameless Hussy Press: for fragments from *Calamity Jane's Letters to Her Daughter*, by Martha Jane Cannary Hickok. © 1976.

Martha Shelley for an excerpt from her poem "Note to a New Lesbian." © 1974 by Martha Shelley.

Simon & Schuster: for excerpts from *Children of Violence* series, by Doris Lessing. © by Doris Lessing.

Times Change Press: for an excerpt from *Momma*, by Alta. © 1974 by Alta. For the line "I am a woman giving birth to myself," from the poster of Pat Parker's poem designed by Su Negrin, © 1972.

University of Pittsburgh Press: for an excerpt from the poem "Mothers, Daughters," by Shirley Kaufman, from *The Floor Keeps Turning*. © 1970 by Shirley Kaufman.

Viking Press Inc.: for an excerpt from *Winesburg, Ohio*, by Sherwood Anderson. © 1968 by Sherwood Anderson. Also for an excerpt from *Les Guérrillieres*, by Monique Witting. © 1969 by Monique Witting.

Vantage Books: for an excerpt from *The Woman Warrior: Memories of a Girlhood Among Ghosts*, by Maxine Hong Kingston. © 1977 by Maxine Hong Kingston.

Yale University Press: for an excerpt from the poem "Looking Out," from *Coming Close*, by Helen Chasin. © 1968 by Yale University.

Contents

and beauty; daughters' fear of repeating their mothers' lives; fathers as objects and competitors; sister-brother rivalry; sister-sister rivalry; the nuclear family as a source of competitive relationships

notes on the cultural history of fatherhood and the institution of patriarchy; social definitions of the father-daughter relation; daughters' perception of and preference for fathers; daughters devoted to fathers; the model for future heterosexual relations; Ida, Judith, and Norman; forgiving and excusing fathers; daddy's girls; sexuality between father and daughter; incestrape; mother-daughter bond excluding fathers; mothers abandon daughters for fathers; fathers interrupt the mother/daughter relation

patriarchal tradition; matriarchal cycles; reluctance, fear and crisis in daughters and mothers; going away to school; "the real world"; getting married; daughters' desire for independence; mothers' responses to daughters' going; daughters want to go back; mothers who leave their daughters; mothers' deaths; metamorphic matricide

the "maternal instinct" argument; socialization toward motherhood; the "decision" to have a baby; choosing not to reproduce; having babies to please our mothers; having babies to prove womanhood; grandmothers; preferences for sex

of children; pressure on women to bear sons;
"my daughter is so different from my mother";
impact of the women's movement

Preface

Nine years ago, as I began to consider "women," trying to understand what feminism, women's liberation and political consciousness actually are, I was struck—almost physically—by the thought of my mother. The introduction of my mother into such considerations was so unusual and, I see now, of such importance, that I remember exactly where I was sitting, how the sunlight fell across the wall, what the air felt like that early summer day in 1970, when my mother first appeared to me as a woman in my life.

I have come to find that all of us must confront the reality of our mothers, as the women they are, and as they live in us—even if they are thousands of miles away or dead. Whether we come to the truth of our mothers through our politics, the guidance of therapy, or the revelations of dreams, we need that truth to break down both the generally false concept of "mother" in this society, and whatever specifically false stance we hold relative to our own mothers. For mothers and daughters to relate to each other in truth—even sporadically—is a terrible struggle for both women.

To a great extent, I wrote this book to advance and enlighten the particular struggle between me and my mother, Ida Rosenfield. She and I have grown in love and mutual understanding through our work on this book. My mother transcribed the taped interview series I made for *Our Mothers' Daughters*—an arduous and time-consuming task. As she listened and typed, for more than a year, we talked about the interviews, finding ourselves in many of them. I could not have made this book without her work and support.

My grateful appreciation goes to all the women who talked to me about their relations with their mothers. Our hundreds of hours of conversation, punctuated by weeping and laughter, are the core of this book. I interviewed 120 urban American women, aged 14–68, primarily from the working and middle classes, of diverse ethnic and racial backgrounds. Some of their mothers were dead; some were missing; many were a daily presence, physically or spiritually, in their daughters' lives. Throughout the book, I have quoted the words of these women; together we have written *Our Mothers' Daughters*. In this manner, women pass on knowledge; whatever our age, older women are our mothers, younger women our daughters.

I am thankful to many other people for helping me to write this book, including virtually every woman I've spoken to in the last four years, all of whom responded emotionally—if not always openly or gladly—to the notion of studying the mother/daughter relationship.

My father, Norman Rosenfield, encouraged both my mother and me, especially in the earliest months.

My dear friends, Pat Murray and Jonathan Arlook, read and criticized each chapter as I completed it, creating a collective editing process.

I appreciate Janie Friedman Isackson's suggestion that I do some of this work through the master's program at Goddard College. I did so, and worked with Alan Walker, who helped me to create and follow a discipline, and to take the M.A. in Women's Studies.

Pauline Bart, who served as my advisor in the Goddard program, consistently gave me encouragement, praise, and support—introducing me to both people and literature which enriched my life.

My working definition of daughterhood came out of a three week session during a Columbia College midterm. The fifteen women who were the students in that group gave me, and each other, a sense of the social role of daughter as it is lived by most of us.

That definition, and the rest of these words, would remain stapled pages of handwritten and poorly typed text, were it not for Linda Turner, queen of the keys, who typed this manuscript. Linda, possessed of a mother and daughter of her own, has been one of my most enthusiastic supporters during the final months of writing and rewriting.

There have been others, including Flora Faraci and Nancy Finke of the Jane Addams Bookstore and Bakery, Arlene Kaplan Daniels, Barbara Emrys, Alta, the women At the Foot of the Mountain, Mary Howell, Phyllis Chesler, and Carol White, who have given me encouragement, advice and criticism in these years of working on *Our Mothers' Daughters*.

I am particularly indebted to my women's group, which has sustained me through the travail of the writing process—Belinda, Lois, Mara, Omie, Pat, Pauline, and Stacie, and to my partner, Jonathan, for the care and love he gave me throughout the writing and living of this first book.

One year ago, my son told me that his group at school was discussing women's work—naming the kinds of work that women do. He said that his contribution had been to point out that women are writers. Wondering if he knew the names of any literary women, I asked, "And did you know any women writers, Daniel?" He laughed, and said, "I know *you*, mom." Thank you too, dear.

Judith Arcana
Chicago
Winter, 1979

Introduction

This book aroused my deepest longings. *Our Mothers' Daughters* is about Woman's stormiest love affair: the one all daughters have with our mothers.

You know: the woman who gave birth to us and/or raised us; the woman we had to compete *for*, against fathers and brothers, losing, losing because we were like her, we were women too; the woman from whom we fled, in wounded adolescent pride, headlong into the arms of men—and children—in search of *Her*, our Mother. The woman we don't have much in common with. The woman who will always mean "home" to us—in all its wrenching complexity.

After I read an early draft of *Our Mothers' Daughters*, I delayed returning it. *I wanted my mother to read it first.* Maybe it wasn't too late. Maybe this book would break the silence, the stand-off, between my mother and me. Certainly, this book gave me the courage, the mandate, to re-think this "unfinished business" in a new way: with less fury, less despair,—and without that falsely triumphant, "Blame-Mommy-it's-her-fault" explanation, so popular—so useless—today.

I took this book home to my mother.

"Please mother read this book. It will make everything—*everything*—clear. Then, you'll say you love me. Only me. For my strength. For all the ways I'm *different* from you. Then, we'll embrace. Prodigal Daughter, Prodigal Mother. We'll speak only words of love to each other. Nothing superficial will ever pass our lips again."

"You're so melodramatic," she says. Putting on her glasses.

(This conversation didn't take place. But we're closer to it every day, my mother and me.)

That's the kind of book this is. Drives a woman to hope. Drives a daughter to kneel once again at the feet of La Belle Dame Sans Merci, heart beating . . .

And it's the kind of book that explains honestly, compassionately, why we can't go home again; why we don't live "happily ever after" with our Mothers.

The book is revolutionary in suggesting that we try. That we at least consider: why not? The book is feminist in portraying the anguish, the powerlessness of *both* Mother and Daughter.

Judith's book confronts the most painful questions: How can we ever forgive our mothers for not *preferring* us to men? How can we ever forgive our mothers for trying to bind our feet, cripple us "for our own good"? How can we face what patriarchy has done to most of our mothers? How can we live with the possibility that we may not be able to rescue our mothers? How can we as feminists, learn to love our mothers, *learn to accept the love we already feel:* understanding that no one else but us will do so?

This is a major book among other major books, all painfully recent, that touch on, or explore deeply, the Mother-Daughter bond: my own, *Women And Madness;* Esther Broner's *Her Mothers* and *A Weave of Women;* Dorothy Dinnerstein's *The Mermaid and the Minotaur;* Nancy Chodorow's *The Reproduction of Mothering;* Susan Griffin's *Woman and Nature;* Adrienne Rich's *Of Woman Born;* and my own forthcoming *Journal of Pregnancy and Motherhood.*

Only I know it's not just "my" obsession. It's not personal: it's political. As this book makes so clear.

My thanks to Alta for publishing this book. She is a large, generous woman. Funny, too.

My thanks to Judith for writing it.

Phyllis Chesler

"Mother, may I go out to swim?"
"Yes, my darling daughter.
Hang your clothes on a hickory limb,
And don't go near the water."

"A son is your son 'till he takes a wife;
A daughter's your daughter the
rest of her life."

1
Daughter and Mother: Learning the Roles

A woman is her mother.
That's the main thing.
— ANNE SEXTON

My mother's whole education and upbringing
had convinced her that for a woman the
greatest thing was to become the mother of
a family; she couldn't play this part un-
less I played the dutiful daughter. . . .
— SIMONE DE BEAUVOIR

It is generally assumed that mothers and daughters are natural enemies. "Clytaemnestra and Electra are clearly mother and daughter, and therefore should have some sympathy, though perhaps sympathy gone wrong breeds the fiercest hate."[1] Where is it that the sympathy has gone wrong? How is it that most mother/daughter pairs maintain guilt, hostility and superficial "affection" as their primary connection? Do we want love from our mothers; do we want to love them? What keeps the mother/daughter relation from functioning as a source of love and support for both women?

The oppression of women has created a breach among us, especially between mothers and daughters. Women cannot respect their mothers in a society which degrades them; women cannot respect themselves. Mothers socialize their daughters into the narrow role of wife-mother; in frustration and guilt, daughters reject their mothers for their duplicity and incapacity—so the alienation grows in the turning of the generations. Women must rediscover our history and our strength, so that we may honor the mother/daughter relationship as a source of love. We must accept our mothers

1

and allow ourselves to learn from them the truth of their lives, unhappy and frightening as that truth might be; and we must all accept the responsibility to *mother* daughters—daughters of the spirit as well as the placenta.

The "profession" of motherhood is one of low status in our society, witness that standard index—money: mothers are unsalaried. Despite flowery seasonal tributes and nostalgia, mothers have a bad reputation; they are blamed for nearly all social ills by everyone, including their own children. While mothers—"Earth mothers," Mother Machree, Mammy, etc.— are lauded in greeting card verses and sentimental songs, and policemen, smiling benevolently, stop traffic on busy streets for pregnant women to walk across, the popularization of Freudian-based psychology encourages each of us to condemn our mothers for thwarting us, repressing us, raising us for selfish purposes, refusing to let us go, even dominating our emotional lives after their deaths.

Much of this negativity stems from the specific misogynism of Freud, but the depth of hatred and resentment of mothers is created by the basic sexist premises of this society. Women are the source of evil; we are degraded; at best, we are inferior—to men, who are both the standard and superior. Our mothers, every one of them women, are pressed into the scapegoat role as they are pressed into maternity. In this book, I have examined the mother/daughter relationship as it exists within a society which has systematically and institutionally devalued women, preventing mothers and daughters from relating to each other with mutual love and support.

In all the classes I've convened in women's studies over the past five years, every subject we've discussed has brought us back to our mothers. Whether we begin by discussing vaginitis, primitive kinship systems, or women driving fork-lifts, we wind up talking about our mothers—and usually swapping complaints and jokes. The coming of feminist consciousness threw my relationship with my mother into sharp relief against the rest of my life; this new vision, this comprehension of the world from such a strikingly different attitude, caused me to struggle through viewing my mother as my oppressor, to try to appreciate her as a sister woman. I looked down my life at all the women I've loved, lived with, tried to grow with, and saw, of course, mother.

Every one of us who tries to shed the contempt and competition, to search for herself in other women, should turn to her mother and offer her what we try now to offer each other. "You can't have two women in the same kitchen," the saying goes, though one of my dearest childhood memories is of all the women—aunts, sisters and cousins, mothers and grandmothers—filling the kitchen before and after holiday meals, talking and joking, working together. The prevailing myth is that we all ought to be isolated, each in her own kitchen, instead of gathered in a house of women; but we belong in our mothers' house.

If I am to see myself, and all women, in this new way, if I am to love myself—love women—what about my mother? The answer to this question has been slow in coming. When I, and the other women in my classes, went to the libraries and bookstores, even in women's centers, we found either no material at all, or literature which furthered the old lies, strengthened the "blame your mother" school of thought, and kept daughters apart from their mothers. Recently, women have begun to consider and investigate the relations between daughters and their mothers, but we have a great deal of work yet to do. For even now, one most recently published and publicized work on the subject, Nancy Friday's *My Mother, Myself,* merely revitalizes old concepts in new language. Friday's work, despite her occasional comments about how things are changing, reinforces only the resentment and anger many women feel for their mothers, and is heavily weighted with the words of gynecologists and therapists.

She believes that our sexuality, and our mothers' denial and fear of it, are at the base of women's problems. I find Friday suggesting that our mothers' "silent and threatening disapproval" of our sexuality leads to rape fantasies, though later, in actuality, "it is not the rapist . . . whom we fear." It is mother, of course, "the real root" of our "sexual anxiety." The fact of rape, and its frequency, are given no weight in causing either our mothers' fears or our own. Friday feels that

4

"most women want to be mothers"—though *she* does not*—
and seems to be describing a society in which everyone is
middle class and heterosexual, and certainly going to get
married. Her analysis evidences no political context; in her
book it is as if our mothers, in their perversity, somehow
decided to socialize us to our detriment. This kind of analysis
is not what women need. What we want is a telling of truths
about women.

Of all the roles women are required to fill in this society,
daughterhood is universal. Being born, every woman is
another woman's daughter. Should her mother die, or leave
her when she is a child, she is yet raised up by the society as a
"daughter." Even if she becomes a mother, she remains a
daughter. And, of all the roles women are required to fill, the
one we are least often excused from, that we least often relinquish, is that of mother. Even women who do not bear children are required to learn and practice maternal behavior.
Some few thousands are still exempt on the grounds of religious devotion or physical incapacity, but there are enough
individual exceptions known to each of us to make their
uniqueness obvious. Such women are often estranged from
society; "women who refuse to become mothers are not
merely suspect, but are dangerous."[2]

Male culture has separated us from our mothers with its
definitions of "mother" and "daughter," in this first of a
series of alienations, woman from woman, women from
women. Nor Hall regards this alienation as a wound, and
speaks of healing it by "an internal conjunction, by an in-
tegration of its own parts, by a re-membering or putting back
together of the mother-daughter body."[3] Women must
redefine the relationship, basing the new definition on
realistic expectations and acceptance of actual needs, so that
expectations may be met, needs be satisfied.

Many ancient peoples called all females "mother"[4] in their
reverence for the wonderful capacity to create people—a
miracle all women, and only women, are able to perform,

---

*Or, at any rate, says she has accepted her husband's statement of
"their" decision not to have children.

whether we do so or not. These people revered woman as the Mother, the Goddess. Here and now, though motherhood is considered "good" for the individual woman, and almost always garners positive reinforcement for her, it has no glory. Mothers are no longer hailed as the bringers of food and light, the holders of beauty and power. Our culture defines a mother as a woman who bears a child out of her body and/or raises a child or children, a woman who alone performs for those children the social functions of mothering—nurturing, healing, teaching, serving. "In primitive society, motherhood was a *social* function of the female sex; thus all women were . .

the 'mothers' of the community. As adult women, all were equally responsible for the provision and protection of the children."[5]

The satisfaction of being women and mothers has gone, as has the collective responsibility. Contemporary definitions have been, ironically, taught to us by our mothers, but created by the culture inside of which the mother/daughter relation develops. Thus, as our culture is male-created and dominated, our expectations have been based upon men's experience and desires. As Adrienne Rich makes the distinction between motherhood as experience and institution,[6] so we should distinguish between those expectations in the mother/daughter relation which grow from the woman-bond, the closeness of like bodies, spirits and experiences, and those which are fostered by the oppressive culture in which mothers socialize their daughters as they must, not as they might. The relationship is structured, at present, upon assumptions and conclusions that are false to ourselves and for each other; that is why so many mother/daughter relationships are filled with pain.

As daughters, our learned expectations of our mothers are of great proportions: "Mother-love is supposed to be continuous, unconditional. Love and anger cannot coexist."[7] We hold the belief that mothers love their daughters by definition, and we fear any signal from our own mothers that this love, which includes acceptance, affection, admiration, and approval, does not exist or is incomplete. Since these

signals must be constantly apparent to fit that definition, we
all assume that we've gotten a "bad" mother. So many of us
prefer the mother of a close friend, the one whose home and
habits seem to reflect the kind of care we've been taught that
mothers are supposed to give. We want the mother who does
what the books, starting with *Little Women,* lead us to expect.
Mothers of perfection—the ones whose understanding and
sympathy never fail, whose only desire in life is that we be
happy, and who never make us feel guilty because that is their
only reason for existing. In the luck of the draw, when the
mothers were distributed, how many of us resigned ourselves
to bad luck, poor distribution? This resignation, and the
dissatisfaction it masks, is based upon our having learned that
mothers are angels, beautiful and soothing presences who
have no human needs or flaws.

Moreover, we learn that it is mother who "is held accountable for her children's health, the clothes they wear, their
behavior at school, their intelligence and general development . . . she and no one else bears the guilt . . . in the eyes of
society the mother is the child's environment,"[8] and in the
eyes of her daughters as well.

*It's very important for me to have mothering, which was also
important for her. She didn't get it from her own mother and
she tried to get it from me, and I try to get it any way I can. It's
real hard to get. I think everybody wants it. It's a scarce com-
modity.*

*My mother was a liberated woman and I wanted a less
liberated woman as a mother. Frankly, I would much prefer
her home baking cookies.*

*I would like to go home and see the house cleaned up. And I
would expect my mom to do it. And I like to have a nice meal
when I come home and I expect her to make it. I don't know if
that's because she's a mother or because it's the kind of thing
she's always done.*

*I used to come home from school and have something I
wanted to talk to her about, and she'd be so busy with all those*

other eight kids, that when I'd walk up to her—and she was a darling; she'd "listen"—I knew she wasn't listening. She would be standing right there, but even as a child I knew she was only doing what she had to do. I went through my whole life trying to talk to her.

My mother worked nights so I hardly ever saw her. When I got home at the end of the day, she'd be leaving for work. I missed her; I missed knowing her.

This view of motherhood, featuring mother as constantly available and nurturant, despite economics, number of children or desire for personal expression, allows for every male fantasy from "M is for the million things she gave me" to "momism." We daughters take our perceptions of mother from father and brother, frequently condemning those mothers who don't act the now falsely sacred role.

I was surprised to discover, in the course of convening a seminar on daughterhood, that the role of daughter is simply woman. This may seem obvious, for all women are daughters, but it was a revelation to me, in that, by necessity, being a *good* daughter depends on how closely we hold to the current standards for women. That is, no matter how loving we are, or how supportive—even financially—we are not meeting the expectations our mothers hold for us if we aren't proper women, in the now well-identified mode: passive, submissive, "pretty," not-too-obviously intelligent, and (at least potential) mothers and wives. These qualities may carry regional, class, race, ethnic or family-specific modifications, but the basic pattern remains the same throughout the culture, notwithstanding these years of impact from the women's movement.

In the daughterhood seminar, we identified the role of daughter in terms of what we had learned as we were growing up. Here is that definition: As daughters, we are to give to our families, especially our parents, unconditional love and respect, and display our affection for them, maintain a certain "acceptable level" of physical appearance, marry, stay married, re-marry if necessary, and bear and raise children.

Further, though these are optional, depending on social differences, we daughters must also be people who "do well in school," sometimes to the extent of being trained in a profession; we do housework and/or childcare—this is called "helping your mother;" and we care for and about our parents as they age and die. This view of daughterhood is also held by our mothers, of course, who are our primary sources when learning the role.*

I don't really know what she thought of me, and that is the mystery. That is the biggest mystery. I could never find out. It was something that I searched for; I always wanted to please my mother, and many of the things I did did not please her. But my mother set up high standards that I could never come to. Maybe it wasn't that they were so high, but it wasn't in me to fulfill that way.

Mothers and daughters have problems because they are a lot alike; they see themselves in each other. My mother cared how I turned out because she identified with me. I guess it's a real affront if your daughter doesn't turn out like you, doesn't care about the same things. It's a real rejection. Mothers are too attached in how their daughters turn out.

They have these expectations for us. Maybe they have expectations for their sons too, but they feel more in our lives because we're both female. They want us to do it right. If they think they've done it right, they want us to do the same. If they think they've done it wrong, they want us to correct their mistakes in our lives.

God only knows what she wants me to be. She wants me "to be

*In the New York Times Magazine article, "Patty Today"—April 3, 1977, by Lacey Fosburgh, Patricia Hearst is called a "lovely daughter figure," once more in the "appropriate relationship to the world around her—that of the proper, well-mannered, compliant, and unassertive daughter.... she has reverted to the role of dutiful child in the family circle." She is "at home with Mom and Dad, more dutiful and loving and gracious than she ever was before."

happy." But she also wants me to be married, to have kids, a house, and a car.

Mothers have real expectations of where our lives will go, especially in terms of the men we live with and marry. My mother doesn't want her daughters to go through changes— divorces, unhappiness, struggle. My relationship with her has a lot to do with satisfying her projected needs, like my having a "good" marriage. She can't relate to me as a person without my being married—but she's having to learn.

We learn the roles of daughter and mother both sequentially and simultaneously. All women are daughters and all women are expected to be mothers. When we are very young, the daughter role is the framework within which all of our woman behavior is learned. We are encouraged to play at being grown women, especially as wives and mothers, so we are daughters being "little mothers" during much of our childhood, and we internalize both roles at once.* Almost all of the women I interviewed were raised primarily or exclusively by their mothers—so we are daughters observing and adopting the mother role as we grow. The culture is filled with cues and rules for little girls to learn from—but the core of role representation is in our mothers.

We unconsciously pattern ourselves after our mothers, even if we rebel against them, ignore them or abuse them, find other models, or even "take after" a man. Some daughters spend all or most of their energy trying, usually futilely, to be as different from their mothers as possible in behavior, appearance, relations with friends, lovers, children, husbands. Sixty-three percent of the women I studied said that they consciously tried not to model themselves as women after their mothers.

---

*Even those little girls who are allowed to be "tomboys" still are undergoing the inexorable process of socialization as proper women. The process "takes" to one degree or another, but, in the main, is highly successful.

She was a negative model. I thought, "When I grow up, I will not be like this; I will not do as my mother does." As a teenager I kept a list of ways I would treat my daughter differently than my mother treated me.

I never wanted to be like her. I always thought it was awful to be like that, like my mother. My father ruled her and she didn't have a mind of her own. She always would do what he said. And she wanted to do it. If she had fought against him, that would be something, but she liked it; she liked to be dominated, and I hated it. And I said never, there's no way that I could ever be in that situation. I just hated it.

I rejected her as a model consciously, and followed her unconsciously. I took it as a hidden agenda; I surrendered awfully quickly when I got married. I worked until I had a child and really that was the end. I must have absorbed it in a hidden way, though I was always aware that I didn't want to do it the same way. I was consciously aware that I wanted other things, though I wasn't so successful at getting them.

I've devoted my life to not being like her, which is a very difficult and negative thing to do, and it has really put me into the wrong way. . . . I've been trying all my life not to be somebody, and that is my mother. I'm just getting around to learning who I really am, and at 58 it's pretty late in the game.

She was just like the mirror image of a role model—I wanted to be exactly like she wasn't. I remember thinking even before I went to school that I was never going to be a nurse, that I would be a doctor. (laugh) I felt that if my mother was a nurse, nursing wasn't something worth doing. I didn't want to be a housewife either, and it was mostly because of the spirit in which she did her work. It was so clearly a drag for her to cook three meals a day, keep the house clean and do the mending. There were always socks to be darned and she hated it.

Some daughters complain that their mothers are reluctant, refuse or are incapable of filling the mother role properly. They say their mothers are immature, irresponsible, emotionally unstable, "too strong" or "masculine," or simply absent. Absent mothers are at work, dead, hospitalized, drunk, drugged, or have left their child(ren). Some mothers are spiritually removed from their families, or at least from motherhood, even when they are present.

I have some sad feelings about my mother. I went through some old pictures and looked at her. I have the sense that something happened a few years after I was born, where she turned off, not totally but a lot, and so I never had the chance to know the woman who I saw in the old pictures, the woman who collected the poetry books. Once I saw my mother dancing at a party—the only time in my life. I don't know where she went to, but I don't think I knew her. . . . Sometimes she was so angry with me that she was not there. Like I would have a scene, and I know mother was there, but I felt abandoned. I now account for it by her inability to accept her own anger in relationship to me or what was going on. She had to be the perfect mother; when she couldn't be, she "went away."

Some of us have sought or fortunately discovered other women to emulate, especially those of us who've considered our mothers unacceptable, even when we were small girls. "Many women have . . . split themselves—between two mothers: One, usually the biological one, who represents the culture of domesticity, of male-centeredness, of conventional expectations, and another, perhaps a woman artist or teacher, who becomes the countervailing figure. . . . exemplifies strength and pride in her body, a freer way of being in the world, . . . alive with ideas, who represents the choice of a vigorous work life, of 'living alone and liking it.' "[9]

There was a woman I met when I was seven. I identify with her; she made me what I am, not my mother. She had a white picket fence and a dog, and I used to sit with my feet through the picket fence petting the dog. She opened up the gate and said, "Why don't you come in?" She was loving and open with me; she would give me honest answers to all my questions about anything, like sex. She would never throw it in my face. She had the gentle hope that I would go to college and graduate cum lauda. I did, thanks to her. If she would have said magna cum lauda, I would have graduated magna. She worked in industry, and she was very strong. I found out when I got older that she had been divorced after 18 years of marriage. She told me that right before I got married, and she advised me not to marry the man I did. She thought he was domineering, and she was right. I never saw her with a man.

Others admire their mothers, even idolize them, but don't want to live their lives the way their mothers did. In answering positively the questions about mothers as role models, most women said there was a distinction to be made between the woman (whom they variously liked, loved, admired, or at least found unobjectionable) and the life role (which they most often rejected, in part or totally).

I had hoped I would be like her as a housekeeper, because she was an extra-wonderful housekeeper, but I worked all the time and for a long time, so I never could. Her relationship with her husband governed me in my marriage, though. I catered to my husband too.

I considered my mother a strong woman although she did accept her lot in life; she wasn't passively accepting it. She knew it was something she was stuck with and had to do. That part of her was a model.

She's the complete role model mother. Incredible. Dynamite with children, and she's doing that now with the grandchildren. The children—my god—that's her whole life—the family. Sometimes it got to be a guilt thing with me—like, "I'm never going to be like that." Now, it's, "I'll never be like that;" my god—I don't think I ever will.

I didn't want to have her life style. I wanted to be like her, as good and as fair as she was; she never did anything wrong, always the right thing. I wanted to be like that. But things are different now, so I am different.

What we learn is what our mothers do, not what they say. The example of a mother who is independent and strong is more effective than one who says, "Don't do what I did"—or one who tells her daughter to have aspirations she has not had or realized herself—to work for her living when the mother is supported by a husband, or hates her work because it is degrading, boring, or underpaid—not to have children (or to "wait"), to have only one or two children when the mother began childbearing quite young and had four, six or even eight children. We learn from, and repeat in our own lives, our mothers' daily reality, whatever their dreams might have been. No matter our passionate vows to reject the model, the majority of us play out the role we learned. "A mother's victimization does not merely humiliate her, it mutilates the daughter who watches her for clues as to what it means to be a woman. Like the traditional foot-bound Chinese woman, she passes on her affliction. The mother's self-hatred and low expectations are the binding rags for the psyche of the daughter."[10]

The thing that my mother used to say that would make me crazy was, "What do you want from life? You want too much. You're never going to get it. Life is going to be a heartbreak for you, for someone who wants too much." That was like saying to me, "Don't try to do anything." I have struggled with that a lot—to go out and get something I really wanted.

My mother undercuts me a lot. She doesn't want me to be too successful or happy. It is because she feels unsuccessful; it would be too hard for her to have me be successful. She would say things to me like, "You shouldn't expect to be too happy in life," that kind of stuff.

"Many daughters live in rage at their mothers for having accepted too readily and passively, 'whatever comes'."[11]

I didn't realize until I got older how she had cheated herself. She put us first where she shouldn't have. I thought she was a perfect mother. I have a lot of anger towards her, because she neglected herself.

When she got married, it was just the thing to do. I don't think she ever thought about it. Everybody did it. Then she went and had the kids ... didn't really have too much to say about it ... just did it.

In recent years I have asked her, because having so many children seemed such a burden, I asked her why she did it. Her only answer was, "just because it happened." It was not something she wanted; *it just happened to her.*

There are, too, daughters who've learned from men, usually their fathers, what they ought to be as women, how to properly fill the roles of mother and daughter. Often these women identify with their fathers and/or prefer their fathers as they grow up.

My father was the biggest influence on the way I live my life today. He paid a lot of attention to what my life was about. Interestingly enough, he was the person who told me about having periods and sex, and he was the one who encouraged me to go beyond just graduating from high school and getting married.

My father said to treat my husband like a king and he would treat me like a queen. It took me five years to discover that no one had told my husband that.

When I was a kid he used to say this thing about the stars—be open to anything, explore. He was imaginative and encouraging of my curiosity. Then, when I got older, the message was, fill the wife role, support your husband's efforts, be a good mother. In other words, he said, "Forget the stars." When I finally said to my father, "I'm unhappy; I want a divorce," his response to me was, "Once you have children you are not allowed to pursue your personal happiness in life."

What daughters expect from mothers, even if we are mothers, and, therefore, should know better, is absurdly non-human—a total commitment. Often we have greater expectations as adults than we had as children. We want not just loving—which many of us withhold from our mothers—but mutuality of interest, even childcare, cooking, cleaning, nursing, money-on-call—all of which most of us would resent *even being asked for* by our mothers. One of the daughters I interviewed described her mother in mostly positive terms, praising her as the self-sacrificing young widow who went to work, raised four children by herself, etc. This mother and her second husband waited until all of her children were grown before they married, because "she didn't want us to have another father," which sacrifice her daughter considers appropriate and correct. "I figured I didn't have a mother anymore; she took him over all the kids who disagreed about her getting married," when she finally did marry her long-time friend. This marriage so displeased her daughter that she was only mollified—though incompletely—by her mother's telling her that "you always come first."

We learn to make these demands of our mothers in childhood, when our mothers, whether they are actually filling the role or not, teach us that motherhood requires these services and sacrifices of them, in a non-reciprocal fashion. Moreover, there is no form for the mother/daughter relation other than that which serves when the daughter is a child, so mothers continue to desire dutiful obedience from their grown daughters as they continue to martyr themselves. Our mothers struggle to satisfy our demands, and we daughters to do our duty, each contrary to her nature, to get the approval and affection we need from each other.

The martyr mother and the dutiful daughter emerged as special types in the process of my interviewing. They seem to be heightened forms of self-denial and total internalization of traditional woman roles—really not so much different from other mothers and daughters as they are extensions of the roles most of us live. Mothers are *supposed* to be martyrs; daughters are *expected* to be dutiful. It is only when women go too far in accepting the roles we're given to play that we become comic figures, family problems, or, ultimately, mental patients, as Phyllis Chesler points out.[12]

I stayed home for a much longer time than I should have; I'm not sure I should have stayed that long. It's sort of like a divorce—staying together for the sake of the children—that's what I was doing. I thought I was a solid base for my siblings, but in many ways it might have been better for everybody if I had left.

When I was in school I used to write to my mother every single day. Every day I would write. When I was married and moved away, I would write a couple of times a week and call. It was expected. Now my parents are very old, and though I don't particularly enjoy being with my mother, I call her every day, and see them a few times a week. I do it because I feel it's an obligation.

I married Cy on one of her trips back here for a visit. When I look back on it now, I know I was trying to please her. I married again because I knew she wanted me to; she felt bad that I was alone. So I married under the pressure of one of her Chicago visits. Both of my marriages were made under pressure from my mother, and to please her.

She taught me about being a martyr; she's constantly fighting not to take that martyr role. She's real good at doing it, and has to force herself not to. She did give up a lot for her children, but she carried it to extremes when she didn't have to. Like she went for years without buying herself a dress and that's just ridiculous; we weren't that poor.

My mother was super-proud and wouldn't let anyone know she had a need, never.

My mother is passive. She has a tendency to let my father push her around. At one time she stood up to him, but then she became a mother, and he was the breadwinner, so she was insecure. She became a martyr.

My mother and I even competed to see who could be the best martyr. Who could be the goodest, who would do it right.

My mother gets hurt very easily, and whenever I become more independent, she becomes more hurt.

To a certain extent, my mother likes suffering from me. She likes complaining that I don't do things the way she wants them to be done. There's a part of her that always wanted to do what I do, so I'm fulfilling that desire for her. Probably she's secretly satisfied with me.

Many women I interviewed want to transcend/destroy the institutionalized roles of mother and daughter. We want to relate to our mothers as women in shared circumstances. We recognize that the roles are imposed by society, that they have little connection with the deep feeling and abiding tie that exists between us and our mothers. We realize that even if the roles as they are now defined are functional when daughters are small girls—which is questionable—these roles are unnecessary when both women are adults.

Some of us have tried therapy to break down the barriers that the role structure creates. The daughters I interviewed have used Freudian analysis, transactional analysis, co-counseling, Gestalt therapy and dream interpretation. They have worked in couples, large groups, one-on-one sessions, mixed groups, and women only; they were out-patients, inmates in mental wards, seen at home by visiting therapists. Some deliberately sought therapy to work on the mother-daughter conflict, to work through the hatred, guilt, competition or resentment they felt for their mothers. Some found that though they hadn't meant to deal with their mothers, "it just came out," or "it turned out to be pretty important." Although this revelation reflects the common bias among therapists of all persuasions which leads them to raise (often negatively) the issue of "mother," in any case, it still indicates that a good number of us* have dealt extensively with our relationships with our mothers in therapy.

Those of us who are feminists are examining the lives of our mothers as we are our own. Since adulthood, I had always viewed my mother as an antagonist, at best an ironic problem.

*Seventy-three percent of the daughters in the study had been in some form of therapy; 37 percent had sought therapy specifically to talk about their mothers; 13 percent of their mothers had sought therapy to talk about their daughters.

I came to see that we shared oppression—that she did not socialize me negatively out of her own head—that she was not the originator of the misogynism I learned as I grew.

I reviewed what I knew of her life: In the middle of WWII, a 33-year-old woman who'd lived with her parents all her life, she married a widower, giving up a well-paying job (far more lucrative than her new husband's) to become a housewife and the mother of his two children; my brother was six; I was two-and-a-half. These, of course, were only my preliminary recollections and a bare beginning. My mother's life became a story to me, as have many hundreds of women's lives now that I seek them out, to read, to hear, to share. One day she was self-sufficient and a major financial support in her family home, the next she was dispossessed: a stranger in the kitchen of her mother- and sister-in-law, and a step-mother to children who had already transferred their devotion to aunt and grand-mother. So began the story I told myself that first time, the first time I thought of my mother as a woman, a person, my peer. Since that beginning, I have entered into the struggle to know my mother, to have her know me.

I'm identifying much more with woman now; I would like to be able to identify with her.

If my father would die, then I might be able to get along with my mother. Politically, I think it is incorrect for me not to be able to get along with my mother.

I have a lot of negative, hostile feelings toward my dad, and I think I got more sympathetic toward my mother when I was in college and got into the women's movement. I can under-stand and see her life differently. It's just an intellectual thing, though; emotionally I still don't feel warm towards her.

When I was in a women's group in Oregon, I started to think about what her life had been like, and especially what she had done for me. I mean there was a long list I had been carrying around for years of what she hadn't done for me, but I have started to understand the limits of what she could do, given the life she was living. She was getting up and going to work

*at seven o'clock. We never saw her really because when we
would get up for school she was already gone. After she came
home and would make dinner, she would fall out, wasted. I
began to understand what a tough lady she was and what a
hard life she lived, and what she had given up to keep me and
my brother going. . . . Her own mother killed herself. She had
talked to me a little bit about that, how her mother had come
and told her that she really felt like doing it, and nobody
thought it was serious, and she felt guilty, and she really
understood what her mother's life had been like. . . . I wrote
her a letter in which I said, "This is what I'm doing with my
life, and I'm doing it because I feel it's the right thing to do. I
know it's very different from what you're doing, but that
doesn't mean that I don't respect what your life is about and
what you've done for me." It was just an acknowledgement of
her own and my life, and to say I dig you and I respect you, and
the only thing I ask of you is that respect, even though I'm
different. She wrote back this amazing letter saying, "I understand what you're doing and I think it's terrific and I love you
a lot." So that was the turning point in our relationship. We
accept the fact that we have a right to influence each other's
lives. The whole thing came out of a conscious decision on my
part after exploring those feelings with my women's group.*

We can transcend the roles only by first understanding that
they exist—that we as mothers and daughters are not acting
freely when we relate to each other, but are unconsciously
maintaining structures into which we have been fitted. We
must recount our own and our mothers' stories to see what we
have been. Much of the bond that holds us to our mothers is an
unspoken recognition of our sameness, the sameness of our
lives, that repetition so many of us fear.

After spending a notably pleasant afternoon with my
mother, and thinking about what might have been the reasons, the circumstances, that allowed us to do so well, I
suddenly realized that, in fact, we were *not* friends. Friends are
generally people who share a point of view, their politics,
and/or share activities and interests, people who seek each

other out of mutual fascination. The reason my mother and I attack each other's tastes and ideas, argue and criticize, is that we want to be more alike—so that we can be friends. (Of course, much of the criticism is based upon profoundly different politics, but the point is, we wouldn't bother to engage, to raise the issues we do, unless we wanted to come together.) We give each other such a hard time because we haven't stopped wanting to love, to share. I want her to agree with me, to live like me. And she, since my childhood, has attempted to effect that change in me; that is what her raising of me was for—to set me into the life she was preparing me for: the life *she* lived.

It is also true, however, that some daughters do not want to transcend the mother/daughter roles—several women I interviewed made this quite clear. Most often the issue was discussed in terms of "friendship"; there is criticism of mothers who want/try to be friends to their daughters. The daughters feel that their mothers are shirking, not fulfilling the maternal role. There is an attendant feeling of unease, almost embarrassment, on the part of these daughters; their mothers' behavior is disturbing to them. Mother/daughter relations and friendship are seen as mutually exclusive.

Throughout my growing up she was trying to be my best friend, so that when it came time for me to need her to be my mother, it scared the piss out of her and she ran. When she was angry at me, that's when the mother came out.

I didn't want my mother to be a friend. I still don't. There are certain things I don't want to share with her. I don't want to be my kids' friend. I want to be their mother, and I think it's because I always wanted my mother to mother me more. My mother actually said to me, a long time ago, "I never thought of you as my daughter, but more as my best friend." I just died. And yet I realize that I don't need a mother anymore, not like when I was a kid.

I think she would like a lot of attention; she would like me to spend a lot of time with her. She said to me one time, "Be my girlfriend." I remember saying, which probably wasn't very nice, "Mother, I have girlfriends. I need a mother." I don't think she understood what I meant, and I think I hurt her feelings.

She's always tried to depend on her children for support, the support she had expected to get from her husband. She never tried to seek out other people. She never had friends other than her sisters. She never had peers for friends, and she tried to draw most of her support from us.

There is a distinction between those mothers who want to be their daughters' friends *as well* as their mothers, and those who do not mother their daughters. Obviously, most of these daughters sustained a lack of mothering when they were girls. Their resentment, well-founded, has kept them from bonding to their mothers in friendship, and gaining the sustenance of mutual nurturing that such affection brings. They are tied to the old mother/daughter roles, even though, as one woman points out, they don't *need* "mothers" any more.

Some daughters only allow their mothers to relate to them in specific ways—determined by the daughters. Most of these require a superficial relationship, but consider this "normal" or "OK," and even call it "love." Often our mothers are in our lives only minimally because we live far from them, and really cannot know them fully. Others of us restrict our relations with our mothers to a very narrow set of times and circumstances, essentially to keep them away from us. Some women have deeply buried their affection for their mothers; others only consider their mothers left-over social obligations. There are daughters who've been rejected or abandoned by their mothers; some have accepted that status, others rage against it yet.

Our relationship was horrendous. It always looked good on the outside, but on the inside there was a whole lot of hostility, and a real lot of anger. Since I realized this, it has gotten better and better. I'm no longer allowing myself to get hooked in places that I used to get hooked by her. I'm not allowing myself to feel guilty where she used to make me feel guilty. She's going to love me because I am her daughter and the person that I am, or reject me.

Well, there really hasn't been all that much contact between us. Occasionally there have been phone calls from her, very pathetic, wanting to renew the relationship. There was one time I actually went to a family dinner, which was very hard, and I said I would not do it again. Never.

I see my mother maybe once a month or once every six weeks even though she lives 30 miles away. I'm always amazed at families that get together once a week, or women who talk to their mothers every day. The reason I don't see her more often is that I had always assumed my husband would be transferred, and I thought the separation will be horrible for us; it's going to be terrible for my child, terrible for my mother. So the best thing to do is just keep at a distance now, so it won't get to be a pattern.

I'm fairly close to my mother; we're pretty good friends. I'm not a friend in the sense that I'd confide in her about my feelings, thoughts, personal problems. I don't do that, and I don't encourage her to do that with me. When she starts, I tell her to go do that with somebody else. So it's a pretty superficial relationship. I love her but it's more superficial.

It's a friendly-type distance; I feel that I have a superficial relationship with her. I don't feel like I'm getting into anything deep. I don't want to share my emotions with her. I don't want her to know when I'm happy, when I'm sad, because she's so concerned about it—that's why I don't want her to know. Also, she seems so omnipresent.

It's much better when you see each other less frequently. Holidays are always strange, so literally the month of January I don't see my mother. Our relationship benefits from lack of frequency. But we have a good relationship. I feel like she feels freer in talking to me now. I still feel quite guarded and often nervous. I can deal with my mother very well, and I have for a good many years. Even as a young child I could push the right buttons on her.

Her thing was, you hire a maid, and you get your mother-in-law, and you buy a house with a yard and push the kid out the door. There was not a whole lot going on between us. The raising—it just wasn't there. The conversations—they weren't there. I picked up on that real young, and I don't expect it anymore.

I remember when I was 18, my mother was sitting and hemming a dress for me, and she didn't seem to resent it. And I remember crying and thinking that my mother hadn't done anything for me without my feeling that she resented it for five years.

My mother and I were pretty much at odds, I would say. She didn't seem to have a lot of affection for me personally. I remember one time, sitting on the stairs and listening to my parents fight, and my mother, as part of her divorce threat, said, "I'll take Steve and Madeline, and you take Fran and Robert"—that's me and my older brother. And I thought, "Well, thanks a lot. Just sign me away. What's wrong with me that you don't want me?"

When I was about eight months old, my mother had an operation. I don't know what it was because she would never talk about it, but it had something to do with reproduction and it probably was the result of her pregnancy with me. I was sent to live with my aunt and uncle for two or three months. She stopped nursing me then. A few weeks after the operation, she brought my brother and sister home, but I stayed because I was an infant. . . . Maybe rejection started then. I've always tried to find out what was wrong with me, so I sort of attached myself to that, thinking that maybe the tie between my aunt and me, which hurt her feelings and maybe made her jealous, was the reason, thinking, "Maybe that's why she doesn't like me. It's not my fault and it's not fair, but maybe that's it."

Many daughters want little to do with their mothers beyond the basic social requirements—which we often feel we cannot escape, but a substantial number want to take care of their mothers. This role reversal is a common phenomenon among the women I studied. Frequently it occurs after the daughter reaches adulthood and/or the mother reaches menopause. The daughter begins, perhaps for the first time, to feel responsible for her, to want to help her, or protect her—and, in the case of daughters who are feminists, we want to bring them with us, to raise their consciousness, to change their lives, to help them be free and strong. Some of our mothers do abdicate much of their position, relax into being taken care of; others resent the reversal, reject the caring, or are incapable of giving over the old role, especially in cases where the husband is an important figure in the mother's life.

My own mother's refusal to accept my guidance sends me into rages of frustration. As in my adolescence, I want to kill her, but now it is because *she* won't do what *I* think *she* should do. I know that I'm right; I even know I'm more experienced. She, of course, tells me not to underestimate her—which is probably what I'm doing—but the feeling persists. Moreover, when a mother finds herself (often rather suddenly) being taken care of by her daughter, she is liable to assume that the daughter feels she is incompetent—*she*, who ran the lives of all her children for years—with no help at all. We ought not to forget that the only real power most housewife-mothers ever wield is over their dependent children, and their reluctance to give up that shred of authority can be best understood by acknowledging the increasing powerlessness of women as they age.

Conversely, there are mothers who actively seek maternal behavior from their daughters, who want to live with them, spend time with them, who ask for their assistance and affection. Unfortunately, the daughters who want to care for their mothers are most often those whose mothers refuse their offers of support and/or companionship; and the mothers who seek it find daughters who want none of them. This disparity results when mothers who have not satisfied their daughter's expectations in performance of the mother role, unaware or unable to consider the daughter's bitterness, begin to solicit nurturing behavior in that same expectant manner. Essentially, these daughters are saying, "Where were you when I needed you—when *I* needed some mothering?" Few of us are capable of the forgiveness necessary in such situations.

A theme which appeared early in the interview series was that of mothers who were going through a rather early, even for this culture, physical/mental "decay" process—mothers not even 60 years old, some under 50, seemed, to themselves and their daughters, to be old, sickly, unattractive, incompetent, waiting in isolated boredom/senility/drug-induced vacuity to be done with living. Several mothers described this way are institutionalized and/or on drug maintenance "therapy," lithium being the most popular control mentioned. Some of these mothers had "gone down" after their last child (or last daughter) left home, or the husband left, some after a move to a new home, or a hysterectomy, mastectomy, or what passes for "natural" menopause in this society.[13] A few had made attempts at divorce, job-hunting or changing, even suicide, before subsiding into what their daughters see as nothingness, emptiness, or "marking time."

I think of her as being a pathetic woman. It's sad. She obviously was never given a choice.

She didn't take care of herself; she was much too involved in her kids. She didn't have a life of her own, a life away from her family.

When I talk to her, there's always a problem with one of the kids, and it's so terrible. Any time I talked to her on the phone, it was always negative, crying, complaining and depressive, and I really can't handle it. I have these memories and feelings of the years when we were close, and this just wipes me out.

My mother is depressed. She appears to be very shallow because she doesn't put much of herself out. She's real thin, like paper; that's about as far as you can see. She comes across as dull, self-centered, and very infantile.

A tragedy—I would describe her as a tragedy. I think that sums it up.

She's dull, very boring. I wouldn't be interested in knowing her if I were not her daughter. She's not interested in much.

She doesn't put anything of herself in what she does. She's just a puppet, and the strings are being pulled by images of "them." There's not much life in her.

She's sort of sad, not very together, real nervous. She's always trying to please other people, to be proper. Very sad.

My mother's been so out of it that it's easy for me to see—a pretty classic case. I always called my mother to tell her things—what was going on. I was her contact for things outside the house, politics, murders, neighborhood events, whatever. I would shop for her and have things sent to her. When she moved away my brother and I packed up everything for her, moved her, fixed up her house, etc. When she was deciding to live down south, I told here she could come and live close to me, here in the city. I would help her get re-established, and do everything I could, and help her out financially. But if she decided to do down there, I wasn't going to come and see her, and I didn't want to hear about it. She was at a turning point, and I was going to back her up if she decided to hold her ground. She had always threatened to leave my father, but it was always at some point in the future. Finally the thing she said she would never do, move down to this extremely rural poor area of the south where my father came from—that's what she chose to do. When the time came to choose, she went down there, and she's been there ever since. When I talk to her now, it's just a matter of hearing her complaints. She takes a lot of pills, uppers, downers—and lots of times she doesn't make any sense; she's just out of it. I feel great pity for her; I really do.

These mothers are the most obvious victims of a society which devalues women at all times, but utterly rejects them when they no longer can fill the narrow role defined as desirable for females: child bearing and raising, serving as a sexual receptacle for men. Maturity, wisdom and experience are not values attached to women past 45 (if any age). Some of their daughters attempt to politicize mothers, bully them, shame them, or beg them to break out. But even many of these daughters have given up, though we still feel guilt at not being able to rescue our mothers, to keep them with us.

I need to take care of her some, teach her some stuff. Sometimes when she's feeling bad, she'll call me up and I'll do a counseling thing with her. One of the people that lives in my house said to me once, "You really surprise me when you talk to your mother. I expected that she would be able to push you around, and it's almost the reverse, because you become the parent and she is the child." I'm doing some parenting on her now because she really needs it.

I don't want anything from my mother because very early I realized that she couldn't give it or was unwilling to give it. I am concerned about her. She's like a tragic figure really. I call her up and write her letters. She looks like she's been institutionalized for years.

One reason my mother and I had so many difficulties was that when I got older, rather than just accepting what she gave me, I wanted to start giving back. I was afraid, though. I would lie; I felt like I had to protect her. I just felt like she couldn't understand—what I would say to her, or what I was doing. I had to keep that hidden to protect her.

I was real excited when I started getting into things I believed in. I started trying to free my mother. (laugh) To show her the light, you know. I would send her books to read for years. Now, suddenly, everything's changed. She has cataracts and she can't see well. She's afraid to have the operation, for fear she'll go blind. So she just sits in the house. And she just had a hysterectomy. It's been a long time since we talked, and I think I'm losing the battle. She was really coming along. It looks to me like she's just giving up. I feel like I need to get hold of her. I'd need to be there, to really help her. The only support she gets is from my father, and you can just imagine that: he'll say things like, "I'll take care of you" and "you're still the most beautiful woman." So she's just like a doll, that sits there. She needs to get up and walk.

There are others of us who give up after years of struggle, bitter from years of frustrated love and resenting our mothers still; we turn away from those mothers, freeze them out— having been ripped off one time too many, having been sucked dry and/or double-crossed by a mother who cannot dare to stop playing the old games, who cannot imagine or understand any other way to operate.

Our relationship has always been bad. I've spent the time trying to get from her what I never got, and living in rage and hatred of her because I couldn't get it. It's better now because I won't let her trap me, but I have some sadness, and even compassion for her. Nonetheless, I do not want to see her; I do not enjoy being with her.

There is no relationship. I always wanted to have it, and I guess I used to try, but I felt no matter what I did or how hard I tried, it just didn't work. I've felt the most comfortable just not seeing her because when we're together we don't get along. If she were anyone else besides my mother, I surely would never see her.

The thing with my mom is that a lot of times you would say something to her completely innocently, and then she would use it against you at a later date, distort it, so it sounded like you were doing something wrong; so I think all of us have learned not to tell her anything really important.

I wanted a sister relationship with my mother. Three years ago when I was writing a lot of poetry, I would write her poetry. I wanted to discuss my relationships with men and my trials with my children, but my mother would shut off at certain points, and not want to go any further—either because she didn't understand or didn't want to. So it was too painful, my opening up to her and getting no response. . . . I think about her a lot; she needs a lot right now. I wrote her a letter saying that if she was feeling terrible, and things weren't going well in her life, I would like it if she would write to me, and I could write to her about my life. I got back a letter that so-and-so did something at the church bazaar, so evidently she didn't want to go into that.

The way I found to resolve my problem, the way I can handle my mother best, is to have as little contact with her as possible.

It came to the point where I said, "I can't let you do this to me anymore. You're mean. You're cruel. You're telling me that my friends are no good; you're calling me names, being nasty. If I were to say that I love you, you'd say you've had nothing but hatred from me all my life. I can no longer talk to you about anything I have not spoken to her since then. I can't discuss anything with her until she treats me with respect, as an adult. I cried a little on the phone, which upset me because I wanted to be strong and stubborn and removed. But I wasn't. The phone rang after that and I thought it would be her, but it wasn't.

She doesn't even listen. It's so funny. I would start talking, and my mother has this filtering agent in her head—if a word comes in that she can deal with, then she'll ask. Then she said to me yesterday, "You don't think your mother cares about you."

I just started realizing that whenever I talked to her I had to talk about what she wanted to talk about. And when I wanted to tell her something she wasn't particularly interested in, she didn't want to hear me. I became extremely critical of her, though I was never able to tell her so. Her complaint is that I'm very secretive, that I don't tell her things about my life. So I pointed out that when I'd tell her she didn't listen. She said, "Oh, that's not true." She's always got an excuse.

And there are the daughters alluded to earlier in this chapter, who say their mothers were *always* incompetent; that because of alcoholism, immaturity, prolonged physical or mental illness, numerous pregnancies, they had to reverse the roles of mother and daughter.

Most of the time, as I was growing up, I resented her explanation of why she wasn't giving me things I need from her as a mother. Her explanation was, "I've got to let you go. You have to do things for yourself." I worked from the time I was 13 years old, and used to give her taxi money so she could run around. It pissed me off. I never got a chance to be a kid.

My mother can't take care of me. I never felt she was competent to do anything for me; I had to put that part in by myself; I had to take care of myself.

When it came to real serious heavy stuff she was not capable of dealing with it. I think there is a lot of child in her, and a lot of adult things that should have been natural for her, she couldn't do. I felt many times in my life that I was my mother's mother, and I've heard my other sisters say that, too.

She wants to be superdependent on me; she wants to be a child of mine. I like to visit her and talk to her because she's still not crazy; she's lucid. But I couldn't handle the dependency. She liked the idea of my divorce because she thought that she would come live with me, that I would support her now. When I got into medical school at the U. of C. one of her friends told her I would be rich, so she became like an octopus. It was just the way she used to approach men—grab one who was going to make a good living. She did it with me; it was scary.

My mother believed she didn't know how to teach me. She was relieved when I would learn stuff on my own and didn't ask her a whole lot. I always got the feeling from her that she thought I was smarter than she was, more competent, and I could figure it out better than she had. I felt she was childish, very immature. When I was about 13 it occurred to me that I was already older than she was, but I didn't feel any confidence in myself and it scared the shit out of me.

My mother moved here, in part, because I was the rock. We were to be close and I would take care of her. I still get stuffed in sometimes to a part that says, "She's incapable; she needs looking after." She really sets me up for that. At least now I know this, and can see it clearly—sometimes I buy into it, and sometimes I don't—but I can see to make the decision.

My mother is so insecure that I felt I had another child to take care of. She never really had to take care of anybody. She didn't take care of her parents because she had left home. She didn't have any younger brothers or sisters. She was the youngest. She didn't take care of us children. When her husband was sick, his two sisters came to take care of him. When he went to the hospital, I went with him. So she never really took care of anybody; she doesn't understand what it means to have that responsibility.

The year between my finishing high school and going to college, my mother was pregnant. She was having a lot of trouble with this pregnancy, so I stayed home and took care of the family. She was bedridden the whole time. She confided in me that there had been a lot of bleeding. I examined her and saw that there was tissue in the discharge, so I insisted that she go to the doctor. It turned out that the fetus had died three months previously. She had actually known this, but she wanted to have this baby so bad that she hadn't done anything about it. So she had a D. and C. to get rid of all this dead tissue—and that all happened right before I left for college.

Most of these daughters carry resentment of the forced role reversal more heavily than any other sense of their mothers. Not only have they had to mother their mothers, but themselves, and often siblings and their fathers as well, performing the physical and emotional tasks of a married adult woman with children when they were themselves yet girls. As a result of these requirements, they were never allowed to be daughters in the usual way. There was no mother to comfort, to teach them, to pattern after. These women were often bitter in their interviews; those who were feminists or were trying to understand the pressures on their mothers which caused them to abdicate the maternal role, had great difficulty putting aside their hostility. Some had adopted an indulgent parental tone; others spoke as therapists, discussing their mothers as "cases"; a few dealt with the situation humorously.

They felt that their mothers' behavior was so undesirable, so inappropriate, that they often were contemptuous of, or disliked their mothers on this basis alone—even if they otherwise found their mothers to be intelligent and sensitive women. For a mother not to mother, in the traditional way—

for whatever reason—is still perceived as a crime against nature, if not against society, and the punishment, of course, is that the daughter, in her own pain and loss, returns no love to her unnatural mother. Given the patriarchal definition of motherhood, wherein each individual woman must be all-in-all to her children, carry the weight of their lives—often carrying guilt and blame as well—into their adulthood, it is no wonder that some of our mothers prove "incompetent," find no help when they seek it, and "fail" at mothering.

When daughters are initiators of role reversal,* more often than not, they are rejected. When mothers initiate, though some daughters will refuse outright, most will accept the change on some level, if not entirely, and will even consider it the natural turn of events.

After I got married things kind of switched. She started calling me a lot and I started to have to take care of her. She called me about her problems. When her sister died, I was the only one who could be with her; she said "You're the one who will give me the most comfort." I figured at that moment that the reversed relationship was established.

I remained physically close to my mother when she became ill, and there was a kind of role reversal, when the verbal communication was gone or confused—that kind of contact where I could touch her hand, or brush her hair, or put a hand on the cheek.

When she was very old and I took care of her, she became like a child. She was very small and very lonely even though we were all around. I remember I would walk with her and felt I was bigger than she was. I don't know if I really was. We would walk holding hands.

I gave my mother information. She had these beliefs like you

*That is, see themselves as the initiators; this is taken from the daughters' viewpoint and my interpretation of interviews.

shouldn't take a bath when you have your period, so I taught her and gave her books on anatomy. She really didn't know anything.

When I was about 15, my mother went through a breakdown. She was then more childlike and I was more maternal, and that has continued.

The last time I was with her, I felt like her mother. Since the time she's been on lithium and has been identified as depressive, I have been feeling a lot more secure about myself. I felt like I was being parental to her.

I am one of those daughters who tries alternately to cajole or coerce my mother into feminist consciousness, to drag her, kicking and screaming, into freedom. An examination of her life in the harsh Chicago winter of 1976–77 really alarmed me: a middle class Jewish woman in her sixties who hadn't worked outside of her home for more than thirty years, her children long ago grown and gone, her husband at home, she began to "get sick." Every month, if not more often, she'd spend three days to a week in bed, with some symptoms of a cold. Her hands, arms and one shoulder suffered pain and stiffness. She would never really get over the illness, remain in a weakened state, and "get sick" again. I was frightened; I saw this illness as the physical representation of the weakness of my mother's spirit, her body finally manifesting the abuse she'd absorbed as a middle-aged housewife, the emptiness of days of "going to lunch," shopping, playing bridge.

One day, when I visited her as she lay in bed looking particularly frail, smaller and lighter than she ought, we talked about alternatives to the life she was living. She told me about a friend of hers who'd taken a psychology class at a local college. She said her friend had been bored, found the class silly, and had been uncomfortable because all the students were so much younger than she. This latter made sense to me, and I could certainly understand being bored in a classroom. But I was puzzled about the silliness. The example she gave was this: The instructor had asked each person in the class to name an animal they'd like to be, if they could choose. My mother's friend, and my mother, thought this was nonsense. I disagreed and told her that I'd done it myself, more than once, and had always chosen to be a dolphin. So I said, "Come on, Ma, think about it—what animal *would* you be, if you could?" She thought for a time and said, "I'd like to be that big yellow spotted cat, you know, the one that runs faster than all the others."

I was so unprepared for this revelation that I could only cry, cry for the contrast between the bedridden woman and the golden cat. My mother the martyr, a woman who put her husband and children before her from the day of her marriage, would be a cheetah, racing over the African savannah. It is for such dreams as this that we desire our mothers' freedom.

The women's movement has created two posters which treat the subject of this chapter: the first pictures a crouching woman, with the words, "I am a woman giving birth to myself."[14] If that is what we are to do, if we must now create ourselves entire, what of our mothers? Are they to be rejected? Are they irrelevant in this era of self-nurturing, wherein a sisterhood of the spirit and body replace motherhood? The second poster suggests an answer: "Our mothers are our sisters," it says, picturing a smiling mother/daughter pair.[15] Indeed, if we aren't *mama* and *little girl* anymore, and we seem not to be friends, if a role reversal is clumsy or incomplete, what are we? In this time, when both institutions and role structures are crumbling, when possibility is a frighteningly vast space, what will we do with this relationship that has lasted beyond its socially defined purpose? Mutual mothering can replace the one-way dependent arrangement that suits only babies and small children. Mother/daughter sisterhood is the consciousness we must seek, to make this basic woman bond loving and fruitful, powerful and deep as once it was.

2
Mothers As Teachers:
We Learn To Be Women

Mother, because you never spoke to me
I go my life, do I, searching in women's faces
the lost word, a word in the shape of a breast?
                                    —MURIEL RUKEYSER

            I learned from you
            to define myself
            through your denials.
                                    —AUDRE LORD

Oh, darling, let your body in,
let it tie you in,
in comfort.
What I want to say . . .
is that women are born twice.
. . .
What I want to say . . .
is that there is nothing in your body that lies.
. . .
I'm here, that somebody else,
an old tree in the background.

                                    —ANNE SEXTON

We learn how to be women from our mothers. They teach us, consciously and unconsciously, what women are. However, our mothers give us very little of the information we come to feel we need, to function as adults. Indeed, most of them do give us some instruction in cooking and cleaning; many of them tell us what equipment we need to deal with menstruation, and great numbers of our mothers advise us in the manner and behavior proper for young girls and women.

35

But we say our mothers never seem to tell us what we really want to know; they rarely tell us the actual details of their (and our) bodies' development, sexuality, schooling, pregnancy and childbirth, marriage and motherhood, seeking and holding jobs, relations with other women, or with men. We say that they don't talk to us about the world, or tell us how to make our lives.

My mother never taught me how to love other people, the most important things you need to know, how to feel good about yourself.

Absolutely not. For one thing, the professions—I had no idea what people did. There was nothing in what she taught me that said you could do this or that—you could be a chemist. I didn't even know women did those things; in a small town you don't know that. I mean, women don't work.

I feel very unprepared to face the world, especially the world I'm facing now—the business world. She probably thought she was preparing me very well; even now she says thing like, "I know you can do it, Tony; have faith." Basically all she said was to have faith, keep the faith and everything will be all right. Giving me that, she feels I can do anything, which may be true, but it's not my idea of giving me a practical sense of what is happening in the world and what I need to do.

She didn't tell me anything. I was completely unprepared for life.

In some instances, the reason for their silence is their own ignorance, compounded by inexperience, shame and discomfort. Generally, however, they seem *not to remember* the painful, frustrating aspects of their living as women. In their struggle, they have lost sight of their doubts and desires, and so present to us the apparent facts of their lives as if that were all there was to see. They've learned to glorify the minimal place women occupy, and offer us sorry vanities or bitterness in place of the information we seek.

There is a forgetting process, subtle and frightening, that

takes place in women's lives. As our bodies weaken, and "forget" that they once could run and climb, so our minds and spirits forget that they were once elastic; that they, however briefly or sporadically, stretched beyond the circumspection of "woman's place." In that forgetting, our mothers lie to us. When describing their lives to girls, to younger women, to daughters, even to each other, the mothers lie. They make the roles they fill seem to be what they had aspired to; they act and speak as if the constriction of marriage and motherhood is what they dreamed of and reached for as they grew.

I always felt she wasn't satisfied with her life because the things she would share with me were a lot of things in her past. She was a professional woman, and she always used to tell me about the wardrobe she had then. I remember she had a dress that was violet, and cosmetic powder that she had specially ground—it was violet color and it smelled like violets—left over from the days when she really looked after herself. I think she was still longing for that independence. She gave up her profession until all the kids were in college, but even now she doesn't work so that she can be available to my father, you know, to travel when he wants to. But she spent all her time telling me that the only thing she loved was being a wife and mother. She never admitted to not liking her life.

Of course there are some who do not forget, but they are relatively few. Those few women who have the conscious desire and strength to break the pattern have been written off as aberrations—negative models, dire warnings to daughters, women who've made dangerous, damaging choices.* Such women may mother us all; we may look to them as blacks do Harriet Tubman, as Jews do those who fought in the Warsaw ghetto—signs that the oppressed state is not native to us, despite the repetition of our teachings. We badly need such signs, for what mothers teach unconsciously, by living their lives bound and constrained, is learned more quickly and

---

*Aphra Behn, Emma Goldman, etc.

internalized more deeply than any words spoken in regret or desperation.

Doris Lessing describes the forgetting in *Martha Quest* and *A Proper Marriage*. When Martha marries and bears a daughter, both her marriage and her motherhood are against her will, though she is not actually forced to go through with either. Rather she does so out of this forgetting, a turning under and burying of her feelings and aspirations, a kind of surrender to the inexorable social forces she can barely feel or see: "somewhere at the back of her mind was the belief that she would never get married, there would be time to change her mind later."[1] Later, "she could free herself, she need not marry him; at the same time she knew quite well she would marry him; she could not help it; she was being dragged towards it, whether she liked it or not."[2] A few days after her wedding, Martha is struck by an "uncomfortable memory." It is of her friend Stella, "roaring with laughter as she told the story . . . of how she had, a day after her wedding, run back to her mother, because she had decided she didn't want to be married at all . . . after some months of marriage, it seemed that Stella found this mood nothing but a joke."[3] Martha's own brief escape attempt is recounted to her husband as an amusing anecdote, "Because, as everyone knows, we girls go through these moments of not wanting to be married."[4]

We may not all have known as well as Martha Quest that we did not wish to marry, but we all knew something, something we then forgot. I, for instance, cannot recall consciously wishing not to marry; but I chose my husband and arranged my marriage, at the age of 21, with a cold-blooded determination based upon my understanding of the fact that I must marry, that I had this young man already under obligation, that he was suitable, and that finding another one might be difficult or even impossible.* These considerations were in no way modified by my very clear sense that he did not want to

---

*I did not understand then, as Ann Landers says, that *anyone* can get married. You just have to want it badly enough.

marry me; that, in fact, he'd rather have hitch-hiked around
Europe that summer; that he was attracted to another young
woman. Upon being married, upon setting up an appropriate
little apartment, I forgot all of this; I believed myself to be "in
love" with my husband; so much so that, four years later when
our marriage was in obvious trouble, I couldn't see what
would become of me if he "shouldn't love me anymore"—I
had forgotten the circumstances of my marriage and the basis
of the relationship. It was not until four more years had
passed that I remembered just how I had gotten married, what
the marriage was for, and what my feelings about my husband
had been.

The forgetting process is abetted by the constant presenta-
tion and reinforcement within the culture of ideas and
feelings women are supposed and expected to have. Daughters learn from early childhood what we should dream and
desire, and how we ought to behave—much of this in
opposition to what we actually feel and think. Long before we
are formally schooled, we learn how and what to be from fairy
tales. With the happy exception of such contemporary
feminist books as *Selene* or *Mi Mamá, La Cartera*, children's
literature remains as it has been for hundreds of years. The
classic fairy tales are told and re-told; they are abridged,
modified, cartooned, even televised, but retain all their basic
elements.* "They delineate the roles, interactions, and values
which are available to us."[5] Fairy tales teach us, as our
mothers read aloud of Snow White, Rapunzel, Sleeping
Beauty and Cinderella, that good daughters are "charac-
terized by passivity, beauty, innocence, and *victimization....*
They never think, act, initiate, confront, resist, challenge,

*The irony of the "classics" being patriarchalized versions of ancient
myths is, unfortunately, lost on small children, who have no idea of
the matriarchal justice of Medea's actions (*Woman's Evolution*,
Evelyn Reed. New York: Pathfinder Press, 1975, p. 449.), the loss of
glory that the three Graiae have suffered (*The Blue Fairy Book*, ed.
Andrew Lang. New York: Dover, 1965, pp. 186–87.), or even that the
Gorgons once were Graces, until they ran afoul of the new order.

feel, care, or question. Sometimes they are forced to do housework."[6]*

Beyond the fairy tales, the good little rabbits and the maternal Kanga of our early childhood, we find magazines, comic books, newspapers, T.V. and the movies—all filled with either no women at all, or women in the same position as in the fairy tales. And, beyond all of this, we find our mothers, reinforcing the now-traditional lesson.

She said a woman shouldn't challenge men; that was very heavy. One shouldn't even challenge her friends. You shouldn't tell your problems to other people. Mustn't wash your dirty linen in public. You must always smile, be clean, look pretty. When I got married she said never to go to bed on a quarrel, that 90 percent of marriage was the woman's. She makes it work. If you're angry, don't fight or confront but go to your room or take a walk.

The message I always got from my mother was that there are certain things you have to do because they *do it or* they *think you should. Lots of shoulds and theys—the public, outside people. She just seemed to be most concerned about what other people thought and that's what I had to be concerned about too. Once she wouldn't go downtown with me because I was wearing jeans with a hole in the back of the thigh and she refused to be seen with me.*

Be nice. One of the most important compliments anyone could pay her about me was that I was pretty or that I was a nice girl. That was real important. It didn't matter too much

*And what must our mothers feel, reading to us of nightmare witches and evil fairies, mothers who abandon their children in the forest, queens who send their princess-daughters off to marry bears, gnomes and strange men, or bargain them away for trinkets? Perhaps for biological mothers it is easy enough to feel separate from these women, to feel, "I am not like this; I love my daughter." But for those who have the bad luck to *be* step-mothers, like my own mother, the going is really rough. Wicked stepmother—what a rap to beat.

*about my grades. In Catholic schools there's a whole deal
about moral conduct, spirit and so on, and you get grades in
that. It was most important that my conduct grade be an
acceptable grade. Be nice.*

The forgetting process is furthered by our fear of being
discovered to be abnormal: that is, not holding the pre-
scribed ideas, perhaps even embodying some aspects of the
witch, now known as a "bitch."[7] We anticipate the reckoning
that surely follows such a discovery—condemnation and
ostracism. Our mothers not only have forgotten, but must
consciously quash any inclination to tell us the fragments
they do remember.

A friend of mine recently convened a Bodies class* at a small
suburban college. One young woman in the group said that
her husband wanted her to get pregnant, to quit her job. She
said she was afraid, wasn't ready, didn't like being around
people who had children; she'd gone off the pill, but gone
back on again despite its dangers, so she wouldn't be
vulnerable to her husband's urgings. A mother of four small
children said to her, "Oh, go ahead; do it. It's wonderful;
you'll love it. I love my kids." The convenor began to present
"the other side," so that this speech would not be the final
word on motherhood in the class discussion. Then a 27-year-
old mother of one small child began to speak of her growing
understanding that she probably shouldn't have had the child
she did, and that, despite her husband's strong opposition,
she would not have more children. She said that she
sometimes felt selfish and that many of her friends even *told*
her she was selfish, but, nonetheless, she didn't *want* to
mother more children. Many women in the group were
shocked at her straightforward admissions; more and more of
them began to speak. Another woman in the group said, "I
have two children; I'm tired all the time; my husband doesn't

*A seminar in which women discuss female anatomy and physiology,
contraception and abortion, nutrition, childbirth, rape, aging, sexuality, V.D., etc.

help me. Sometimes I wish I hadn't had any children."
Whereupon the mother of four again spoke, to say that her
previous statement had not been true. "I'm tired and unhappy
a lot of the time; I'm exhausted. I have no time for myself; I
wish I hadn't had the last one or two of my children." As she
spoke, it was clear that this revelation was as much a surprise
to her as it was to the group. Clearly she was enlightened; she
had never before considered thinking or speaking on this
subject in this manner—frankly and openly. She was very
emotional, struck deeply at this understanding of herself. Her
initial lie, which was a learned reflex, would have been left to
stand were it not for one woman who began the truth-telling,
and the sense of support in the class, where a woman could tell
her feelings about her own motherhood without risking
severe, painful criticism. Our mothers have almost never had
that luxury. They have had to uphold their lies, even—
perhaps especially—in their most intimate relationships,
with sisters, mothers, and of course, daughters.

Women lie, too, because we cannot face the truth. What if
we mothers acknowledged that we don't want the children we
already have? What happens when we come to understand
that we've been coerced into maternity? When wives realize
that marriage is unhealthy for us,[8] that we are constrained in
body and spirit? What do we do then? Most of us take the
blame for our blind acceptance—we know that we must be
weak, stupid, easily led—else how could we have been so
duped? This internalization of guilt and blame further
prevents us from telling the truth. How can our mothers
admit they were such fools? If we, their daughters, point out to
them that they've been trapped, they certainly cannot allow
themselves to see. If we don't live out the female role as they
have, then we are rejecting what they have accepted; we are
rejecting them.

Often our mothers refuse to acknowledge the value of our
struggle to be independent. Having felt the terrible realization
that they were robbed, tricked, they know they never meant to
give up their dreams. Now, as we grow away from them, they
cannot even look back and find the moment in which they

knew that they must forget. Layers of shadow, the lies of years, obscure the moment as they do the truth. When they teach us about woman's role, this understanding is a source of contradiction and confusion.

She was so molded into this woman role that it was her whole life, doing things that women were supposed to do even though it was narrow and she was terribly frustrated. If we didn't do it too, my sister and I, then she didn't have to do it either. Who the hell wants to look at that?

Most of our mothers gave us a blurry picture of motherhood. Though almost all of them were present as examples while we grew up, only 59 percent of the mothers studied actually discussed mothering with their daughters. A small number of these praised motherhood, described it as pleasurable, recommended it to their daughters. The rest of them imparted a sense of acceptance at best, some with resignation, some with humor, some with bitterness. They either spoke against motherhood or demonstrated their unhappiness and frustration to such an extent that we readily took their meaning. But open criticism was very rare; our mothers knew the rules.

Motherhood was very near and dear to her. We were never given the impression that at any time in our lives we had been a burden to her. She has told us over and over again, from the time I can remember up until the time I left her yesterday, that we had been nothing but a source of joy.

She didn't talk about motherhood except to say that she couldn't wait until we had kids so she could laugh.

She didn't say anything other than how hard it is. She did say it was hard to be a mother. She's right about a lot of things.

I remember my mother telling me at the time I was pregnant that it was very difficult. When I was in labor she kept saying to me, "If you want to scream or hang onto me, go ahead." I didn't want to, and that's all I remember. I never associated my having children with her having children.

I was told that your life really begins when you have children; you'll wonder how you ever survived without children—I remember that phrase. And when I had my son and my life pretty much ended, I thought, what was she talking about? I was waiting for this wonderful experience.

She said that motherhood was so fulfilling. My mother, even today, would give you the story that the most important thing in her life is her children, you know, but there isn't one of her children who believe that.

She always used to say that she loved children, she couldn't wait to have children, and then she did have them and she regretted it, regretted having them. She said, "If I had it to do over again, I would never have children."

She talked to me frequently about motherhood, because I was doing a lot of the raising of her seven kids. And she always made it seem real good, until she had the last child. Then she said, "Don't ever have any kids . . . don't have any." I think she wanted to save me from all of it. Now she's back telling me she wants a grandchild; when am I going to give her a grandchild? I think she thought that being a mother was the most important thing in her life. And you know, that's what she expected of her life.

Frequently, our mothers have lied in the mistaken belief that we should be shielded, sheltered, protected. Some keep us ignorant and dependent, even set out to "break" us, like ponies, of our willfulness and pride. Once they've made nice girls of us, dutiful daughters, we are to marry, and, certainly, most of us do—65 percent of the daughters in the study had been married once; 13 percent more than once. Fifty-eight percent of our mothers never talked to us specifically about marriage, but were preparing us for it all along. After all, who is the beneficiary of all this training, this creation of obedient pretty things? To be sure, it is our husbands, not our mothers. They have to pack us off. (Our mothers do receive positive sanction for producing and socializing us, but this must be hollow satisfaction when the fruits of their labor are handed over to strangers.)

She really was much too kind. Her gentleness made it very difficult for me when I became older, to put up with the knocks that you get.

She thought that what she was telling me in my early years protected me, that there were bad things that I didn't have to know, and the right, I mean the RIGHT—all capital letters, big lights on—way to raise a daughter was to shelter and protect her from everything.

Thus, our mothers foster and perpetuate our role-playing rather than nurture our woman-selves. Yet, denied their birthright and oppressed into the wife-mother role, they still try to give us the tools we need to survive—as in any slave culture, we learn our own style of shuffle and grin.[9] We learn what is expected of us; our mothers point out the punishment for improper deportment: no husband-protector, financial insecurity, social ostracism, imprisonment in mental hospitals. Women have built up, in defense, a sub-culture ("sub" in the sense of hidden, underneath) which instructs and protects its own, within the boundaries of the general, male culture; in "a male-dominated society, . . . women condition their daughters toward behavior that is 'safe' and therefore unchallenging to male domination."[10] Basic to the education of oppressed peoples is learning how to get by, get around, get over and get along with the oppressor. At the same time that our mothers made it clear that men are the masters, they teach us that therefore we cannot be honest and forthright with men, but must manipulate and scheme to make our way; so our mothers demonstrate their contempt for men.

When I asked daughters if their mothers talked to them about men, about relations with men, 35 percent said their mothers never discussed men with them at all; of those who did talk about men with their daughters, nearly half referred to men only in terms of sex; almost no mothers spoke to their daughters about men as companions, friends, even as actual people. Primarily, men were construed as sources of trouble and danger, or financial support. This does not mean that our mothers do not expect us to socialize with men, marry men, and bear children by them. They certainly do; the point is that men are objectified by most of our mothers, as basic requirements, prerequisites to living life as proper women.

There is just an attitude in my family, being a family of women, that men are undependable. My grandmother had a husband who drank and didn't take care of the children. My father was nice though he didn't have any responsibility, and my brother was pretty much crazy. The attitude I picked up was that men are pretty unreliable, and that women are the dependable people.

She said that men are callous, or my father was callous, and by implication other men were too. And men are irresponsible; they're like children. She always said that my father was like a child.

Can't trust men. Never trust men as far as you can throw them. Never trust men. I've been involved with a number of fellows and she dislikes all of them. Men are to be used. You just don't trust them. You never open yourself to them. You never tell them anything. That's the kind of burden we have to bear; they're just there.

Men want only one thing; watch out.

One day I came home from school crying that boys were saying nasty things, and my mother said, "Oh, boys, they're all alike. They're going to make a good girl bad and a bad girl worse."

"All they want is to take advantage of you; don't walk near a group of boys." She was real fearful of the city, but she never talked about rape. I'm sure that was one of the things she worried about. "Watch out for men behind cars; watch out for men in doorways; watch out for men. . . ."

Twenty-seven percent of our mothers openly spoke negatively about men,* and a greater number of those who did not, who even praised specific men, contradicted the apparent social value of men by the dishonest ways they taught their daughters to relate to them. We are taught to consider men brutal, insensitive, emotionally inadequate and highly needful of nurturing and pampering, requiring special handling like babies or convalescents; we are shown how to trick them, demonstrate false affection and/or sexual passion, trap them into giving us money and social security. Almost all of us are encouraged to disguise our actual appearance with cosmetics, costumes that reshape our bodies, even surgery; and because men have been schooled to appreciate the false image, these tactics are "successful" with most men.

She taught me to manipulate men. I started dating on a Saturday afternoon basis, to the show, at the age of twelve. She always made sure I had the clothing; she saw that the clothing looked right. These relationships with boys were important; she was going to make sure that I had all the intrigues. . . . Some of the political moves she taught me, as far as men were concerned, have proved to be quite valid.

She said things like, "Don't act too eager, or he'll never come back again." (laugh)

We've had several "getting a husband" discussions where I'll just sit quietly and she'll tell me—I've given up arguing. Like when I told her about beating this guy in tennis, she said, "Why did you do that?" (laugh) She gets very angry when I go out and pay my own way.

She said women should take care of men because that's what she did. I'm pretty sure she said it like this: "Find yourself a good man who will take care of you financially and you do everything else."

She said women had to be manipulative and subtle; that's how you get what you want. You don't ask for it directly. You

*Three percent of our mothers spoke negatively about women.

make him kind of think it's his idea.

She would say that you have to hold yourself back or a man would not respect you. Oh yes, come to think of it, there was a lot of Scarlet O'Hara-type advice. (laugh) You know, tricks, tricks.

She told me that men like petite women and men like sickly women, so that the men can be stronger and the women can depend on them.

I am not suggesting either that our mothers be blamed for this pattern of instruction or that the contempt implicit in this behavior lessens our oppression. We suffer grievously as women, in our bodies and our minds, from relating to men this way.* Such behavior does not allow for respect or affection for men; it is natural that we should learn contempt for those who oppress us. What is unnatural, though "normal," is that we should marry them.

We are to follow the plot of Beauty and the Beast. We learn that men, strangers, are dangerous and that we should fear and avoid them. But for each of us there is one beast among them who will become a prince, in magical transformation caused by our love, called marriage.

She told me that men were dirty, filthy animals. "Stay away from them because they are filthy beasts; if anyone comes near you, you just tell me. Just stay away from them. When the time comes, you'll get married and have a husband. Then you do whatever your husband tells you.

It is not our mothers, however, who teach us to expect the magic. They insist that we marry, but almost none of them tell us that marriage is romance. Fairy tales, love comics, magazines and movies have done that job for several decades.

*A very small number of mothers did give their daughters advice contrary to this majority; "She would say, strive to be independent: you can make it without a man."

It is as if our mothers, accepting the task of socializing us into our subordinate position, have rebelled at this one lie, have refused, have been unable to teach us that kissing a toad is going to give us anything more than warts. Even that most indefatigable of socially correct mothers, May Quest, is unable to deny that her daughter will be sleeping with a stranger. In a quarrel over Martha's need for a trousseau, Mrs. Quest finally says, "Well, at least you should have a nightdress." She blushes as Martha continues to argue. "'My dear child,' said her mother, 'you must. Besides, you hardly know him.'"[11]

In fact, only 43 percent of the interview mothers even talked to us about marriage as we were growing up. They talked about their own marriages, ours, and the institution of marriage itself. All but a very small number assumed we would marry, even if they condemned marriage consistently, even if their own example was disastrous. Few were entirely positive about marriage. And these few, despite their positive remarks, displayed frustration and dissatisfaction. Seventy-one percent of the daughters I interviewed had mothers who were married all through the daughter's first 15–18 years; almost all of these included marriage to the daughter's father. An additional 28 percent of the mothers had marriages which ended in divorce or death during the daughter's childhood. So, whether they spoke of marriage or not, whether or not they advised against it, our mothers were married women. No wonder they assumed we would be too.

The only thing she said was that I was definitely going to do it. It was an assumed thing.

The message was very clear that I was supposed to get married. That's how I was supposed to get along in the world. She also told me that it's just as easy to fall in love with a rich man as a poor man.

She was very concerned because I didn't get married until I was 28. She felt it was every woman's goal in life to get married. She thought that the primary thing in marriage was to get along and please your husband.

I used to say I wasn't going to get married, and she would say, "You'll change you mind. Some boy will come along and you'll fall for it."

She didn't want me to have dates with anybody who wasn't Greek. They wanted me to get a boy from a nice Greek family who had a lot of money. She planned to give me a made marriage. That kind of panicked me.

My mother gets nervous because I'm not with a man. No matter what I would do, even if I would do all of what she thinks is this crazy stuff in my life, if I was married it would be all right. She feels responsible for me because I'm not married. When I get married, then she can relax.

When I was in high school and my sister got engaged, my mother would say, "Ugh, it's the worst thing she could do. It's no bed of roses. It's going to be awful." When I got to be 23 and wasn't married, she became very positive. "Don't you ever think about getting married? Don't you want a home and children?"

Much of what we learn about marriage is not taught by our mothers, but by their marriages. For years I was unable to fight openly with my husband because, in 21 years of living with them, I had heard my parents fight only once. There were other lessons for wives demonstrated: always present a united front with your husband; never disagree with him in public, or even in the presence of your children; always present him, especially to your children, as being superior to you and everyone else; use his superior positon to escape from responsibility for your actions, opinions and decisions; assume no roles, do no chores, that are not clearly marked, "FOR WOMEN ONLY." I learned the form of an upwardly mobile Jewish middle class marriage; other women learn other forms—but we all learn to be married.

She was caught in the whole fifties thing of getting married and getting pregnant. You know, a woman gets married, so that's what she did.

There is a pattern. My mother always got the same men. She pretty much defeated her own purpose, most of her life until just recently. She was always waiting to find the man who was going to be a good husband to her and a father to her children, who would make things right, who would support her. But she always picked total losers that she ended up supporting, that beat us, that raked her emotionally over the coals. Her relationships with all of them were fairly subservient.

I never saw my mother cry and she went through some pretty bad divorces. You know they used to have this thing about how someone had to legally take the blame for ruining the marriage. And being stuck with five kids, that's nothing to laugh about. I never remember her being sad about it.

From the time I was four years old, it was horrible. They were fighting constantly, openly, screaming and saying horrible things to each other. I heard a lot of fights when I was in bed at night. Constant fighting over money which I think was a coverup for other things. When I was about nine or ten I heard them talking about a divorce; my mother wanted a divorce but my father said he would never let her go. They stayed together. I don't think they ever slept together. They didn't seem to care about each other at all. They were just living in the same house.

My mother, even when she was very tired, when my father would come home she would go to the refrigerator, get a pear and wash it and cut it and bring it to him, or bring his slippers. It was a caring way for them. It wasn't like a burden to her. She didn't feel burdened, she felt OK.

When we get married, our mothers still have teaching to do. There's the choice of the husband, the wedding itself, where and how to live, when to have babies, treatment of husband and children; all of these are part of our mothers' responsibility as our teachers. Some of us embrace this further advice and support; some of us reject it passionately. Despite daughters' resentment, mother-in-law jokes and therapists who find the root of all our problems in our mothers—however negatively society construes this phenomenon, it is assumed and accepted, on some level, that this responsibility exists, that it is part of mothering a daughter.

My mother sort of pushed me into marriage in the first place because I had been sort of having an affair with a young man and she was worried that I would become a bum, be promiscuous. So she kept urging me to marry Roger. She told me I was going to be a bum, and of course that really helped my self-confidence. She said, "You should marry Roger; if you don't get along, in five years you can get a divorce." She thought I would be safer married, because she had no confidence in me.

The whole wedding was just a joke. It was her wedding and I just came. I mean it. I walked down the aisle and that was it. I didn't feel that it was my wedding.

At first, she didn't like my husband. He helps me out and we split the housework. We do everything pretty much half and half, and she just couldn't see that. How could I leave the house without feeding my husband? How could I leave without cleaning the house?

She was real glad when I got married. She feels that I should be taken care of by Karl. She says I shouldn't say certain things that I feel, not to Karl. A wife shouldn't. She always liked him and said that he's a real man; I thought that was interesting. She was more involved in my getting married than I was. I get real strong feelings from her about what marriage is supposed to be, my position and Karl's position.

She was the one who brought up my getting married. She said, "Well, isn't it about time? I would really like to have a son-in-law." I think I did it for her, because all this time I really wanted to please my mother.

In times and places where women were respected,[12] our mothers taught us what our rights and duties were: we were tenders of the sacred flame, providers of food and shelter, priests of the Mother, warriors. Our mothers still instruct us in our womanly role. But now they have to pass on the means of survival in an alien and threatening social structure, one into which we do not naturally fit, into which we must be distorted to function "properly." Some of our mothers, victims of this same distortion, give all their energies to shaping us, righteously embracing prevailing mores. Mothers have a great investment in the success of their teachings, for we represent them to the society, and if we are not proper women, they, too, are suspect.

She said a woman should always look clean. You should always be a lady. The only toilet seats you could sit on were at home. Marshall Field's was the only place you could urinate downtown. (laugh) Your slip should never show. Always wear clean underwear. I'm really for clean underwear but it was like some heavy thing.

She judges what I wear by if I look "nice"—for other people you know, because she feels that I represent her. It's so important to her.

Other mothers, who have acknowledged that they are not proper, not themselves dutiful daughters, not filling the mother role as they ought, frequently find their daughters are the backlash that reminds them of their failure.

I'm living with this little girl, Ivy, and her mother, Myna, and we're vegetarians. Ivy wants pretty dresses and she wants television and she loves to eat steak. So sometimes Myna buys her a steak. And she goes over to a neighbor's house and watches TV. Myna says, "I'm raising a straight kid."

Any society prepares its children to perform the tasks ex-

pected of adults—the forms our mothers teach us are those of
contemporary women's roles—they are not, as we so often
assume, the specific ideas, designs, and purposes of *our*
mothers. The job of mothers is to prepare their children to
maintain society *as it is*, so they perpetuate their own
situations. Ironically part of what most middle- and working
class mothers teach their daughters is to strive for "improve-
ment," i.e., upward mobility, so the destruction of the role,
and the pain of the contradiction, is built into the process.

Mothers usually feel that daughters ought to know how to
cook and clean; most of them consciously and deliberately
teach us these skills. The lessons are rarely couched in terms of
self-maintenance; the assumption is that we will be serving a
husband and children as we perform these tasks. Some of our
mothers were reluctant to teach us how to do "women's
work," for then we might become rivals; we might perform
their tasks more effectively than they, exposing their
weaknesses. A small number of mothers in the study refrained
completely from teaching their daughters household tasks
because they wanted more for them than the wife-mother role.
Others were delighted to have the assistance their daughters
could give.

Some daughters are pleased that they weren't required to do
such work as girls, and feel their mothers did right by not
preparing them for domestic chores; some are resentful of
their lack of preparation. Yet other women resent the way in
which their mothers taught them, the attitude of superiority,
the contempt for girlish inexperience and awkwardness. My
own mother would only let me dry the dishes, never wash
them; setting and clearing the table were my jobs, cooking the
food was hers. The hierarchy of the kitchen was invariable;
though I pleaded and carried on, the greatest responsibility I
attained to was that occasionally I might stir up the gravy or
baste a holiday turkey.

*My mother would do things and I would be in the kitchen and
I would be expected to pick them up. She cooked and all of us
learned to cook by watching her. She ironed, and we all
learned to iron.*

She was a meticulous housekeeper; I can remember her saying that she didn't want to be ashamed of me. She wanted me to be a real good housekeeper; that was very important.

She is an excellent cook. She showed me how to cook. She showed me how to make potato pancakes and blintzes. She would clean and I would follow her around learning. She showed me how to juggle a lot of things at once. She's a great juggler; she could be sewing a dress and make a meal for ten people and deal with phone calls and all that shit at once.

My mother hated house cleaning and assigned tasks that my sister and I had to do.

She was consciously and deliberately instructing me in every-thing that she ever did. Everything—she would say it. If I would be wiping the dishes she would say "Let me teach you." If I would be dusting the books, "Let me teach you."

Oh yes. Housekeeping and cooking and doing the dishes right—they were to be stacked neatly, you didn't just wash them and plop them into the pan. And you stacked silverware neatly. You didn't sweep a floor by slinging the dust. You took little pushes.

She taught me to cook and sew and iron. It was very hard for her to teach me cooking and sewing because, after all, we needed her to cook our food and fix our clothes and we could do that for ourselves if we knew how. I think that was an infringement on her powers so she didn't often share. She knew this, and she did it well, and by no means was I ever going to be as good as she was at those things.

She was a good cook herself, but I cooked a lot of things better than she did, and she knew that. When I was twelve I made a pan of lasagna that turned out to be a real hit. Then all of a sudden my mother never made lasagna. Whenever we had it after that, I made it, and I think it grated on her that everybody liked it.

A major source of resentment among daughters is being drafted into childcare, mothering. Many daughters are required by family pressure to take on the role of mother while they are children themselves. Despite obvious financial or medical reasons, or sheer numbers of children, mothers (and fathers) often construe this maternalization of their daughters as training, teaching their daughters to become mothers. Rarely do mothers want to face the fact that they have pressed their daughters into service because there is simply too much work for one woman, or because the mother is working outside the home.

If I could live my life over I wouldn't have my daughter. I spent so many years changing diapers, hanging diapers out on the line when I was a girl myself. I remember once when I wanted to buy a Toni doll, my father said, "What do you need that for? We've got babies all over the place." I was 25 when I had Mora. I have these terrible dreams about getting pregnant again. I can't seem to make the decision to sterilize myself.

When I left home my basic feeling about my mother was resentment. I had to assume a lot of mother responsibilities when I was in high school, because she decided to go back to work. I had to take care of the house and the rest of the nine kids a lot of the time. I resented that. I resented that a whole lot.

Sometimes I thought I was her favorite. She was indebted to me for all that I did for her, and for her children. And she would say to me, "I can't trust the children with anyone but you," and "I'm so glad you can do this," but of course I had no choice, really.

I was responsible a lot for taking care of the younger children, making sure they took their baths at night, that they dressed right for school. I was taught to cook because otherwise, the kids wouldn't eat until very late. This was very early in my life, at the age of eight or nine.

Between eighth and tenth grade I became very resentful of my mother because I was given all these child chores. And my dad wasn't doing anything. The kids were calling me their father

for a while and I hated that. My mother and I would have
arguments about it. I told her I was afraid of hurting them
because of my resentment. She said, "You're hitting them?
I'm never going to let you take care of those kids again." Of
course it wasn't true. If she had only kept her word I would
have been real happy.

We expect that our mothers will be our source of
information about our bodies and sexuality. Despite, or
perhaps because of, the furor in the 1950s about religious
instruction and/or public schools providing "sex education,"
mothers are still supposed to be possessed of all the necessary
information and expected to deliver it to their daughters in a
positive and supportive manner. But mothers, not unlike
everyone else, are only slightly more knowledgeable and
capable than they ever were on the subjects of sexual
reproduction, basic anatomy, the menstrual cycle, sensual
pleasure, and health care for women. Thirty-seven percent of
the women I interviewed said their mothers never talked to
them about their bodies at all. Only 13 percent felt their
mothers had given them good instruction and sufficient
information. The remaining daughters received some information, much of it laced with "hygiene"—tooth-brushing
instruction and the importance of regular baths or showers.
Many mothers were uncomfortable even with this.

Body? What body?

She would say, "Oh, you know all about this," and I would
say yes because I was embarrassed. She was embarrassed to
talk about it.

I have never to this day seen my mother without clothes on.
Never. She would go into the bathroom and close the door to
change her panties. She never told me about menstruating.
I'm sure she thought all this talk was dirty.

When I wanted to know where babies come from, she said to
me, "What do you think the men have that thing in front

for?" That was the only thing she ever said and I was so embarrassed.

In the way she talked about our bodies, there was the sense that a woman's body was not nice; a woman's body was not OK to comment on. Breasts were not OK. Menstruation was certainly not OK. My God! The worst thing you could say about someone was that she had spots of blood on her clothes. I still have that icky feeling about myself.

She knew all the right things. She would walk around without clothes. On the one hand the message was that bodies and sex are OK. On the other hand she cried quite a bit when she thought I was masturbating; when I actually engaged in sexual experimentation she beat me. I was so puzzled. I didn't understand. I had been told it was nothing wrong.

When I first got married, I had trouble with sex. I was really depressed. I asked my mother about it. Her solutions were very passive, traditional-woman oriented, and that was not going to be helpful to me anymore, so I stopped asking her those questions.

When I first got my period I thought I had injured myself, but I took care of myself with rags, as we did then. My mother told me how to do that. Now, I was instructed; I could not go near freshly baked goods or touch the wine or go near the plants, so it must have been filled with horror. I didn't think it was evil, but it was pretty powerful, whatever it was.

My mother was always the source of my information. She showed me how to put a Tampax in. She did it on herself, and always answered my questions honestly. She was very up front with me.

It was a big thing waiting to get my first period. We went out and bought Kotex; I had a special place in the medicine cabinet for all the stuff for when the day would come. Finally when it did come I got to stay up late and drink coffee, and stay home from school and be grown up. She told me a lot. It was all very positive.

Much of what our mothers said to us, when they did discuss these matters, had to do with morals and virginity. Discussing sexuality in physical, biological terms is often complicated by emotional considerations, and, until recently, has been done exclusively in terms of heterosexual marriage, morality, even *duty*. Discussing sex with one's daughter almost always meant talking about men, rather than women, and specifically penis-in-vagina/male ejaculation-type sex.

It was terribly important to her that all of her daughters be virgins. Sometimes I thought she wanted us to be virgins more than she wanted us to be intelligent. I said that to her one time and she said, "Oh, no—I don't really mean that. I just think it's important."

My mother was not a sexually oriented person. She grew up in an era where sex was a dirty word. She always said that sex was like urinating or defecating, and had a place in the physical well-being, but it wasn't a plaything.

When I got into high school she talked about boys being hot and bothered all the time; I thought, "So am I." She would never admit that girls and women could be that way too.

The only thing she said was, "Don't get pregnant before you get married." That was very important to her.

She said you shouldn't let boys put their hands you-know-where. (laugh)

She said, "Don't you get into any trouble. Don't let any boy fool around with you." But who knew what the hell that meant? She never said what the trouble was.

None of the interview mothers had had the benefit of the Boston Women's Health Collective, Masters and Johnson or Mary Jane Sherfey, to say nothing of Betty Dodson. How could they? As we find our expectations unmet, we readily blame our mothers; we criticize our mothers mercilessly. We have all longed for a mother like the one in Janet Ruth Heller's poem, SACRAMENT:[13]

> Gazing at your newly rounded bosom
> And curving hips,
> Your mother smiles with pride.
>
> When you bare the red fountain
> Flowing secretly, painfully
> From the aroused womb,
>
> She embraces you and whispers,
> "This is our shared body
> And this our blood."

But how were our mothers to come to an acceptance of their bodies? Where were they to get the strength to overcome their embarrassment, to tell us—if they knew—about masturbation and orgasm, the experience of childbirth and nursing, the menses? Our mothers, most of whose shame kept them from showing their bodies even to us, many of whom have worn rags lined with discarded newspapers to catch their menstrual blood, who are not conscious of having masturbated in their youth, who had babies pulled out of their drugged bodies, who cannot remember having touched the girls and women they've loved—these women sought to be at ease in their bodies just as we do. But most of our mothers lived most of their lives after the last wave of the women's movement subsided, after 1920; there was little support or inclination for women to increase their self-knowledge.

Perhaps it is because our mothers realize that society holds *them* utterly responsible for teaching us that so many of them do not hold with the seriousness of their daughters' formal education. Throughout patriarchal history, women have been excluded from schooling, granted access to intellectual and professional training only after great struggle.[14] Our mothers have assimilated the fact that yes, now girls graduate from high school, take the B.A., M.A., and Ph.D. degrees, money and class allowing. But they continue to embrace the widely held belief that all this education is somehow "extra"; it is trimming, frosting, window-dressing. We go to school to meet the man who will make it unnecessary for us to use our training; we learn skills so we can patch up our lives should this man leave or die. At best, our education is (all together now, girls) "something to fall back on." My mind runs a continuous cartoon strip of thousands of women falling backwards onto a huge pile of nurses' uniforms, secretaries' typewriters, and teachers' clipboards.

I'm not the woman my mother raised me to be. (laugh) She says, "If this is how people turn out when they go to college then I don't want any more of my girls going to college."

She expects that I will grow up and get married. She seems to stifle anything else. My writing, she kind of laughs at that; as a hobby she thinks it's kind of funny.

She's real proud of some things I've done, but, no; she would prefer a suburban housewife sort of thing, going to church every Sunday, and with five kids.

The concept that women should want to learn because we are interested, because we think, because we want to be recognized for our ideas, or because we need training for the work we choose to do—this is hardly what one might call a popular notion in 1979. Our mothers, as they urge us to stay in school, to graduate from high school, to go to college, to enter university, are giving us what the psychologized language now terms a "double message." The urgency and passion with which some of our mothers send us off to be educated is that same drive noted among immigrant ethnic minorities in the United States in the first half of the twentieth century and among urban third world peoples in this half—to gain status in the society with "knowledge," obtain financial security through schooling. But our mothers get sidetracked, as do we; our way is not clear. College degrees don't sweep the same path for women as they do for minority men.[15] Women are to get their degrees, even their jobs, and then subside. Though women continue to push for more and higher-ranking jobs, though more women work for more years outside of domestic service and maternity, our psychic training, the teachings of our mothers, does not prepare us to do so. Our mothers do urge us to "escape," to make more of ourselves than they have been able to do, but this message is obscured in the years of feminizing, the creation of proper daughters, that is their main goal.

I think mothers don't want their daughters to make the same mistakes they did. It was a priority for me to get through high school; she felt like it was her accomplishment for me to do it.

My mother wanted me to do more with my life than she had done with hers; she felt she was stupid for not having continued her education.

I fulfilled one of her dreams—going to college. My God, she has broken her back to get me through a fantastic school. She was the one who was sweating it out, washing clothes, working two jobs; it meant so much to her.

We daughters receive the message as it is sent: we understand that it is now considered attractive, or even practical, to be educated. We see that schooling, like job-holding, is part of the contemporary social requirement list for women. What is still not being taught us is that there is value, purely, in our minds; that our minds hold great beauty. Thinking is exciting; exercising our brains, like our bodies, is required for health. Our mothers do not speak to us of such things. Intellectual excitement cannot be communicated by a woman whose mindset has been stunted into programmed responses, to be set off by the clamor of other people's needs.

About employment, then, our mothers also have said relatively little, compared to the talking they did about men, marriage, motherhood, proper behavior, housekeeping, even our bodies. Forty-three percent of the interview mothers did not do paid work in the years their daughters were growing up, though many did volunteer work, or worked for their husbands in offices and shops. This partially explains their reticence, but we may be sure their lack of personal experience in the job market did not prevent them from discussing and encouraging employment and careers with their sons. Those mothers who did work for pay, even those who held jobs with very low status (although jobs held by women are generally so defined) often enjoyed either the work they did, the being away from home and children, or the society of other workers.

She was a school nurse, a public health nurse. She needed her own money. She also wanted to get out and have her own life, without any children and husband. She liked what she did.

She worked primarily to support us. She was our sole support. She was a very self-sufficient secretary and proud of her skills.

When I was five years old she started a gift shop. She couldn't just sit home with the kids; the job was all-consuming and it gave her a real place. She is a wonderful business woman and a realist. She's crafty and clever and an actor, so it gave her an outlet for her creativity. I never thought of that before, you know.

She loved it; she abolutely loved it. She devoted her whole life to it. She was preoccupied with the school and she wanted to be highly thought of by the other teachers, the board, and the community.

My mother said one day, "I'm getting tired of just raising kids. All my life I've been raising kids." So she got a job in this real fancy hotel, in the kitchen. She stayed there until she felt they should give her a raise and they didn't, so she went to the hospital, where they gave her a better offer as the head meat cook there. I heard her say for the first time in my life, "I can spend some money without asking anybody." My dad would never let her have an umbrella or carry a purse. My mother bought herself the brightest, reddest umbrella in the store and very proudly carried it over her head.

She always worked whether she was married or not. Sometimes she didn't work as much as she wanted to, or make as much as she wanted to, but it was always assumed she would work, regardless.

My mother started her first paying job when she was 63 years old. That was after my father died. She didn't know what she could do. I said to her that she had always liked to pack things, maybe she could get a job as a packer. Somebody told her about this job at an instrument company in our neighborhood, so she went there. She was there for several years until she took her social security, and nothing ever broke that she packed. She was very proud of the work that she did because she did a good job.

Only one-third of our employed mothers expressed no pleasure or satisfaction gained from their jobs. These mothers were resentful of the difficulty, boredom, and low pay of their jobs, even if they accepted them as unavoidable and necessary. Most of them did not complain, but the drudgery of their labor was plain to their daughters. These women clearly had no choice, but frequently felt guilty about not mothering as they "should," and fostered the notion that women oughtn't to have to work, ought to be able to stay home with their children, "where they belonged." The focus was on finding a man who would marry the daughter and make enough money so she would never have to support herself or create her own life.

She always said that she really wanted to be working but she would always find stuff to complain about at every job she took, and she changed jobs frquently. She also felt guilty about working, guilty that she wasn't home.

Her attitude is that she works because she has to. She resents that. She works in an office. She hates it, has always hated it. She never gets along with any of the people in the office at any job she takes.

The jobs she did were menial jobs; she had no salable skills. She understood the position she was in; she had to make money.

She did people's washing. She was washing all the time; the machine was the rhythm of our house. Then she got a job as a

crossing guard for school children. She was out in the snow in
the middle of winter, freezing to death out there, coming back
in the middle of the day to help my father, who was sick, and
do the washing, and then back out and cross the kiddies again.

Those two-thirds of our employed mothers who enjoyed
and depended on the stimulation of their jobs did not empha-
size the positive qualities of their work. Again, as with
education, the feelings our mothers have are subordinated to,
if not overwhelmed by, the socially correct line. They present
to us a contradiction of their own reality. Moreover, there
were not many daughters of non-employed mothers who
recalled their mothers saying that perhaps they might have
gone out to work; the handful of those who did speak of it
expressed themselves so bitterly or hopelessly that the value of
meaningful work was not conveyed.

When they separated she tried to figure out a way to make her
own money, to get a divorce, but it didn't work out. It didn't
work out because my father withdrew support money and
made constant threats on her life; she had nobody to leave
three small children with. A lawyer, after talking with my
father, said to forget it, she'd have to go back to him. She was
desperate.

She keeps saying, for the last ten years, "I ought to go out and
get a job." She does beautiful sewing work. She always says, "I
could make a fortune. I should go into business." But she
never does, of course.

We daughters are often certain that our mothers have lied to
us, and, perhaps in consequence, not recognizing the
forgetting mechanism, all of us lie to our mothers.
Frequently, not liking the realization that we don't deal in
truth, we say we're "leaving things out," as if that were not
dishonest and misleading, as if our motives, expressed as
being for our mothers' good—"to protect her," erased the lie;
as if we didn't, just like our mothers, lie out of habit, fear,
insecurity, lack of consciousness, inability to take ourselves

seriously, or to take our lives into our own hands. Most of us who say we lie to protect our mothers are afraid of the struggle that would ensue if the truth were told. Much of this shielding is learned from mothers who practiced the same dissembling when we were small, and demonstrates the same lack of respect, in that neither we nor our mothers feel that the other is competent to receive truth.

No, I don't tell her the truth; I shelter her a lot. When I have trouble with Joe, with the kids, or with myself, when I do terrible things because of my temper—it has been my policy since I went away from her to not tell her when something is real bad. I would just rather not hurt her. I don't see the point of it.

It's not that I don't tell her the truth; I just don't tell her everything. My reasoning is that she doesn't always understand. She would be unhappy if she knew, and she might be hurt or she would worry about something she would have no control over.

I lie to avoid hurting her because I do feel kind of protective still. If she had remarried that would have taken it off my shoulders. It's almost like I'm trying to take over the things that a husband or father should do for her. I know my daughter Carol has felt that way about me, very protective. She felt guilty because she couldn't do more.

My mother wanted me to be a virgin. She knew I wasn't but she pretended I was. I lied to her and she knew I was lying. I always knew when my mother wanted me to lie.

Because my mother lies, I try not to. Now I won't say that I don't. I will make up a little story so it's not exactly a lie, but it's the truth in kind of a different way. My kids will tell you that I don't lie.

In the interviewing, many daughters lied to me. The forgetting process was evident in these situations, especially with women older than forty or fifty, who have had a longer

time over which to both forget and maintain the habit of forgetting. One woman of 59, whose 30-year-old daughter I also
interviewed, said repeatedly that her daughter, all of her
children, in fact, had afforded her "nothing but joy" throughout their years together. In the course of the interview, she
quoted her mother as saying the same words to her about their
relationship. When the interview was done, and we sat
together and talked without the tape recorder, it was
immediately revealed that she certainly had experienced the
usual measure of anxiety and pain from her children—for
instance, two of them had gone through divorce in the last few
years. That she neglected to discuss any of the attendant
struggle, even when she talked about her daughter's current
life and work, is a clear example of this phenomenon. I often
felt, in the presence of these women, that they couldn't speak
of the situation without somehow seeming to be critical of
their mothers or daughters, or unloving—neither of which
they could consider, much less accept. One woman I
interviewed was unable to answer any but the most factual,
demographic questions without saying, somewhere in her
reply, "I love my mother," so important was it for her to
appear uncritical of her mother.

Some lied because they have always lied to themselves about
their mothers, and they don't even know they lie; the lie has
become their truth. Sherwood Anderson, in *Winesburg,
Ohio*, has "quite an elaborate theory concerning the matter. It
was his notion that the moment one of the (women) took one
of the truths to (herself), . . . and tried to live (her) life by it, the
truth (she) embraced became a falsehood."[16] Several women
worked very hard not to see what were the obvious meanings
of their mother's words and actions. One woman, who had
run away from home at the age of fifteen because her mother
and sisters decided they needed medical proof of her virginity,
finally visited her mother again when she was married and
pregnant six months later, and only remarked that her mother
thoughtfully never talked about it (the marriage, the pregnancy, or the running away), though she seemed to regret
that it had happened. This daughter repeatedly praised her

mother and pointedly compared her lack of negative feeling for her mother, whom she idolized, despite this amazing story, to the violent hostility her own adult daughter often displayed for her. Some daughters are terribly unaware of their emotions, and thus are rendered incapable of representing the situation truthfully. Some lied just because they weren't about to tell me painful truths about their most intimate relations, despite the anonymity of the interview. This lying was readily uncovered by contradictions within the interview, which was often lengthy.

In those cases where I interviewed two or more daughters of the same mother or a mother-daughter pair, contradictions were also obvious. For instance, I would be told there was no competition between mother and daughter, but examples of competitive behavior would appear throughout the transcripts. Or, one sister would disclose information about another which differed from that daughter's own story. In all this murk, the difficulty of learning what it means to be a woman is further increased. Not only do we find none of what we seek, but the information we do get is inaccurate, filtered and obscured by our individual mother's personal truth, and received by us through our own.

She couldn't face the truth herself so she lied.

She didn't tell the truth; she wanted to keep that mother image. I just learned several weeks ago that she had an abortion when she was younger; before she was married. She wasn't honest about her drinking; she wasn't honest about where she was at. She's very deceptive.

My mother lives to a certain degree in a fantasy world. She's always been a supreme bullshitter. When it comes to her sitting down and explaining things to me, a lot of it I just don't believe. I believe her feelings, her fears—but she lied to me so much when I was growing up, and I've caught her a few times lately, too.

She tells the truth as she knows the truth. Our truths are different. No. She lies to me. The heavier the question, the more she'll lie to me.

I don't believe that she lies consciously but she has a way of distorting the truth.

Sometimes she lies and sometimes she leaves out stuff. She would never say she lies, though. She's "doing it for my own good."

She always told me what she believed to be true.

In many ways my mother was deceptive—a little lie here or there to protect yourself, a lie to avoid a certain situation. I'm fighting that in myself. I can't escape from life anymore.

Ironically, some mothers tell very important truths to their daughters and are not heeded. If we have learned not to trust our mothers, if we have been treated with disrespect, or if our mothers have demonstrated no love for us, why should we believe their teachings? Why take their advice? in the case of mothers who are outside the maternal norm, they are automatically suspect; anything they say is assumed to be false, for they aren't proper mothers; we don't respect them by definition, and all other socializing forces contradict them. Those mothers who occasionally remove their masks, show their real selves to their daughters and repudiate the dailiness of their lives, contradict the truth of these repudiations by their rarity; after all, no matter what such outbursts may seem to mean, these mothers continue to live their lives just as before. What is the teaching value of admitting to your daughter that your husband is irresponsible, unloving, or even brutal, if you remain married to him? These mothers don't follow their own advice; why should we?

Further, we cannot underestimate the fact that much of what our mothers tell us is discounted simply because they are women, whose pronouncements attain to no importance in the culture. Given the traditional view of women, it is not surprising that we are left out of history, and each new generation of daughters must struggle in a vacuum. Judy

Chicago describes her discovery that "many women before me had broken through female role and made themselves into successful, independent, creative people. . . . One historical period would allow women more freedom. They would push forward, overcome the restrictions of female role, affirm their talents, realize their abilities. Then male dominance would assert itself again. The women's achievements would be left out of recorded history, and young women could not model themselves upon struggles and accomplishments of their mothers."[17]

My mother told me everything she knew. She didn't know much.

I don't know what advice she could give me; her life was certainly no example.

My mother doesn't do anything. What could she teach me?

As we integrate our socialization at the hands of our mothers, we learn that *being women* isn't important or valuable; we realize that the teachings of our mothers must not be worthwhile either. This obtains even in cases where we love and admire our mothers; the negative sanction on women is that strong. By definition, the advice of our mothers is *merely* old wives' tales, mocked and repudiated by fathers, husbands, male doctors and teachers, understood by daughters to be of little or no value, except perhaps as "household hints," which are of no importance either.

My mother did deliberately instruct me—what comes to mind are trivial things. Oh, I don't really mean that because it's important I suppose, housekeeping, knitting, sewing.

All that our mothers teach us is what they have learned in the crucible of sexism. They cannot give us a sense of self-esteem which they do not possess. We must learn to interpret anew the experience our mothers have passed on to us, to see these lives in terms of struggle, often unconscious, to find and maintain some peace, beauty and respect for themselves as women.

3
Touching:
Affection and Violence

My mother was well prepared for me
when I popped from her steaming womb
like hot toast,
right into her best bread basket
and into her double bed.

We stayed in bed for eight years
. . .
We never touched.
. . .

—SHELLEY SIMON

That taste you asked about
—a bit metallic—
—like a tidal pool—
is older than buffalo grass
warm as the ocean was warm
in the days when the sun was young
is the taste of your mother

—MARTHA SHELLEY

Growing inside of our mothers' bodies, created of their tissue
and blood, we touch and are touched in sublime intimacy.
Even an unwilling mother's body nourishes her growing
child; should our mothers be among those women who bore
children against their will, their bodies responded to our
foetal needs despite them. Almost all of us were handled by
our mothers in our infancy and earliest childhood, if for no
other reason than that such handling is the job of mothering.
The small girl's physical maintenance is sometimes given
over to a servant, a grandmother, or even a father; but in most

of our lives, the care of daughters devolved upon mothers. However, in seeming contradiction, only slightly more than one-third of the daughters I interviewed recalled receiving physical affection from their mothers while growing up. For many daughters, their mother's pregnancy, infant nursing, and early handling represent the full extent of the physical nurturing their mothers have given them.

There have been numerous studies which demonstrate the need of primate young for physical contact, hands-on-affection, so to speak. They are legendary, from the earliest— Frederick II, Emperor of Germany in the 13th century (he wanted to know what language babies would speak if left to themselves), who ordered a nurseryful of infants to be fed and cleaned with a minimum of touching, and no spoken communication at all—to the best known, the Harlows' laboratory monkeys with their surrogate mothers of wire and toweling. In the former experiment, all the babies died, leaving Frederick in his ignorance about whether human beings might speak Latin or Hebrew "naturally." In the latter, the baby monkeys who got a "mother" of warm towels grew up neurotic and sexually inadequate compared to monkeys whose nursing was accompanied by the grooming and fondling of a real mother.*

We must begin, then, with the assumption that baby girls need to be fondled, caressed, hugged and stroked, in order to be healthy and happy. Touching is a form of teaching—it teaches us that we are loveable, and loved; to be loved is to be secure. Moreover, touching bonds mother to daughter, daughter to mother in a kind of imprinting process. If we are nursed lovingly at our mothers' breasts, or held warmly and smiled at while being fed commercial formula, we associate the pleasures of fulfillment and sensual gratification with the woman providing those services. Babies experience bliss at being rocked and stroked, and they remember the source of

*For excellent discussion of human need for affectionate touching in all developmental stages, see chapters 3, 4, 6 and 7 of Ashley Montagu's *Touching*. New York: Perennial Library, 1971.

that ecstasy. As our mothers are the people assigned to take care of us, we continue to look to them to provide affection as we grow, so bound up is loving with early child care.[1]

Tillie Olsen, in her short story, "I Stand Here Ironing,"[2] wrote that she nursed her first child, as she nursed each of the children, but with the first, she followed the advice of doctors and books, and nursed on a rigid schedule, rather than according to the needs of the baby. She described the agony of enforcing arbitrary rules. Olsen asked herself why she put that information in the story; she wonders if that early treatment matters. It matters, and it explains a great deal.

I went into therapy because of my relationship with Laura, in which I was duplicating the bad relationship I had with my mother. She was seven years old then. Part of the problem was that the anxieties and frustrations I had with my mother got played out between me and Laura. I think that happens a lot in mother/daughter relationships. I'll tell you something interesting about my second daughter, Lilly. This is a theory, but I think there's something to it. I did not nurse Laura, but I did nurse Lilly. I really regret that I did not nurse Laura. If only I had known before what I knew the second time—but you can't go back. Interestingly, that has become kind of an issue with Laura. She resents it.

So do we all, the daughters who weren't nursed, resent it. In fact, almost none of us were "nursed" by our mothers as we wanted to be. "There was, is, in most of us, a girl-child longing for a woman's nurture . . . a woman's smell and touch and voice, a woman's strong arms around us in moments of fear and pain."[3]

It seems that even those mothers who did touch us when we were small, stopped long before we wanted them to. The touching, as described by most of the women I interviewed, decreases through the first few years we can remember, and then stops around the age of nine or ten; most often, it never returns. As adults (over fifteen), very few daughters embrace mutually with their mothers, hold hands, walk arm in arm, or kiss.* Most of us describe, where physical contact does occur, the perfunctory social touching that is public affection, the cheek-laid-to-cheek greeting, the dry pucker exchanged by bodies touching nowhere but the lips. Rich suggests that, "Few women growing up in patriarchal society can feel mothered enough; the power of our mothers, whatever their love for us and their struggles on our behalf, is too restricted." [4] This is so; in fact, however, another reason we feel this is that we are so little mothered in a sensual way. "Mother loved us desperately, but her tireless devotion was not the same thing as petting, her caresses were not given unless we were asleep, or she thought us so." [5]

We always kissed goodnight, and that was about it. It was a ritual. When we'd see each other after separation, we'd hug. It all seemed more like a ritual than an expression of affection. But I always appreciated the goodnight kiss.

I don't remember being cuddled or anything. I remember my mother kissing me when I went away to school or when I came home, or when I got an honor in school. We don't have that closeness now, either.

There was very, very little of that sort of thing. The only time she touched any of us was to hit. I cannot remember being kissed by my mother until my wedding day. Now when she sees me, she gives me a little hug.

Until I was about five there was a lot of it. But when I was about that age, we went to a movie and I put my head in her lap. She pushed me away, and said, "You're too big for that." After that there wasn't any physical attention from her.

Actually there was no close touching between me and my mother. I'd hug or kiss her sometimes after we'd had an argument, but I never could come to her and just tell her that I loved her without feeling that I had done something wrong to her.

*In other cultures, even those quite similar to ours, like contemporary Italy or France, this is not true for mothers and daughters.

She says I wouldn't let her touch me very much. When I was little she used to make a fuss over me. She would dress up me and my sister. She used to do our hair for hours, like we were little dolls. I looked just like Shirley Temple when I was a little girl, with the curls and the whole thing. There was a lot of physical care. As long as the touching was in the range of physical care we could have lots of it.

She wasn't physically affectionate. Maybe if we were sick— once when I was in the hospital, she kissed me on the forehead.

No matter what the successful advertising image of mothering may make us think, most mothers in the daughterhood study did not stroke or fondle their small daughters very often. It's not remarkable that women trapped in the mother role and unable to move freely should be unable to love freely. In addition to the constriction of motherhood itself, we must remember that women grow alienated from their bodies in the patriarchal culture. Part of this alienation has been the rejection of breastfeeding by most American women in the twentieth century. For decades, bottle and formula manufacturers have joined with pediatricians, gynecologists and advertising copywriters to promote the demise of nursing. Functionally, breasts are perceived as sexual objects, designed for manipulation by male partners—a notion elevated to pseudo-science by pop anthropologists who suggest that breast development in the human female is for the purpose of enticing the male into copulation.* Breastfeeding has been denigrated as animal-like, savage, dirty, and even nutritionally inadequate! (One of the relatives visiting my newborn son went through a ten-minute lecture as I nursed the baby, explaining why and how she had found bottle feeding *easier*, because the formula took so little time to mix, the bottles were so easy to clean, etc. This—in the face of my lifting up my shirt for the child to suckle.)

We have come to a time in which women are averse to

*Desmond Morris, in *The Naked Ape*, is one example.

nursing their babies out of shame and embarrassment. Nursing mothers need active and constant support from friends, so that they may overcome their fear of being seen nursing, so humiliating have our bodies and this natural function become. When our babies are older than six months we may be openly accused of destroying them psychologically (sexual maladjustment) or physically (poor nutrition, badly shaped teeth and gums). Tremendous desire and a network of encouraging friends are absolute necessities to the nursing mother of a toddler in this society. Those of us who start by nursing are otherwise easily convinced either that we "should" wean at six months, or some other arbitrary number, or that many babies give up nursing on their own accord, out of "boredom" or "lack of interest." Not many of us learn, as we grow up, that one to three years of breastfeeding had been common practice until contemporary times, and that third world women are even now struggling against the importation of American sugar formulas, in the spreading commercial attack on breastfeeding. Even those of us who come to realize the serious detriment of formula and the natural benefits of nursing may not nurse our babies because of such cultural bias and advertising.

Beyond nursing, fondling and caressing small children is still frowned upon "in excess"—the definition of which state remains beyond me. Mothers are made to feel that they are "spoiling" children or that their own natural impulse to stroke and cuddle children over the age of two or three is somehow based in psycho-sexual problems, or a "neurotic need" to keep their children dependent. Despite the allure of the silken skin of children, and the obvious desire they express for sensual giving and getting, mothers (and others) deprive themselves and the children of the gratification which leads to contentment and well-being.

Moreover, though there is a minority groundswell toward "natural" birthing, nursing newborns, and carrying infants in body slings, this movement is under the control of institutional (male) "guidance," so the number of mothers who escape into a physically easy symbiosis with their baby daughters is probably still measurable in dozens. When American women began, in the last ten or fifteen years, to try to take motherhood back from the army of male "experts" who had stolen it,* we faced the threat, and to a great extent the reality, of co-optation by liberal men. So we find that, generally, independent midwives must practice outside the law, nurse-midwives are subjected to hospital-oriented training and domination by obstetricians, expectant mothers may not give birth at home, assisting and supportive birthing participants may not be selected by mothers, fathers have become "coaches," and pediatricians who now "prescribe" breastfeeding still control it. The fact is that even those of us who manage to break through our socialization and come to motherhood in good ways, cannot fully control our pregnancy and delivery without superhuman efforts—and illegal action.

The physical intimacy we experience while in our mothers' wombs is not comparable to any sort of touching after birth, even nursing. After all, during pregnancy, the two are one body. The separation that occurs at birth is traumatic for both mother and daughter. The infant is propelled from a totally supportive environment into an alien and apparently hostile atmosphere. Reunion with her mother, incomplete as it will be, often does not occur for many hours, or even days. Meanwhile, the mother has been subjected to the dismal experience of giving birth in the standard American hospital.

The average woman is hospitalized, and after laboring in isolation and being drugged, is made to lie on her back on a narrow platform, often strapped down, and has her child pulled out of her body; or, more and more frequently, [6] her body is cut open and the baby taken out in Caesarean section. She is kept separate from her daughter, sees her only at scheduled intervals, is encouraged to feed her sugar water from a bottle, and is discouraged from touching her baby "too

*Obstetricians, gynecologists, psychiatrists, psychologists, pediatricians, abortionists, formula, baby food and contraceptive manufacturers, public school officials, etc. Also see Rich, *op. cit.*, Chapters VI and VII especially.

much." The infant not only undergoes the trauma of leaving her mother's body, but is handled brusquely by strangers, put in a plastic box, sees her mother rarely, and, on these occasions, perceives her in terms of low energy and an awkward physical presence, both the results of her mother's abuse at the hands of medical practitioners.* In fact, to the nursery-dwelling American newborn, her mother isn't even a constant supply of nourishment—sugar water and commercial formula are usually dispensed by others. [7] Birth separation is magnified and augmented by these experiences. The baby is terrified and insecure; the mother is filled with contradictory emotional responses, heightened by induced ill health and negative results of anesthesia. To their great credit, and the incredible good fortune of their daughters, nearly thirty percent of the interview mothers came through the brutal experience of American hospital birth with good words for their newborns. The daughters were not seen by these mothers as the cause of their suffering.

It was an easy birth; you popped right out; there was no pain.

It hurt a little, but it was worth it.

I was so excited, because I wanted a girl very much; I had you against the doctor's advice because I wanted a daughter.

It was a very short labor; you were the healthiest and biggest at birth; my others were problems.

It felt good; you were right on time; it all went like clockwork.

Some mothers who had contradictory and conflicting responses to the birth experience still tried to give their daughters a positive sense of their births. Despite such contradictions, these mothers attempted truth with their daughters.

Your birth was very important for me, though it was very painful.

*Of course, this applies equally to male infants.

It was a good experience, but I would rather have stopped at four. (Daughter is fifth child.)

I was sick during the entire pregnancy, but you were an easy delivery.

You were an easy birth, but a troublemaker afterwards.

Thus there is a very shaky base for a healthy physical relationship; but, amazingly enough, some mother/daughter pairs overcome this frequently horrendous beginning and find warmth and comfort in cuddling while the daughter is very young.

I was never down. I was always in the arms. She told me that she rocked me to sleep until I was three, when my sister was born. She told me that even when she was pregnant she rocked me all the time. We hugged and kissed a lot, and I still kiss her.

We used to cuddle together, and when I was scared at night I used to go into bed with her and sleep. There was lots of hugging and kissing.

There was always a lot of hugging and kissing and rubbing; she would play with us—throw us down in the grass and carry on like that.

My mother was always very close with us. We touched and hugged and it stayed with me. I found it to be quite a handicap in the north because northerners aren't used to people touching. We're still a touching, hugging, kissing family.

I think we were very affectionate. She was like a mother tiger and we were cubs. We were always hugging each other. That is still the case; the whole family is physically affectionate.

There was a lot of touching. It was a bath every night, powdering and getting your hair combed. My mother would do an elaborate braiding thing with our hair that a lot of people do now. It used to be just for little kids, the corn rowing used to be a rite at bedtime. I'd go through the whole ceremony of getting my hair braided for school the next day.

There was a lot of touching with that.

Then, just as mothers are obscenely taught that touching and kissing with their little boys of five and six years old is inappropriate, so mothers are discouraged from touching and kissing their daughters—though at a later age. With this additional suggestion of prurience, society further separates mothers from their children. Daughters and sons are prohibited from seeking mother as a sensual comfort and pleasure source, and she them. "Looking back on my uncuddled childhood it seems to me a sad mistake of my heroic mother to withhold from me the petting I so craved, the sufficing comfort of maternal caresses."[8]

Children of both sexes are taught to wait until the designated age, then seek sensual gratification with "opposite" sex partners, ultimately within a marriage. But the cessation of mutual sensuality in childhood ill suits all of us, for even what passes as sexuality in most marriages. Boys, in being encouraged to be heterosexual, can more or less pick up where they left off,* while daughters are required to develop a sexuality which is much less easy for them: exchanging physical affection with men. Girls first experience sensual pleasure through their own and their mothers' bodies. Young women are expected to "switch over" to boys and men under complicated circumstances. Though the mother's body is only available early on, it remains the only body to which most young girls have access; other people, especially men and boys, rarely assume the nurturing role in our society.

As the mother's physical contact recedes, the little girl is often admonished against touching herself as well, and certainly most children are forbidden sensual contact with each other. (The fact that they do have such contact, and do masturbate, does not remove the negative sanction upon the activity, or therefore, upon their consciousness.) Then, at menarche (onset of menstruation), girls are thrust into "acceptable" though negatively presented contact with their

*A boy child's "sense of being 'other' makes separation from the mother more plausible—he may come back to her in every woman he meets." See Hall, p. 18.

own bodies and expected to begin preparing for sexual liaisons with boys and men. This sudden and remarkable change is required after several years of taking in complex negative social messages about bodies, especially female bodies. Additionally, as the young woman grows through her menstruation, she is ever more strongly admonished to have no physical contact with males. At the same time, mother-daughter touching has disappeared. The lesson is so well and consistently learned that both mothers and daughters accept the curtailing of physical affection as natural. One of the women I interviewed realized while speaking that she was drawing many comparisons between her mother and her now-divorced husband. We talked about her feeling that she was often attracted to "feminine" men, and her conclusion that the affection and approval she wanted, but didn't get, from her mother, was potential (in her eyes) in this man—so she married him seeking maternal affection. Yet another daughter said of her now-divorced second husband, "If he's like anybody, he's like my mother, infantile and needing instant gratification, dependent. He's competent in his work; he's infantile in his emotional life; he needs somebody to take care of him—just like her." We are required to seek physical satisfaction from men; yet what we lack, so many of us, is physical affection from our mothers. It is no great wonder that men, who are bred to the antithesis of maternal behavior, are so often unsatisfactory in this role.[9]

Much of the impetus for this cessation of touching seems to come from daughters; there were several women in the study who specifically said that they couldn't feel comfortable hugging or kissing their mothers. Some of these did allude to the sexual aspects of the relationship; others simply spoke of uneasiness.

It was all very loving; as a family we all used to lie in bed together. In my adolescence I used to lie in bed with my mother, lie in her arms and tell her all my problems. We used to kiss a lot, which was really wonderful. Now it's gotten more stilted, probably on my part.

I don't think there was much touching after I was grown up enough to know what touching was.

My mother was very demonstrative and affectionate until I rejected her, and one day just said, hands off. I didn't want her to come near me. I was about 12 or 13 at the time. When I grew up I had the same feeling; I felt bad about it and wanted to work it through, but it was just too uncomfortable. I felt some kind of sexual overtones and I was real uncomfortable after a certain point.

My mother has gotten into a kissing thing lately and I can't stand it. She wants to kiss me all the time. She's never touched me before and this is so alien, I don't know what it means. I feel like saying, "Please, get away from me."

When I was around 12 or 13, the only closeness that occurred between my mother and me was when I was forced to share a bed with her. The only times I lived with my mother I was forced to share a bed with her, and the closeness and the touching were very seductive. I rebelled against this, and to this day I can't stand being touched by my mother.

When I was younger my father worked nights and I would ask my mother if I could sleep with her. She was big, and I would get into bed and just feel her body like a big bear, and I liked it. But as I grew older we didn't touch. I kept her at arm's length and she did the same. She was in the hospital a few years ago, and I couldn't touch her; it was like a strangle. She said, "Aren't you going to give me a kiss?" and I just had to force myself to kiss her. There was a big stone in the middle of my heart, that I couldn't touch my mother.

Those women who sensed sexual feelings coming from their mothers, or who themselves regarded their mothers in sexual terms, were vague on this subject and reticent after the subject was raised. The incest taboo is still powerful against mother-child sex (though it appears ineffective against many fathers*); in this study it is no doubt heightened by fear of

*See Chapter 5.

lesbianism. It may be, in fact, that our learned fear of lesbianism is the base, heightened by the power of the incest taboo. Moreover, given the power dynamics of the patriarchal nuclear family, mothers may not feel that they can exploit their children as fathers might; certainly mothers understand the limits of their power, where many fathers believe that sexual use of their children is their "right."

At any rate, the breaking off of physically affectionate behavior appears to be mutual. In most of our lives, as we have seen, either from distaste or inhibition, under social pressure, mothers cease fondling their daughters just before we begin to menstruate. We, also under social pressure, sometimes personally disinclined, break off with our mothers by about the same time. By adolescence, usually by menarche, we have lost the comfort of our mothers' bodies. Deepening this loss is the fact that the touching stops at the time we experience the first menstrual flow. This is a time of poignant need for our mothers' bodies, as evidence of what is beginning in our own. Not only would our mothers' bodies mirror ours, but we crave comfort and support as we pass through "the intense confusion and disruption of sudden dramatic changes. . . . A young woman experiences sudden highs and lows, she may burst into tears 'for no good reason.' She becomes a stranger to herself. . . . "[10] Weideger further emphasizes what many of the women in the daughterhood study made plain:* most of our mothers do not provide us with facts about menstruation, or information about sexuality and reproduction, and shun the subject and/or their daughters, at this time. A woman who cannot bring herself to deal with menstruation—hers or her daughter's—may well be unable to touch her newly menstrual daughter.

She gave me a book, and said, "Read this." She was real shocked that I didn't know it when she thought I was getting my period. I went to spend the week-end with my grandmother, to adjust to the whole thing, I guess. (laugh) I didn't get the idea, but that's what they did with me.

*See Chapter 2 of Weideger.

84

Not a word. You would think that it didn't exist. No comment passed between us when I started having my periods. As far as she was concerned, it never happened.

She told me I couldn't wear Tampax until after I got married. One time, when I was 13 years old, I asked her while she was washing the dishes, "Why do I have to wear pads? Why can't I wear Tampax? Is it because when you're married, you're used to having something in there?" She said, "Shut up."

Our mothers, who are themselves objects of the taboo which keeps menstruation secret and unmentionable in this society, and victims of the fear of competition with younger women, do not embrace us as we join them, massage our bodies to ease our cramps, hold us in their arms as we begin to bleed. Should they, most of them would be rejected, with the violent emotion attendant upon a newly-menstrual woman's psyche. The mother, herself filled with shame and embarrassment, gives her negative body sense to the daughter, who internalizes it and, thus, cannot go to her mother for comfort and knowledge.

One constant in women's search for validation and higher consciousness is the discomfort we feel about our bodies. Most of us trace those feelings to the time of menarche, that realization that the business of women is looking and acting "feminine," responding to boys and men as potential "boyfriends," and to women and girls as rivals. This is a complex and crucial moment in the physical and social development of a girl. She stops running and climbing, and begins to clothe and move her body in uncomfortable ways. At the same time, she has begun to menstruate, *and* she and her mother cease whatever touching has passed between them, strengthening the sense of isolation and alienation of that time and for her future.

For most of us, it isn't until well into maturity or the advent of feminist consciousness that we reconsider the bond we felt with our mothers, if we come to such reconsideration at all. That bond is at least partially the result of physical contact, even for those of us who've had horrendous relations with our mothers, who've been estranged for years, whose mothers are dead—the bond is there yet*—we wish we could have had closer ties to our mothers; we regret the pain and separation.

I'm trying to get in touch with my need for my mother. I repressed that early. I know every kid wants her mother to love her, and I never was conscious of that in my whole life. I feel like it's in there somewhere and I want to be able to feel it, and to be in touch with her.

Until the last three years we had a very distant relationship. Part of the change is that I left and then came back and it was a voluntary relationship. Also, I just decided to take her on a little bit more. I looked at her life and understood it better. Our physical relationship is still limited.

I really regret dealing this way with my mother—being estranged—and I feel sad about it, but that's just the way it is; I've accepted it. I envy women who have a good relationship with their mothers and seem to get along and have mothers who are supportive.

I feel bad about my relationship with my mother. I wish I could be closer. I don't totally blame her; we miss a lot. I would like to be able to just pick her up and take her out for lunch.

Of the small number of women who stated that they felt no bond to their mothers,† four-fifths recall no maternal physical affection. Of the more than one-third who were touched and held by their mothers, all but one feel strongly bonded to their mothers. Moreover, one-third of the daughters in the study were women who describe their mothers

---

*Many daughters, when asked to define the bond they feel with their mothers, would say things like, "she's my mother"—as if that alone could explain the intensity of the mother/daughter relation, as if no words could describe it.
†Thirteen percent.

primarily in negative terms, with contempt and disdain; fully three-fourths of *these* women are among those who did not receive physical affection.

Most of us both feel and express contradictory emotions in dealing with this issue. We are wary of the strong pull toward our mothers; we fear dependency (theirs *and* ours); we don't trust our mothers or ourselves to keep a safe distance—though what we actually may want is a strong love relationship with no distance at all. These contradictions were often scattered throughout whole interviews; there are some responses which contradict themselves within just a couple of sentences.

She writes me a lot. She wishes there wasn't so much distance, so she could see the grandchildren and she could talk to me. I would like to see her more. I only get to see her once or twice a year and sometimes every two years. We keep minimal contact, living so far apart. I wish she could see her grand-children. I would like to talk to her once in a while—for her sake mostly. (laugh)

I like her a lot. I would like to get to know her better. I have tried to establish a more physical relationship with her. At first she would call me. I would visit her about once a week and we would talk on the phone fairly frequently. Now, during the last six months, I rarely see her, maybe once every two or three months. I talk to her once a month maybe. I think she would like a lot more of me and will not ask for it.

There's no way I can be around her. I am still enough of a coward where I cannot bear to be with her by myself for any length of time . . . I do want to try to make her happy. When I remember to, I write letters, though I just hate writing letters. I'll love someone madly when I'm with them, but when we're separated, that's it. The same way with my mother, though I'm very comfortable with her.

Some of us are able to make physical contact with our mothers despite a lack of touching in our girlhood or a style of behavior which is strongly at variance from our mothers. To do this we usually have to overcome both our own attitudes *and* our mothers'.

She's kind of disgusted with the whole thing. I've asked her if she comes; when I goof around with her, I'll touch her tits sometimes, and she backs away when I hug her and get physical, but she doesn't really get pissed.

Now I kiss my mother occasionally, and I hug her, and when we play around, when I'm teasing her I'll contact her physically, put my arm around her. When I was a teenager, adolescent, I don't remember being as in touch with her as I am now.

I was not physically close to my mother. Now my daughter, being more open than I am, would complain, and then I would have to deal with it, but that was very hard for me to do. Verbally, she's more open. It's only in the last couple of years that we hug and kiss when we get together. I put it to her, too, because she's very aggressive that way. She'll just fall on top of you—and I put that to the woman's movement. That's really helped me, too, to reach out to her physically. Her complaints about me were the same that I had about my mother.

The struggle to reach beyond our socialization—and to take our mothers with us—is further complicated by the fact that not only have we not received the maternal caresses we desired, but we've been physically abused by our mothers as well. Just as we may try to overcome the loss of physical affection we suffered, we also attempt to understand and work out the anger at our mothers' physical violence against us. Some of the maternal violence perpetrated against girls and young women is born of our mothers' role as cultural educator. We learn what Andrea Dworkin calls "the technology of beauty. . . . Mother teaches daughter to apply lipstick, to shave under her arms, to bind her breasts, to wear a girdle and high-heeled shoes. . . . What must any daughter/child feel toward the mother who forces her to do painful things to her own body? The mother takes on the role of enforcer: she uses seduction, command, all manner of force to coerce the daughter to conform to the demands of the culture . . . . Pain is an essential part of the grooming process, and that is not accidental. Plucking the eyebrows, shaving under the arms, wearing a girdle, learning to walk in high-heeled shoes, having one's nose fixed, straightening or curling one's hair—these things *hurt*."[11]

Obviously, since most of us learn from our mothers to abuse our bodies in the quest for "beauty," we feel our mothers as the source of this pain. Even if we come to accept the idea that we must contort and disfigure ourselves to suit the socially described ideal, we have learned that our mothers brought us the hurt, and we remember the hurting; we add it to the running total of crimes against us our mothers have committed. Those of us who ultimately reject the idea that "no price is too great, no process too repulsive, no operation too painful for the woman who would be beautiful,"[12]* are again in the position of having to reject our mothers' teachings, and, since they subscribe to them, our mothers as well.

But most of the violence our mothers visit upon us is more direct than this, although it, too, is born of the proper role our mothers play. Almost all of us were hit by our mothers as we grew up, primarily between the ages of two and twelve. This hitting usually took the form of spankings, slaps, "smacks," or "socks." Sometimes our mothers used weapons, most often straps, belts or hairbrushes employed ritually, as in a formal spanking, but occasionally they'd use household objects— hangers, wet dish towels, electric cords—seized in passion.

What kind of question is that? You mean you know women whose mothers never hit them? Yes, she hit me. She never beat me.

*Read in *V*, by Thomas Pynchon, the chapter which describes the surgical process of a "nose job"; also see the October 1977 issue of *Ms*. magazine, for photographs of women who've undergone "cosmetic" surgery on their breasts.

Oh yes! Sort of like socks, usually in a burst of anger, probably when something else was bugging her and I happened to be there.

Well, she would smack; she never whipped. It would be just a lick in passing.

She did it with a switch on the legs. The only mark she ever left on us was streaks on our legs. We always knew why she was doing it—it was for a specific thing, not just on the spur of the moment.

She would hit me, and I would say, "That didn't hurt," and she would hit me again.

Mother would give you a clop on the side of the head before she would explain to you. Her instinct was to hit first and ask questions later.

Sometimes she would get angry and give me a swat on the bottom, but one time she became very angry and hit me across the face. That was 19 years ago; I remember it.

She only did it rarely. It always happened when she was real angry. She would do it, and then she would feel awful about it and apologize.

Most of us have assumed that this hitting of children is not too serious, certainly "normal," and an ordinary aspect of family life. This latter, of course, it is. Rare is the American family in which physical violence is never used against children. We need to understand, however, that there exist, and have existed in the past, cultures in which children were never struck. The poet Alta, in her book *MOMMA*, points out that "when indians saw white people spank their children,/ they thot at first that whites hated their children. . . ."[13] Margaret Mead's study of the Arapesh affords us another example of non-violent child-rearing,[14] as does Ashley Montagu's discussion of her study of the Balinese.[15]

Some of us have included in our ideal—if not real—picture

of family life a rule against hitting children, especially by the mother. One woman I interviewed, when I asked if her mother had hit her, replied, "Oh no; my mother was Jewish." This Jewishness, she later revealed, did not prevent each of her parents from physically attacking her at least once in her adolescence when she was suspected of sexual transgression. In middle class families, where physical violence is not supposed to occur, its occurrence is simply denied. "Normal," we must remember, only refers to frequency; behavior is "normal" if most people do it. This frequency has no connection with what is good for people, in this case, for small children and their mothers.

How might it be construed as unimportant in describing any relationship between two people, to say that not only is one person two, three, or four times the size of the other, but that the larger one uses physical violence, threatened or actual, to enforce rules of behavior or control the expression and attitudes of the other? Obviously the smaller one is a prisoner. This is part of the definition of "normal" parent-child relations within the patriarchal nuclear family.

When small girls are hit, the experience locks into the pattern of their socialization. It is one more aspect of the training which puts down their natural impulses, cripples their egos, stunts their body movement and curiosity. In hitting any children, we foster their feelings of impotence and inadequacy. Small boys are encouraged to be violent themselves; little girls are rarely encouraged even to hit *back*, to defend themselves. Hitting their daughters is one of the ways mothers, albeit against their will or understanding, enforce society's oppression of women. Our mothers are the agents of this process; spanking or beating are the physical representation of the psychic education they deliver. How better to impress submissiveness upon us than to force us to submit?

Though discipline and punishment have traditionally been associated with the father's role, most physical punishment, like almost all of the responsibilities of parenting, falls to the mother. Even beatings are more frequently administered by mothers than fathers. Only seven percent of the daughters in the study were beaten by their fathers, but seventeen percent were beaten by their mothers. These serious beatings or punishments are distinguished from ordinary hitting, but were occasionally minimized by the daughters who related them. This minimalization is like "forgetting," in that it serves to remove from the picture of family life those elements which are not "supposed" to be there.

She battered us around in times of great anger; she would use an implement, such as a strap, or a piece of rubber hose. Whatever she had in her hands landed on someone's head.

She used to hit me pretty hard, pull my hair and slap my face a lot, and it hurt. But I wouldn't say I was abused. I mean I didn't have welts.

She always hits with her hands. Sometimes it seems like she'd hit me almost continuously. I could almost call it beating.

She had a strap on the kitchen door that she used whenever anyone got out of hand, and there was the threat of the strap there all *the time.*

She would periodically burst out in some bizarre temper and smash me with the telephone receiver, or a frying pan, and once she chased me down the street with a belt, but this was infrequent; it was not constant.

She had this red leather belt that she used, and she used her hand a lot. She used to do things like if I was getting up and leaving the table before eating what she wanted me to eat—I didn't like to eat a lot—she would tie me to my chair with cords. I struggled for a while and then gave in. I wouldn't say I was beaten. I was hit quite a bit, but not as much as my mother when she was little. She used to tell me stories of my grandmother hitting her every day. You know the old cliché, if my grandmother didn't know what it was for, my mother would. So my mother got hit daily; I would say I got it two or three times a week.

92

In her chapter titled "Violence: the Heart of Maternal Darkness,"[16] Adrienne Rich delineates the causes of maternal violence. She demonstrates that the violence our mothers vent upon us, far from being deserved by us, or even aimed at us, is a product of the frustration, pain, rage and desperation which the contemporary institution of motherhood creates and then seeks to suppress. It is not only the children whom the media now call "battered" who suffer the violence of the institution. These are only the most obvious, the proverbial tip of the iceberg. Below the water are the rest of us, daughters and sons, "the children desperately pushed, cajoled, manipulated, the children dependent on one uncertain, weary woman for their day-in, day-out care and emotional sustenance. . . ."[17]

> i walk past those homes
> & hear the
> mothers striking the
> children
>
>> (i am one of those
>> mothers
>> striking
>> the children)
>
> & the screams, the screams
> of us trapped animals
> striking one another
> & screaming
>
> & screaming.[18]

By the time my son was four years old, it was clear to me that he was physically afraid of me. Though I had never spanked him, and prided myself on not using physical discipline, I had used my strength and size to frighten him, my voice to intimidate him. I had grabbed him so violently that I could easily have broken him—that surely must have been what I wanted to do. And I have used the facade of "hitting him back" to really hurt him, out of my frustration at my rule never to "hit" my child. The guilt that seized me on these occasions was devastating. His face, at two, three and four years old, would fill with anxiety, and his body would cower as if expecting the whip. What am I, I thought, that this baby should feel such fear at the sound of my anger, that my child should look at me so? I felt a hypocrite, cruel and foolish. It was then that I began to understand the complexity of maternal violence. Not only the beating of small children, the apparent nastiness and outright viciousness of mothers in supermarkets, at the movies and in the parks, but infanticide I understood as well.

And I—white, middle class, college degreed, possessed of a growing feminist consciousness, I, who was fired from a teaching job for my radical attitudes about children and education, now working part-time and having one small child for whom I had industriously organized play groups since his fourth month—I began to imagine: what if I had three or four children, all under the age of eight? If my child's father never sent me money or did child-care? What if I had no job, or worked an eight-hour shift every 24 hours, with none of the facility and knowledge of the world that my whiteskin/ class privilege has bought me? I multiplied my son's fear and my rage by these factors—and realized that it is only through the destruction of the mother's ego, the internalized degradation of women, that this society manages to keep any children alive. If women were not programmed to sacrifice ourselves to maternity, it, and the species, would cease.

With this new understanding of violence in mothers— gained by being one I reconsidered my mother. She had always tried to repress her anger, not just at her children, but her husband and others as well. When her anger emerged, she suffered tremendous guilt and no relief. I recall myself at the age of 16, standing by my mother's side at the sink after dinner. She would wash; I would dry. My father and brothers were downstairs, reading newspapers and watching television. We would stand there together every night, unless I could get out of it, and often we would fight. We would talk, and the talk would grow into an argument. It seemed to me that she could only criticize me, and I expressed great contempt for her. My contempt was rarely masked; I drove her to exasperation. We screamed at each other; I would cry more readily than she. When she could restrain herself no longer, she would try to slap my face, or would lash at me with a damp towel. Sometimes these struck, and hurt; more often she never got that far, or I fended her off, or there was no pain from the blow. Rarely, she would shout at me to get out, to get out of her sight. I would go to my room, but neither of us was free then. We couldn't escape from the cyclone of feeling we'd released in the kitchen. I don't remember ever leaving on my own accord; we were both tied there; we had to stand at the sink. I don't even remember what we fought about. In my room, I would rasp whispered curses at her into the mirror, watching my face distort with frustration. I don't know what I thought would happen if she heard me, but I was raised in a family where it was forbidden even to refer to our mother by the pronoun "she"—such "respect" was mandatory, and was enforced by immediate guilt. The physical sensations of my own grief and rage were suffocation and strangling, great heat, and severe muscle tension. Only after much sobbing would there be a release. My mother, left standing at the sink (she had to "finish the kitchen"), undoubtedly swallowed her anger, floundered in her guilt, and repeatedly agonized over the fact that her daughter, whom she adored and continually sacrificed for, had come to hate her. The hatred and anger we both felt had a common source—that rule which tied us to the sink, which gave her false power and me none at all. Unable to see the real source of our mutual pain, we blamed and hurt each other. She had discovered me to be a traitor; I regarded her as a tyrant.

Sometimes we manage to rebel against what we perceive to be our mothers' tyranny; and sometimes we are successful in that rebellion. Charlotte Perkins Gilman, in her autobiography, tells of her mother issuing an ultimatum: either apologize to a neighbor (for something young Charlotte had not done) or "you must leave me." Gilman says that, "Never before had my own conscience come squarely against hers," and her answer to her mother was, "I am not going to do it— and I am not going to leave you—and what are you going to do about it?" Her mother, "horrified beyond words . . . came over and struck" her.[19] This produced in Charlotte an understanding of physical coercion which she retained all her life, and the realization that, in order to end such coercion, rebellion is necessary. For most daughters, such a scene is repeated many times, only ceasing when the daughter is "too big to spank" or is no longer living with her mother.

4
Competition: Some Data and Definition

Through every night we hate,
preparing the next day's
war.

—SHIRLEY KAUFMAN

I danced for Herod, yes. My mother's eyes,
Watchful and wary, followed as I danced.
I never dropped my veils, but swayed, advanced,
And tripped the steps she taught me, maiden-wise.
. . .
I sought to please my mother as I danced.

—LEONORA SPEYER

when I watch you
you wet brown bag of a woman
who used to be the best looking gal in Georgia
used to be called the Georgia Rose
I stand up
through your destruction
I stand up

—LUCILLE CLIFTON

It is axiomatic that women compete with each other; mothers and daughters compete intensely, primarily for the affection of the husband-father. Most of the women I interviewed made these assumptions, whether or not they were substantiated in their own lives. But only 49 percent of the daughters in the study had a sustained competitive relationship with their mothers. Fifty-one percent of us did not regularly compete with our mothers; a smaller percentage would have been sufficient to disprove the given social assumptions. In addition, there are other forms of competition revealed in the study which weigh heavily on the mother/daughter relation: competition between mother and father for the daughter's allegiance, competition between the daughter and one or more brothers or sisters for mother's attention, and competition between daughters and mother's husband for mother's affection.

Some of the competition between daughters and their mothers is over the performance of "womanly" tasks. Can we cook and clean house, dress and act the role of gracious lady as well as, or better than our mothers? Though they are generally the source of our skills and knowledge in these areas, often we, and/or they, feel that we have surpassed them at being the proper woman.

I was definitely categorized as the housekeeper, the cook, and the one who did the laundry. When my mother's mother was dying and she wasn't there, I did everything she did. Unfortunately, I did it better because my mother didn't like housework and would read a lot. I could really whip up that house in ten minutes, and it looked like a target the first thing in the morning, so you'd think I was real together. So I used to win points that way.

Certainly I was a better cook. In fact, I have found out now that my mother used to like cooking and it was just something I have taken over; I am the family cook and she doesn't even want to cook any more. (I was always encouraged by my step-father in this.)

For one thing, she would never let me cook. My father would insist that it was all right for me to do it. So on Sunday morning he would say, "She wants to make breakfast; let her make breakfast." But my mother didn't want another woman in the kitchen. That was her domain and she didn't want another woman in there, especially her daughter. Believe me, I was no rival. Not that I was going to take over her job or anything, because she was by far the better cook.

She always said to me, "Daddy says I can't buy any clothes

*unless I take you with me because you're the only one who has
a sense of style." That kind of thing—she'd never admit to
being jealous but it must have annoyed her. It would annoy
me incredibly, if I had to take my daughter with me to pick out
my wardrobe.*

*The way I competed with my mother—well, my mother tends
to be not very meticulous about how she keeps her home. My
mother always piled things up all over. She never was big into
house cleaning. I didn't like it, so the way I competed was to
tidy up, was to be the good girl doing the right things. I
always got positive feedback on that from my dad. In recent
years the way I competed with my mother was to go to visit
them and, since both of my parents were working, I would
cook all the meals while I was there, thinking it was my share
of the work. I was a hundred times better cook than she is. So
my mother lived for weeks with "It's too bad you can't cook
the way Nancy does." Just recently I realized how blatant the
competition was.*

Since mothers often must play that role as the sole basis for
their identity, when a daughter usurps that place, the loss
prompts or furthers disaffection and alienation between
mother and daughter.

Others of us competed with our mothers in the areas of
intellect and conversational wit and power. We tried stacking
up accomplishments against our mothers' totals, or belittled
our mothers' lack of credits. I can remember disdainfully criticizing my mother for not being politically astute or well-read
while she was keeping house for a family of five, including
three school-age children. Here, a minority of us felt superior
to our mothers, and intellectually identified with our fathers.
But, more often than not, in the interviews, daughters would
say that no matter how hard they worked, or how "smart"
they were, they lost the contest.

*In terms of who's the smartest, yes, there's continuous compe-
tition. I'm supposed to be really smart. I'm daddy's little girl.
I'm mommy's little girl. I'm a National Merit Scholar, I'm a*

Betty Crocker, I'm this and I'm that. But my mother resents it tremendously. I worked very hard to be much smarter than she was but I was never smart enough in what I did to satisfy her, and she would always work to be smarter than I was no matter what. You had to change the subject to be smarter. There was that constant demand that you had to get smarter and smarter, and do things better and better. "No matter what you do it's not going to be good enough because I'm smarter." It can be really confusing. You keep doing it and doing it and doing it and it's still not good enough, it's not good enough.

Not on her part. I always felt that she is a very intelligent, very refined woman, and I've always envied that. I felt I couldn't be that kind of person; I couldn't have that patience, and I used to envy her. But as far as her feeling goes, envying my beauty or brains, I doubt it.

I felt jealous of her but I don't recall her ever saying she was jealous of me.

It does bother me, seeing that she's such an independent person, and she goes through a lot of trouble to let people know she's very strong and very independent. I feel like I should be stronger than I am.

Ever since I can remember, I could never quite do anything correctly. I remember when I was a kid I was forced to stay up all night to do one math problem. I was always told, all the time, that I was extremely smart—this was in front of company. When we were alone I was a dumb, stupid kid, and how come I couldn't do that? She knew that I could do that— whatever it was. It was a direct competition to some degree. When I was learning the piano—which she performed on— when I was about 11, I finally gave up having her teach me anything, because she was just outrageous, just a monster.

There were a lot of tensions between us that I think probably were competitive, but I felt that my mother disliked me so much that she never gave me the idea that it was something she cared about. I just felt that she resented me because I was this other way. I never had the feeling that she wanted me to be like she was, but perhaps that was there; wasn't that competition? According to our family folklore about mom and dad, she was the dumb one, dumb but beautiful. My father was smart but she secretly felt that she was smart too. I was another one of the acknowledged smart ones in the family, and there probably was competition there.

Some of us feel that the competition is for the attention or affection of other people. No matter who—the daughter or the mother—initiates the rivalry, the fear is that one's rival will appear a more appealing woman.

Sometimes I'm jealous of the relationship between my mother and my daughter. They get along real well. In the earlier years there was a lot of conflict in that my mother wanted to be my daughter's mother also. That was a very hard thing for me, for all of us; for the three of us it was very hard. She's now gotten to the point where she's willing for me to be the mother, so that's a big plus and it's much easier for me to handle the situation. It's better for me to be the mommy and for her to be the grandmother.

In relation to my children I think there's been competition. It's not overt at all. I think it's not conscious on her part, but I see changes in her behavior when my children are around, trying to compete for their affection.

I know I felt that the competition came through her being really a little girl. I hated her for that kind of thing. She could always get her way. She was a cute little red-headed, stamping-her-foot child, and father loved her, and clearly she came first, before my sister and me.

I started college, and the first week of school I became ill. My mother came up and stayed in my room. It was the first week of school and I had to stay in the clinic. I hadn't met anybody and she stayed in my room and got to know all of these people at school before I did. I felt she was more successful in my life than I was, and I was real angry at her for coming.

It is commonly assumed that mothers and daughters compete to see who is the most beautiful or sexually desirable. This Snow White/Wicked Queen rivalry was rarely mentioned by the women I interviewed. Those few who did allude to it seemed to feel that they, regrettably, could not compete with their mothers for beauty—that their fathers and they, the daughters, found their mothers to be beyond competition in this respect. Perhaps these women wished that they could *be* their mothers, rather than depose them.

As I was growing up, I used to run around in her bras, I used to run arund in her panty hose, get all dressed up in her stuff and wish I was her. . . . Oh yeah, I sure do consider my mother good looking.

There were a few daughters who felt that their mothers initiated competition with them on the basis of "sexiness" or "desirability"—in terms of responses from men. These women certainly resented being set up in this competition, felt it was inappropriate, and refused to compete.

After she left my father she got super-sexy and really got into tight clothes and short shorts—what we call hot pants now— and that used to bother me, because people would say "Look at her." She went through that stage as I was just entering puberty, and later, when I was 16 and started having boyfriends of my own, she would try to seduce them. She had used me as bait before. I eventually didn't bring anybody home or date anybody. A lot of guys would think I was easy because she was. I really was a virgin for a long time.

After my father died and I was in high school and she was dating and I was dating, there would be competition on Saturday nights as to who would have a date and who would be home. I felt she was competing with me. I remember being home one time on a Saturday night, and she was going out and I was moping around the house—not feeling that she's going out and I resent it, but just moping like 16-year-olds tend to do—and she said to me, "You're jealous because I'm

*going out and you're not going out." I remember thinking it
was very far from the truth. As a matter of fact, I used to like it
when she went out because then I had time alone; she was
always happier when she went out, and when she was home
she was depressed.*

There were, of course, daughters who found their mothers
beautiful, made no reference to the sexual aspects of their
appearance, and displayed no concern about being less
attractive than the mothers. Fifty-one percent of the studied
daughters found their mothers to be attractive women, and,
for most of these, the acknowledgement of mother's beauty
was a source of pride, and part of the pleasure they felt in their
mothers.

Many of us have felt that the competition is initiated, or
wholly carried on, by our mothers. Even when we express ourselves ambivalently, it is clear that we believe "she started it."

*I would say sometimes she gets jealous of me and my brothers;
my brothers and I have good relationships, and she does not
seem to like that because she feels I'm taking over their
affection. She thinks maybe I'm telling them things about her
and actually I'm not.*

*From the time I was about ten years old when my friends
would come over she would make a point of trying to
dominate the conversation with them. I remember at my
eighth grade graduation she had a party for me, and my
friends weren't invited. It was all her friends. There was this
big mirror in our dining room and she had taken pictures of
herself out of photograph albums she had, and put them on
this mirror, so I felt it was a party for her. I really felt put out
because it didn't seem to be any kind of celebration for me. For
my high school graduation she did the same thing, invited her
friends, older people who would give me money. It wasn't for
me.*

*The competition between me and my mother started when she
started taking my clothes. It was mostly after my first job*

when I was 16. She started taking my clothes, and every time I would buy something—it was such a joy to have money you know—she would get real mad, and she would be upset unless it was something she could sneak out and wear. I got mad at her once, and told her that she was jealous of me. There was a big scene over that. I thought she was competing with me and I felt real uncomfortable about it. I don't think I was competing with her.

My mother always had to feel that she did things better than I did. Things like cooking that she did real well, she'd always tell me I couldn't do that. I thought there was competition there. She was competing with me; I don't think I was competing with her.

I learned from her, and I passed on to my eldest daughter, the competition to be the kid. Who was going to be the child, who was going to take care of whom. I did not feel competitive with her; I felt she was competitive with me.

My mother is a highly competitive woman, but I can't think of a situation in which I competed with her. She knows that I'm also competitive and she encouraged all of us to be so, if we were comfortable with it. She liked that, and if we were competitive she enjoyed it—she was excellent in sports and some of us were very good also—so I think she encouraged it, but I don't know that I competed with her.

There was always a lot of competition between my mother and myself. Yes, my mother was a fiercely competitive person. I don't feel that I'm like that, and what it did to me was—I backed off. A lot of people think I'm very aggressive; I do get my points across. I guess I do. But I work at it real hard—it's not an automatic thing. It's not easy for me and I do have lots of doubts afterwards. You know what I mean, it's not an easy thing, it does not come naturally to me. I feel like my mother was jealous of me because my father was very fond of me. I feel that later in life, as I grew older, I was much more of an anchor for my siblings than she was, and I think she was jealous of that. And I feel that continues to some degree.

It is apparent, however, that competition is mutual in most cases. Our mothers fear our maturing into women who will not only not be their little girls anymore, but will simply be younger competition—especially when so many of us begin to separate from them by criticizing them and throwing off their advice. Much of what they do in competition, their strongest weapon in fact, is to remind us of our "weaknesses." For our part, daughters compete to surpass our mothers— perhaps out of that fear we have of "being" our mothers over again. We compete to go beyond our mothers, so that we need not *be* this other woman, particularly if her life is not what we want for ourselves. For most social purposes, we learn, women are interchangeable: in the dark they are all the same. When we perceive the role, demeaning as it is, we reject it; this 49 percent of us who sustained competition with our mothers reject the role through competing with our mothers to bypass them, to best them, to succeed where they have failed—*we* will be exceptional women; *we* will not be this degraded creature, woman.

Was my mother a role model? God, no, except in a negative sense. I didn't want to be like that.

No, never. It's the last thing I want to be, the last thing.

I knew I would be a grown woman some day if I was lucky, but I knew I wasn't going to be like her.

I didn't want to be like her, and I was real worried. I can remember saying to myself, "I'm not going to be like her."

And yes, the competition is conscious. Daughters may repress such consciousness, may deny it—but it emerges in our (often rabid) fear of the similarity between ourselves and our mothers. Though many of us who engage in mother/daughter competition do acknowledge it as such, even those who don't will talk about the fear of reproducing mother's life pattern and idiosyncrasies.

I think who I am now is a lot in response to her, a negative response. I'm still sometimes scared that I'm going to be like her, that I am like her, and there are some parts of me that are unthinkingly opposite of her, and if I thought about it I wouldn't necessarily want to be so much like that. I've just been a total slob all my life because my mother is so fanatical about keeping stuff clean. I still have to struggle to realize that I like to be a neat person and don't like mess and clutter; that I don't have to be a slob because my mother taught me not to be.

You know, I think I would have liked my mother a lot more as she was 20 years ago when I was five years old. When she hadn't been married for long, you know. We used to have real plants in the house. Now they're all plastic. It's very far away, it's very far away from life. My uncle reminded me that my mother was a rebel when she was young, and she was real wild and rebellious and talented and wanted to do her own thing. And God, that's what scares me.

I think when I was a young mother and my kids were coming up, I was a mother in the negative ways my mother had been, concerning my fears, my needs not being met, and my being unsure about whose role was what, who was the mother and who was the kid. I was however aware of this and my mother wasn't. It was extremely painful. That's why I started therapy. It was very frightening to me; I was determined not to be like her, and fought against falling into the repeat, but didn't have the tools to do it successfully. I knew what was happening and wasn't able to deal with it until later.

Oh God (deep sigh) I always wanted so much not to be like my mother (laugh). In some ways I think I am like her. I worry a lot and I'm insecure a lot and that's the way she is too.

My worst parts, my weakest, my most scared, doubting parts are like my mother. All the negative parts of me are like my mother.

My mother would always say I was just like her, and then she would say how my son, she and I were alike. Well it scared me because I thought I was being programmed to be crazy like she was too. It was very scary.

I remember one thing that she did and it used to make me physically uncomfortable. She would put her red hair over my forehead to cover my black hair and claim I looked like her and that bothered me for some reason.

Shortly after I had my son, I went to spend a week with my mother. That week was something that had never happened to me before and it was very frightening. I came away feeling like I was my mother. I acted like my mother and I talked like my mother and I was nervous like my mother and it was frightening because I never realized that I was so much like my mother. It was a process that was going on for my entire life and I never realized it. What that did to me was that for a long time I wouldn't let her near me. I was afraid to be with her. I didn't want that to happen again because there are a lot of things in my mother that I don't accept and I didn't want to be like.

I look like her. When I see a picture of myself or particularly in film it's shocking, but we actually do look alike. Tantrums. My mother is a big tantrum person, and I also have to go to bed when I'm feeling upset—which is what my mother always said, she was sick and had to go to bed. And I do that too, but not anywhere near as much as my mother. The parts about myself that I like are not like her.

I used to be a lot more like her and it scared me. I used to react to things the way she did, and I would get angry at my husband. Sometimes when she got angry at my father she would scream and rant and rave. Oftentimes she would get real quiet and curl herself up in a ball and go off in a corner and I did that often too. Sometimes I used to feel that my attitudes about sex were the same as my mother's. I felt that she never enjoyed it. For a long time I didn't enjoy it. She never said things like "it's an obligation and something you must do when you get married," but I knew.

If our mothers have been institutionalized, or are on maintenance drug therapy, we assiduously note traits in ourselves which might make us suspect; we toe the societal line with care, and generally disavow affection for, or connection to, our mothers. If our mothers are alcoholic, the tendency is to perceive ourselves as being quite different from them. Even though there is no reason to compete with a mother who has so obviously "lost," we struggle to rise above the failure, lest there be some discernible point of comparison. Our mothers share these fears, especially if *their* mothers have been institutionalized.

There is a fear of that in my mother. She talks about it a lot because of what she saw when she was being raised. My grandfather could be a very violent man. He had beaten her mother, he would get drunk, he would come in and do crazy things. He was the one who finally hanged himself during the depression years. My grandmother was unstable for many years because of that, institutionalized for a while. My aunt goes off once in a while, my aunt who used to live with us; my mother says she goes off the deep end once in a while and gets put away. She has her breakdowns. My mother has said from time to time, "I'll wind up like my mother from you kids," and that kind of stuff.

My mother worried about it. She was afraid of going crazy. She was afraid the pressures in her head would cause her to flip. She used to use the word oblivion.

My grandmother, my mother's mother, was in an institution. When I was 4, 5, or 6 years old, my mother took me shopping, and while we were gone my aunt and uncle put my grandmother in a mental institution without telling my mother. She had lived with us only for a short time. They put her in. Nobody would go see my grandmother but us. Sunday mornings my mother and I would hop the bus and go see her. My grandmother was schizo. We finally got her out and at least she died with us. I think this bothered my mother. My father used to throw up to her, "You look like your mother and you're both nutty and squirrely."

Given the acceptance of Freudian hypotheses as fact, and

the use of Freudian jargon in ordinary conversation, it is no surprise that a distinct group of daughters label their competition with their mothers as "the usual thing," "a classic case," "very Oedipal," and "your standard Electra complex."

She won. From the time I was a young woman on, and certainly in the last years of her life when my mother was an invalid, I wanted more of my father's time. I wanted to share with him. He was fun to be with. I loved going to a museum with my dad. It was an event that very rarely occurred. There was no question that she won, first and last, and all the way around the block. She may not have been in competition. I was. I'm aware that I wanted more of what she had and there just wasn't any way I was going to get it.

There was for sure competition for my father's approval at certain ages. Off and on, now and then. He thought my mother was stupid so he used me as an example, that I was smart. I think I did get extra attention by saying things to my mother to prove that in fact she was stupid.

I'm sure I felt it angrily and strongly as a little girl, and I remember the feelings well. I remember one time saying to dad that I was marrying him when I grew up and I gave him an engagement ring. And this was young enough, open enough, between mother and father; it was obviously a little girl kind of thing to do.

We competed for my father's affections. I was not conscious of doing it but I feel my mother was worried about me as a competitor. I don't know why I feel that way because actually she had him and I feel pretty bad about that. He always told me what a wonderful woman she was and I guess I resented very much that she had him.

We competed for my father's attention. She always won, or most of the time. She was so pretty that I didn't think I could make it on that level, so that's why I decided to go for the tomboy part. I could ride my bike better than she could, go to baseball games, go horseback riding, but I could never compete with her for looks. I'm sure that's why I didn't try for many years. I think she was aware of the competition when it came to wanting to get in bed with them. Sometimes she would look a little strange when I would go to a ball game with my father, like she was aware that I had won. Also I could win with my logic. He appreciates logic.

You know, it's a real queer thing. Little girls are usually in love with their daddies and want to x out their moms. One of the hardest things for me to cope with was when my parents were divorced—I had worked out a lot of those triangular feelings about my parents—I walked into therapy and said, "My God, I've won," which sounds horrendous, and I don't really mean that, but it just flashed through my brain. There was competition when my mother came up here last year; she was on a steady downhill drunk all summer long. She propositioned my husband in front of my kids. The interesting thing is that she's competing with me because I've got all the things she never had. That was hard at first, real hard.

These comprise the strongest stereotypical competitions. But the father's role in competitive family situations is not simply that of love-object, the cause of sexual rivalry between mother and daughter. Quite often, the father competes with the mother for the daughter.

I was the focal point in most of their arguments, frequently bitter—all through the years.

I guess I've put a lot of this on my mom, but there were a lot of things my father did to provoke her. He was a real asshole, but somehow I see her as being an awful person. I think a lot of it has to do with the fact that she's alive and my father's dead.

When I was around 15, in the court scenes, there was heavy competition between my parents for me. A lot of court scenes. (laugh) It really was like that—just what one imagines.

There was intense competition between my mother and father for my affection and allegiance. She seldom could come out in

*front and fight for it which is exactly why I think she cared
more for my brother than for me. There was a breakdown
when they split up. Somehow I was his and my brother was
hers. He bought me a lot (laugh) and I would go and spend
week-ends with him. Sometimes—my father was a drinker—
they actually were physically battling over me, him driving
me off in a car, and her pulling me out of the car because she
knew he was going to take me to bars, and she didn't think I
was supposed to go to bars.*

In those situations where the father competed openly, showed
a preference for his daughter and criticized or ridiculed the
mother, the daughter usually preferred him. Though several
of the women have changed their minds, a majority of
daughters whose fathers competed for them were "won over"
by this active campaign, no doubt aided in their father's cause
by the apparent social "fact" of their mother's inferiority.
This also sometimes resulted in a determined identification
with the father.

*My father criticized my mother, saying she was dumb or My
father critized my mother, saying she was dumb or irrational,
worried too much, that kind of thing. And I agreed with him
mostly, and I think my mother was as he said; she was not that
together as a person, especially dumb. Now I realize my
mother is real smart. She's irrational and she doesn't do things
the way I would do them, but she's real smart.*

*Well, the way he would do it with me is he would get me alone
and say, "What do I do with her? She can't learn how to iron a
shirt and I showed her how. What would you do with a person
like that?" and that kind of thing. He preferred me I think
because I was young and voluble. He wanted me to be the
perfect girl, so all the stuff she refused to learn how to do, he
tried to teach me—this is the proper way to iron a shirt, this is
the proper way to wash a dish, this is the proper way to mop
the floor. He was so hyper-critical when he realized she wasn't
going to learn how to do those things that he turned all of that*

on me and he was a real nit-picker. He wasn't satisfied with my performance either because he didn't like my attitude.

I think she knew that my head and his worked the same way. I was a compulsive reader as a child, and the only time I'd lie was when I'd say that I'd go to sleep at a certain time, and I wouldn't read any more. I couldn't help myself and I read the book every time. So if mother was going to hide my book I could never find it. If daddy hid my book I found it every time, so there was some kind of recognition in the family that we were a match.

I think my mother probably resented a lot of the closeness that the kids in the house had with him and didn't know what to do about it so she just let it be. Because she let it be, sooner or later everybody came to the knowledge of what the truth was, and all the children shifted to her as we grew older. They began to understand and respect her. When we were small my father used to call her stupid. He used to treat her like she was the most ignorant person around. Yes, he used to treat my mother like an imbecile. He still tends to think of women as a subordinate race. He's got seven women in his family and they're all very bright and he thinks they're dumb.

I preferred my father because he wasn't around much and she was the one who had to scream at us and do the shit work, and that's why I didn't like her. I even went into the court to live with him, when they were divorced. My father tried to break up the relationship I had with my mother. I do remember, when I was 12, I think, or 11 maybe, and we were visiting my grandparents. My father and I went for a walk in the evening. My parents had just had a fight and he was telling me how he was going to divorce my mother as soon as we were grown up. He did things like that when the custody fight was going on; he said, "Your mother's a witch." Before I lived with him, he prompted me to run away and go live with my grandmother. He said, "Oh, do it, do it, do it," and he drove me over, threw all my clothes in the car when she was gone one afternoon, and we just sort of moved out. (laugh) I was just sort of thinking that when I was a little kid he always got the chance to *play nice guy to me. He was like the good guy.*

When mothers openly tried to enlist their daughter, competed directly with the father and/or asked the daughter's support, the daughter either rejected her, or, unable to deal with the pain of the choice, avoided choosing.

My mother tried to keep my father and me apart, and I think that was competition. I wasn't aware of it until I started talking to you today. It came out very loud and clear when I was 16 and she went with me and my brother to visit my father. She said something like, "I would like you to love me. Don't love him." She wanted us to prove it. I got up and walked away from both of them and went home in a taxi, because I couldn't handle that, being torn. Obviously I have feelings for him somewhere.

When I was in junior high school, probably around 7th or 8th grade, they were fighting at the table and it was one of their usual knock down-drag out kind of fights. My mother said, "Well, if you want to leave, go ahead, but the kids will stay with me," or something like that, and then she turned to me and said, "You tell him that," and I left the table.

When I'm having a conversation with my father, and she wants some attention, instead of going into the conversation she'll talk about something else like, "Those are nice shoes you have on, Delia." Like she's totally irrelevant verbally.

I think my mother has a tendency to say certain things to us, her daughters; you know all her children are women, and there's an allegiance right there. I think she has a little tendency to say things to my sisters that are a little bit against my father. That's because of her own problems, not because she's a mean woman.

This is the other half of the situation; i.e., daughters will not align themselves with the obviously inferior position of the mother if there is a choice offered. Only a few of the daughters who spent much of their childhood and adolescence preferring their fathers seemed to imply that, if only their mothers had given them the attention or affection they desired, they'd have thrown over their fathers, who were chosen by default.

I never felt that my mother cared to compete with my father, but that could be wrong.

She always sort of felt that my father had more of a way with me; I was striving to get her attention, but there would be more times when she would accuse me of wrapping my father around my little finger.

There were about an equal number who felt that their fathers would have wasted time and effort in such competition, for the choice of mother was not open to contest.*

My mother had it all along so there was no competition.

There was no competition because my mother had won early in that game. It was just their type of arrangement.

A small number of daughters felt that they had to compete with their brothers for their mothers' attention and affection—again a situation where the socially-defined "superiority" of males dooms us to lose before we start. Most of these daughters understood that boys were considered more valuable. That is, these mothers did not necessarily prefer particular male children *for themselves,* as individual people, but for their maleness. It was their being male that made them more important to their mothers, and therefore favored. Here is one classic story that may stand for all daughters in this position: †

---

*See Fathers chapter for more on the mother-daughter-father triangle.

† The mother raised her two sons with such care that each of them, in adulthood, believes himself to have been his mother's favorite child. Their sister, obviously, has no such thoughts.

My mother kept me in my place—the bottom of the heap—I had the least importance in our household. As the years went past, now and again I'd doubt this, perhaps trying to convince myself it wasn't true—the way my mother had treated me. But when I became pregnant, she said to me, "Oh, I hope it's a boy. Boys are so much better to raise than girls, so much nicer; girls are so difficult." So I know. I knew I wasn't crazy. She had been doing that to me all those years.

My brothers were treated with respect; their lives had more value than mine; my achievements were belittled. But I never gave up. I didn't try to talk to her, to change her mind—I brought the fight to my brothers. I competed directly with them. It was an ongoing fight, in sports, in academics. And I knew that it was woman against man. For instance, I said to my mother, "I'll do household chores if they will." Of course they never did—so neither did I. And the result? My mother would set the table for dinner each night with one place missing—mine. She was setting the table for them, my father and brothers. She'd iron all the men's clothes. I ironed all my own, but I wouldn't do theirs. Her basic attitude about me was, "You're impossible; you're just impossible."

This wasn't just a feeling; it was explicit. Every night after dinner, she'd clear the table, wipe it clean, and light the lamp for my older brother to do his homework. He'd bring all his stuff and spread it out—the whole space was for him. I could do mine in the bathroom, on the porch, in my bedroom. She'd say all the time, "Ted is such a reader"—the intellectual. My test scores were higher than his—she was called to school and told this about me—yet she'd talk to me about him that way— no words for me.

And my younger brother—well—there was a rule in our house, no eating between meals. But for him—she'd order the pizza, she'd make the sandwiches. I'd come home from school and see George drinking a bottle of the special juice my mother bought especially for herself. Right in front of her. I'd say to him, "What are you doing?" He didn't care. He'd even say, "Aw, let her have some, Ma," but I wouldn't touch it.

She even helped them with money to go to college—I never got a dime; she assumed I'd get by. I knew in my heart I was superior to them, and in their hearts they knew it too—but nobody would give me a break. She never came through for me.

Such mothers have accepted sexist bias to such an extent that they do not see, not only how outrageous it is to act out and display this preference before their daughters, but what a rejection of their own selves such preference indicates.

Some daughters, like myself, saw the disparity of treatment, but never experienced lessened affection. My mother always made it clear that her only daughter was special; she said that every woman should have a daughter; she told me, "A son is your son till he takes a wife; a daughter's your daughter the rest of your life."

Because of my lack of "real" sisters, I was ignorant of the possibilities for competition between them. It seems that, for some women, my mother was more than right: every woman should have a daughter—but just one—for the pain of sister rivalry is intense. Dismal enough to try to meet your mother's expectations and fail, without having to compete with another young woman, your sister, who seems to suit your mother's dreams and needs quite comfortably. In these situations, we not only lose our mothers' affection, but cannot love the sister-rival who has found it.

When my mother remarried, I got a step-sister who is ten months older than I. The two of us were more or less united, but when we were together, my mother seemed to prefer Melinda, who played up to her more. Melinda was much better at not showing her true feelings than I was. My mother also competed with both of us, and then she would compete with me, I think, to get Melinda's allegiance.

I don't think she wants me to outshine my sister. My sister is married, she has two kids, she's been married for about 12 years—she got married when she was 19, to a high school sweetheart (laugh). And she has a master's degree in math and she teaches in the junior high in the suburbs. She's not a very successful teacher and she's real overweight. And my mother was outshone by her *younger sister, and she's real resentful about that, so she was real concerned that I shouldn't outshine my older sister.*

I gave my mother a feminist poster for her birthday, and my sister gave her a trip to Disneyland or something, and I was very disappointed that my mother, who is a political, intellectual, cultural elitist, did not understand that my present was superior to my sister's. My sister is very competitive.

My parents never went to visit my sister after she married without bringing gifts. I mean my mother worked for three weeks buying enough things to take. And what did I get— nothing. We went to New York one day and she spent the whole day buying things for my sister and not once bought me anything. I had a nice little party for my parents when they came to visit, because I thought it would be the thing to do, and my mother spent the whole night talking about what a nice party it would have been if Joanie had given it. . . . In highschool, I wanted to sew and she said to me, "I spent nine years teaching your sister to sew, and she never learned, so if you want to sew, do it when you're 25 years old and I don't want to hear a word about it." That was it, so I never sewed at home, ever. I wouldn't dream of it and I wouldn't take any advice. She tried once, saw something I had made, and quickly wanted to give me some advice, and I refused to listen. . . . I always thought my mother identified with my sister. My sister looks like my mother did when she was young, was attractive with the boys as my mother had been, and she excelled in sports. I felt that my mother had my sister to identify with so she didn't need me. I wasn't important. My victories or defeats weren't important because she had gone through that with my sister. I think the telling thing is the big wedding. My sister had a big wedding, so we didn't have to do that anymore. And it's the same with everything throughout my life. I didn't need to do this because Joanie had done this. I should have gotten my thrill through Joanie. I just wanted to have acceptance so I tried to do what they wanted me to do, and she just did everything the opposite, and still she's the one that got the affection and I'm the one that got the sluff.

Competing with a sister may be far uglier than mother/ daughter competitions. After all, in most cases, mothers have given us nurturance and support at least part of the time, and our sisters may never, given the structure of the nuclear family, have related to us in a way that positively binds us.

Discovering the falsity of our assumptions about competition between mothers and daughters has strengthened my conviction that our sociopolitical system is maintained through a network of lies. Moreover, it is clear that the nuclear family is based in competition. No one family member may receive love, attention, admiration or support without draining it from the emotional reserves of another. In order for deeply felt emotions to develop and be expressed between two people, time and energy have to be devoted, in a rather exclusive fashion, to that specific relationship. Particularly in the case of women, especially the mother, that time and energy are never available, except at someone's loss. That loss, by definition, is *always* the mother's, but other members of the family lose too. No mother can possibly fulfill all the requirements of her role at the same time. In order to "properly" mother one child, she must slight the others. To give her intellect, sensuality and strength to her husband, she must deprive the children of those qualities. Because the institution of motherhood in this society requires the continual stunting of either the mother's growth and expression or the child's, there can be no ease to the tension between mother and daughter. The uncompromising tightness, the stranglehold of the nuclear form, is directly responsible for the competitions that exist among mothers, daughters, fathers, sisters and brothers.

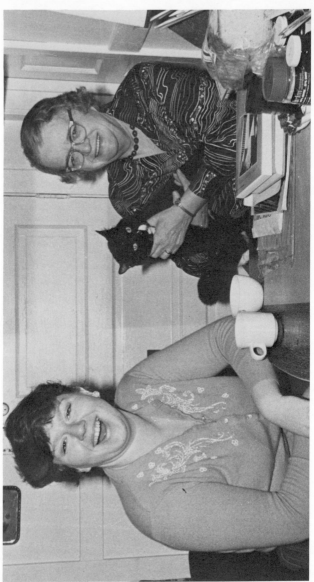

Jo Ann Arduini

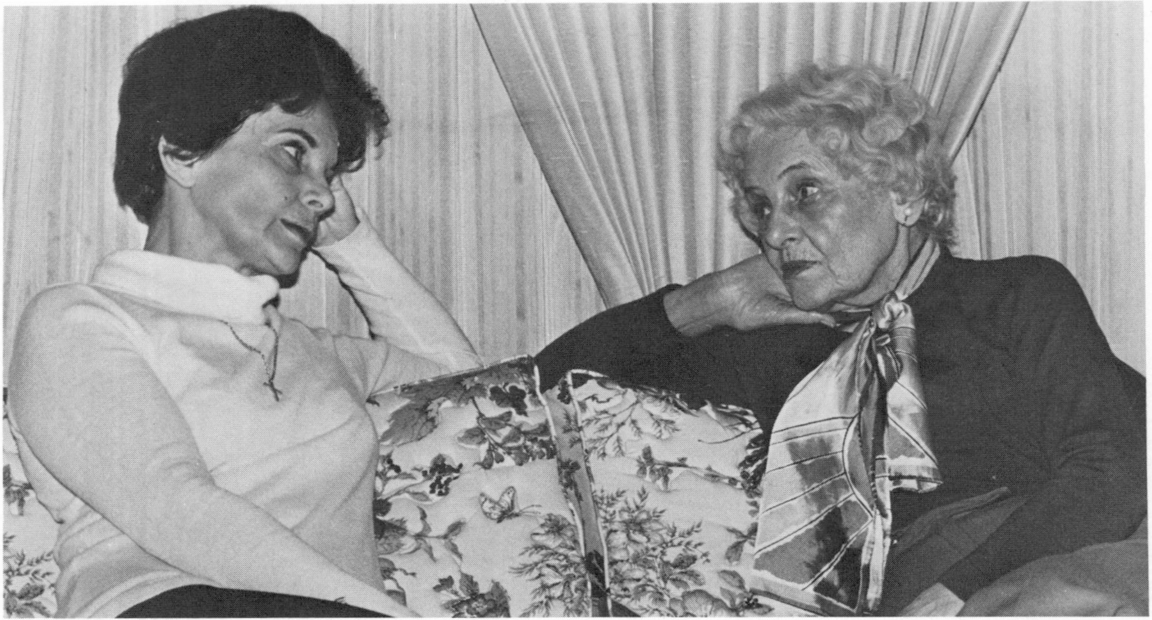

Jo Ann Arduini

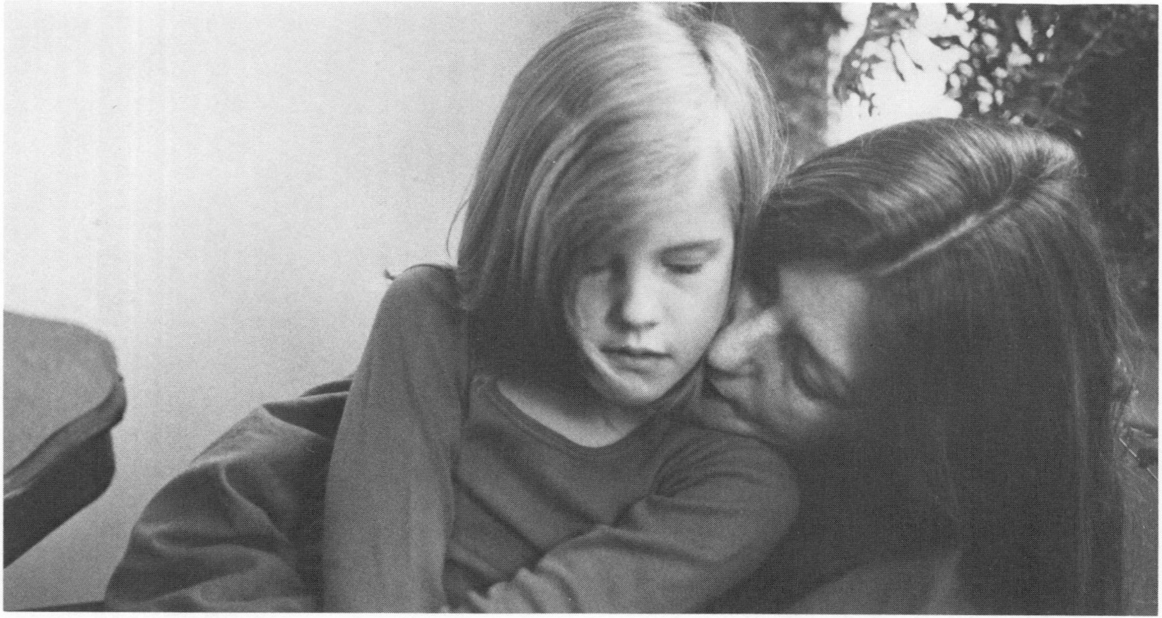

Signe Varco

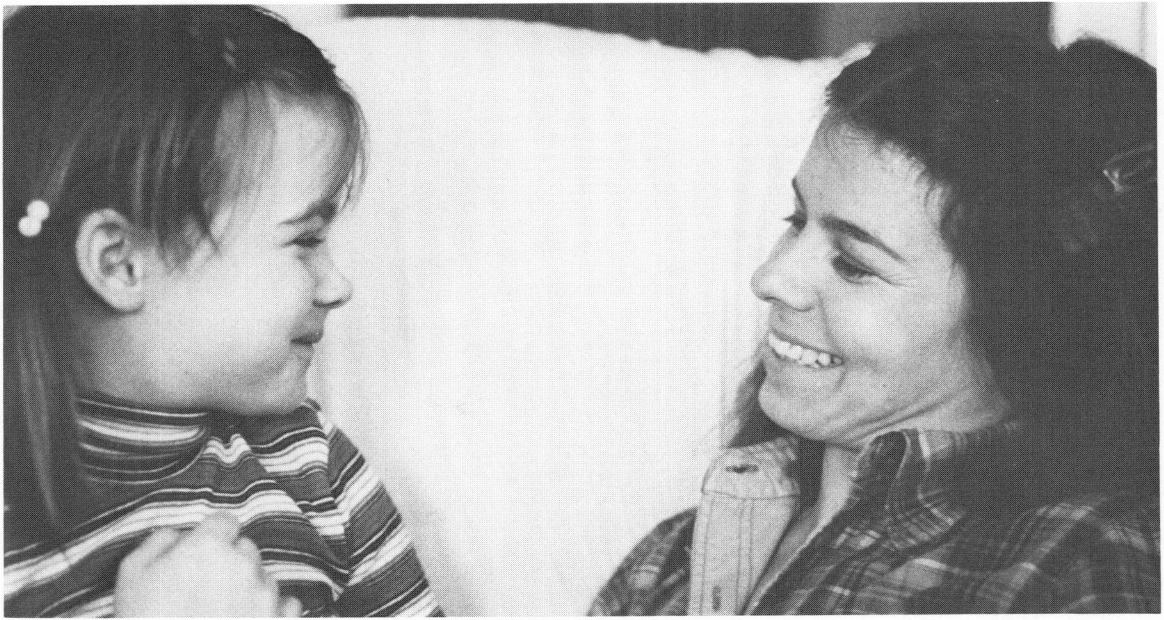

Omie Daniels

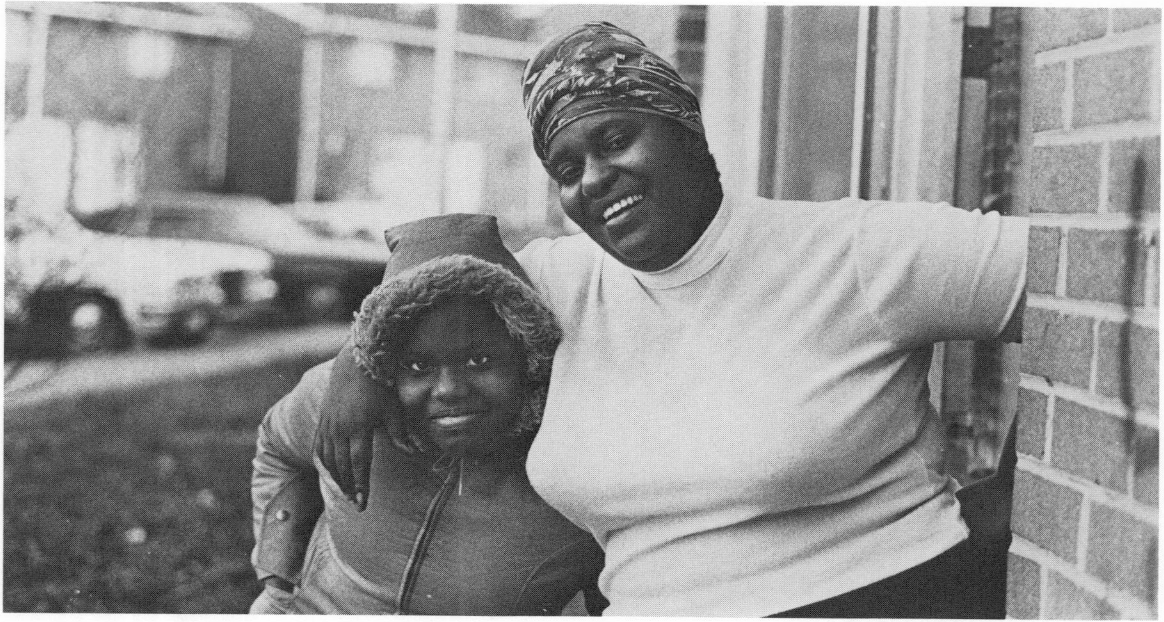

Shirley Parry

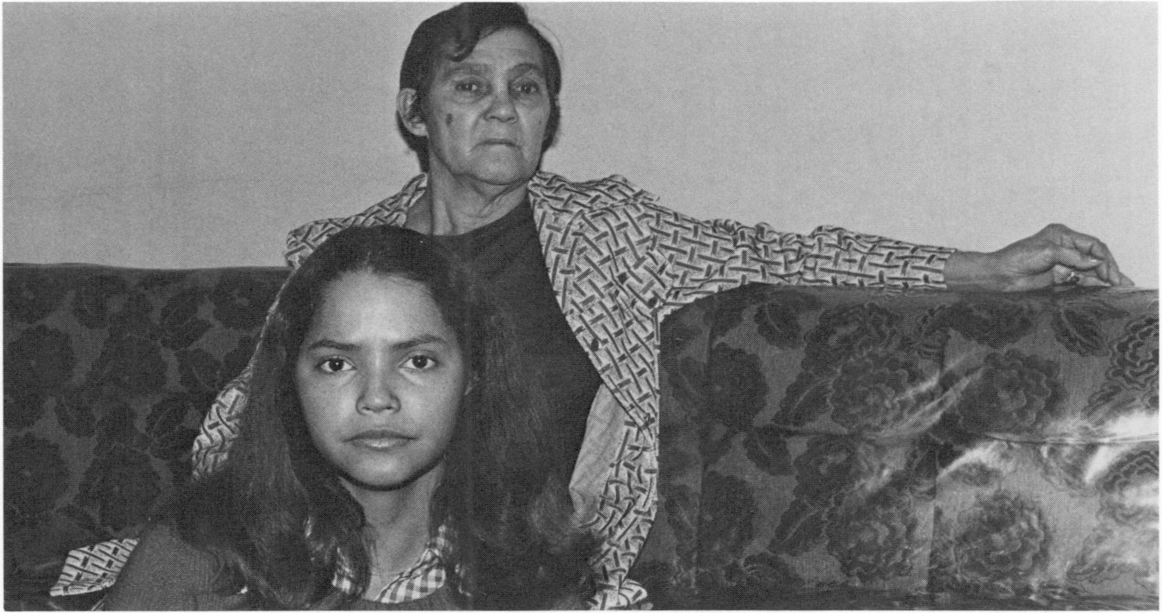

Jo Ann Arduini

5
Fathers: The Men in Our Lives

Daddy, daddy, you bastard, I'm through.
—SYLVIA PLATH

To hold you again,
Dear father!
I should gladly water all the garden
With my blood.
—HEIDI GITTERMAN

Contemporary mother/daughter relations are consonant with the existence of the patriarchal nuclear family. Both the alienation and distrust which daughters feel, and the fear and resentment of mothers, strengthen and perpetuate the current social structure. Fathers are the repositories of patriarchal law. Individual mother/daughter pairs have, each in the person of a husband-father, a representative of the power structure to whom they relate on an intimate basis. He sees to it that the rules of the society are followed by his wife and daughter, neither of whom have as much interest in maintaining the status quo as he does. Such maintenance reinforces his authority and power.

Fathers have a shorter cultural history than mothers. For most of the thousands of years human beings have existed as a distinct species, the role of the father in the creation of children was unknown. "Before the idea of biological paternity can be grasped, it is necessary to understand that sexual intercourse between a man and a woman is the indispensable first step toward conception. But primitive people did not know this. . . . They attributed conception to various causes, not one of which was connected with sexual intercourse. They thought women gave birth spontaneously through their magical powers, or through something that entered their womb, or through something they ate, or were given to eat, perhaps by a man. If a man was involved at all, it was through food intercourse, not sex intercourse."[1] Reed goes on to describe the ritual of "couvade," which established the right of a woman's mate to perform for her children what had previously been exclusively maternal functions. Couvade explains the origin of fatherhood; "it made the man . . . a 'male mother'. . . . The central feature of couvade is the imitation by the man of a woman in childbed. . . ." The woman, "directly after giving birth, goes about her daily activities without further ado." The man "takes to his hammock or bed, 'lying in' for a time. He is treated as an invalid and subjected to strict taboos and rules of avoidance . . . . Old women minister to his needs, supervise his observance of the taboos, and assist his recovery. . . . Couvade allowed him to have close association with his (mate's) child, to hold it in his arms, nurture and care for it. . . . Couvade testifies that the father does not enter history as the biological male parent of a child, but through a ritual giving him social recognition as the father."[2]

It is an irony that fatherhood as defined and practiced in patriarchy should have evolved out of these original attempts of men to join in the tender and loving relations they observed between women and their children.

Even after the patriarchy had developed and given rise to those cultures which are considered the primary sources of western civilization, Greece, Rome and the later European nations, the actual role of the father in conception was still inadequately understood. Clearly, the error was in favor of the patriarchy; i.e., the notion was that the sperm was not a complement to the ovum, nor even a seed, but that the female was merely a receptacle which held the growing child (the "homunculus") that had been deposited by a male. This gave over to the concept of "planting"—as late as this century, male doctors, ministers and politicians in the United States would speak of women as being the "soil" for men's "seed" when describing conception and pregnancy. They were arguing that women do best when left to lie fallow between plantings; that voting, attending school and holding jobs—to say nothing of engaging in intensive intellectual and political activities—were damaging to women, would overwork them, would wear out the soil.

Patriarchal capitalism, the general politic of contemporay American culture, defines both women and children as property belonging to the husband-father. Thus, a daughter is twice over her father's chattel. The father-as-owner's purpose is served by facilitating his daughter's socialization. His role is to maintain the present order. He is supposed to protect his daughter, support her until she marries, and oversee her training as a woman through the agency of his wife and whatever schooling he sees fit.

The folklore of father/daughter relations also asserts that there is a fondness, affection, a doting and even covetous attitude on the part of fathers toward daughters; this is the acknowledged emotional stance which describes intimacy between fathers and daughters. Sixty-nine percent of the fathers in the study took no active role in raising their daughters; many of them were barely present. The supposed protection and affection are remote; our fathers certainly are not present in our daily lives to the extent that our mothers are.

He was the man. A provider. We were his girls, both my mother and me. It didn't have to be said; it was right there, that he was taking care of his girls. He loved the fact that we were both his girls. He didn't want a boy for anything. He loved it.

My dad went away mostly to work, the harvest, any kind of work. This was during the depression. When he wasn't working my mother would say he was "chasing the honey pot and the butter tree." He was away from home a lot.

It was an odd situation, because my mother was the middle man and she would say, "Pa says," or we would tell my mother and she would relate the message to my father. My father was the supreme being at that time. He made the decisions and we actually were afraid of my father, what his reaction would be to anything we said or did. My mother was the one who told us what he expected or accepted.

If I'm real upset I go to my mother. When I'm really upset I don't go to my father unless my mother is not home. . . . My father is a very good friend and we share things. We kid around a lot and go bike riding generally every day. We do a lot of things together but they're not really anything in particular that we share. It's more just for fun.

He was there all the time. He doesn't seem to have an important part to my whole life.

Nonetheless, daughters consider their fathers "special." Not only do we see that men are powerful and dominant, but that our fathers are particularly so. Daughters are supposed to hero-worship their fathers, idolize them, fear them if necessary, but to assume an automatic measure of respect. Just as we learn about the roles of mother and daughter, so we apprehend "father."

We are schooled in daughterly respect and admiration by our mothers, and their training is enhanced, again, by the same tales and legends cited in Chapter 2. Andrea Dworkin points out that fathers in fairy tales are mostly kings, noble and rich. (Even if they are poor, they are noble-hearted; often they are deposed monarchs.) "They are never responsible or held accountable for the evil done by their wicked wives. Most of the time, they do not notice it. . . . Cinderella's father saw her every day. He saw her picking lentils out of the ashes, dressed in rags, degraded, insulted. He was a good man. The father of Hansel and Grethel also had a good heart."[3] When his children returned to him, there was a joyful reunion, despite his having been a party to their abandonment in the forest. "Do not misunderstand—they did not forgive him, for there was nothing to forgive. All malice originated with the woman. He was a good man.

"Though the fairy tale father marries the evil woman in the first place, has no emotional connection with his child, does not interact in any meaningful way with her, abandons her and worse, does not notice when she is dead and gone, he is a figure of male good. He is the patriarch, and as such he is beyond moral law and human decency."[4] From fairy tales to contemporary TV programs is no noticeable jump, for all the daddies from Ozzie Nelson through "Father Knows Best" to Archie Bunker are patriarchs just the same. Wise or foolish, they are the kings of their respective households. We see them as romantic figures, even in their negative aspects.

My father had real problems with my mother. My father had real problems with coping with life, and the way he dealt with most relationships was to be passive. My father would have been very much in the mainstream of life today—he'd be out in Wyoming, living off the land. He would be very much into the values that I see today; there would be a place for him today. There was no place for him in 1930.

I don't want to admit it, but John Wayne reminds me of my father. He's the kind of guy dad was; he always wore a ten gallon hat and boots. Looking back at it now I can understand how he got to be that way, but as a child I couldn't see it. I remember two times in my life I saw him drunk and I said I wish he'd stay drunk all the time. I wish he'd been an alcoholic because he was a really beautiful person. He became very gentle; he'd wrestle with us kids, he hugged us. One time we were waiting for him to come home—we looked down the street and here came daddy just drunker than a dog. He'd taken his whole paycheck—we'd been living in this coal mine shack—and he'd bought my mother a pair of gold threaded drapes and a lemon meringue pie. Drapes in one hand, big lemon pie in the other. We had a big party. Mother acted like we were living on Nob Hill; she put the curtains up, and we cut the pie, and we had a party.

I think I was kind of romantic about my father. Then, when they were going to get a divorce, and he said he was going to

124

*take me, I realized he was no good. Faced with the facts, I saw
that he was not my best shot.*

Frequently our mothers buttress this image of our fathers. If
they do criticize the father, it is rarely straightforward, and
often not in his presence. If they eschew criticism and follow
the traditional mode, they often go out of their way to create or
shore up the superior position of the father. My mother
always presented my father, to my brothers and myself, as the
ultimate arbiter of truth and judgment. When my own child
was born, I had the opportunity to actually see this process
worked out. Even in my son's infancy, his grandmother
would give him up to her husband, saying as she did so, "Go
to your Papa; all the children love Papa." By the time the boy
could walk and talk, he readily understood, from her own
words as well as other social cues, that Grandma wasn't as
interesting as Papa, nor as much fun; perhaps when he was
older, he would "appreciate" her. When we discussed this
self-effacement, my mother told me "the same thing
happened with my mother; none of the grandchildren would
go to her until they were much older; they always loved my
dad." She had learned the technique from her mother.

The socialization process that presents the parental pair of
the good father and the self-effacing mother is reflected in the
population of my interview group. For instance, though only
31 percent of us had contact with our fathers that could be
construed as their "raising" us, 48 percent of us preferred our
fathers to our mothers as we grew up.*

*They always kidded me that I was his favorite child, and I was
daddy's girl. I would sneak in the car and go off with him. I
was like his sidekick. I respect and love him; there are times
when I do get scared that I love him more than I do my
mother. I sympathize with him in a funny way.*

*It is testimony to the strength of the woman-bond in the mother/
daughter relation that 50 percent of the daughters preferred their
mothers, despite anti-woman and anti-mother bias in our socialization. (Two percent demonstrated no preference.)

When I think about being little I can remember running up and jumping into my father's arms, and I can't remember doing that with my mother. I know that I was held by her but I can't remember it.

I show a preference for my father actually because I can't talk to him. I will always bend over backwards to try to talk to him about things in the news and all the things that he's interested in but he ignores me continually no matter what I do. So I've always tried to show a preference for him outwardly, because mothers, they just love you; they don't care.

When I was a kid I wanted my father's attention. I wanted him to do things with me and wanted him to approve of me and I didn't admit to caring whether my mother approved of me. I gave her a hard time. She was an interference.

I think my father was capable of spiritual exploration. My mother was disinterested. My father was exciting and his head was like mine. He was interested in the arts. As far as talking about ideas and fun things is concerned, it was easier for me to make the contact with him. My mother was somehow, by her choice, not as turned on to things. In the last years of my father's life he took to painting, became passionate about it; he was talented. My mother was already sick and most resentful of this. Whatever equivalent would have been for her didn't happen. I think I didn't like it that she resented my father's blossoming.

Some of us prefer our fathers to such an extent that we give our lives to them. Daughters are expected to marry, but there is still a tradition which decrees that there be one daughter who takes care of her father, who remains single to assume her mother's role as it becomes necessary, or who marries only when her father dies. Virginia Woolf's father, Leslie Stephen, was one who required such service from his daughters. When their mother died, the oldest daughter, Stella Duckworth, took up the care and nurturing of her father, but escaped into a brief marriage and an early death. Vanessa Stephen then began her term as the dutiful daughter. Virginia is quoted in

126

her biography as having said that Leslie told Vanessa, "when he was sad, she should be sad; when he was angry . . . she should weep."[5] Vanessa and Virginia were released from this pattern by their father's death. Vanessa, who had bridled at the outrageous conduct of her Victorian father, had done her duty, but "complete and self-effacing devotion was what he demanded and this she was not ready to provide. . . . She had seen her mother and elder sister wear themselves out and die; she did not feel inclined to follow their example."[6] Vanessa had never preferred her father and considered his death a liberation. Virginia had loved him deeply and felt sad and guilty after his death. Yet, later in her life, she wrote in her diary, "His life would have entirely ended mine. What would have happened? No writing, no books;—inconceivable."[7] Lest we allow ourselves to assume that such self-sacrificing fidelity passed with the Victorians, know that a number of daughters in this study expressed similar devotion to their fathers.

I guess I loved him very much because I used to feel that if my father hadn't died—you know he died when I was 17 or 18—I would never marry; I would never marry because I never would have left him.

He wanted to be taken care of until he died. He got it. I didn't marry until I was 38. I didn't marry until after he died.

I was tied to him because I felt a lot of responsibility for his welfare. He would say that if I left him he would kill himself; he was going to drink himself to death. When I got it together to break off with him, he would try it sometimes on the few occasions we would be together. He would say, "I'm a lonely old man; come and stay with me; be my little girl." But I was able to escape the guilt when I got a better attitude about myself, and understood the sexual aspects of our relationship.

Though we are not all so devoted, and, in fact, may have serious problems with our fathers or actually dislike them, the majority of us excuse them, make allowances for them, deny those aspects of the relationship which don't fit the social

stereotype of father-daughter relations. It is this attitude
about our fathers which we transfer to other men, usually
stereotype of father-daughter relations. It is this attitude
about our fathers which we transfer to other men, usually
husbands, when we are adults. We have learned that despite
their failings or even their absence, we must give them our
affection and service. There were fathers in the study who beat
their daughters (7 percent), were alcoholic (12 percent), or
were harsh disciplinarians.* Among those fathers who were
less obviously problematic, there was a large number who
paid little or no attention to their daughters, shared no
common interest with them, hardly ever spoke to them. Yet
their daughters usually continued to seek their affection,
continued to express "love" for them.[8]

It takes nothing in the way of research to understand that a
great number of relationships between adult women and men
who are their friends, lovers, or husbands fit this same description. Thus, many women learn that they oughtn't to
expect comradeship, tenderness or sociability from men. It is
incredible to see the extent to which we excuse our fathers for
behavior we condemn in our mothers, female friends, or even,
sometimes, other men.† We pity them, rationalize their faults,
see their flaws as being caused by other people—their parents
or our mothers. We accept behavior from them that is
unacceptable, and we call this acceptance love.[9]

*I feel like he cares about me a whole lot; like I'm one of the
most important people in the world to him. We never talk
about things of substance, like about our feelings. We talk
about stuff like my car, or photography. It's not about feeling
stuff; I wouldn't feel comfortable telling him something I was
upset about. But I really feel he cares about me and I'm real
fond of him. I do have some resentments against him for not
having paid more attention to me.*

*Often daughters of these men preferred them to their mothers, or
idolized them, romanticizing the beatings, the drinking, etc.
†In fact, it may be an axiom: Daughters will excuse their fathers
anything, even beatings and rape; daughters will never excuse their
mothers, no matter what the mitigating circumstances might be.

He said to me once, "Some women never get married and you're one of those women." (laugh) I don't know whether it was because he wanted me to stay at home with them all the time, or whether he thought I was way too smart to be satisfied with the men in that small rural communty, but he just thought I would never marry. He loved me very much and still does.

He gets real threatened because he knows I'm smart and he's insecure about his own intellect. I don't like to show him how smart I am so I suppress myself. But he does love me and he talks to me a lot and I love him.

Our relationship is distant. (laugh) I have had great affection for my father but I never felt it was returned. My father was a very sensitive man but was unable to reach out at all. I have this tremendous love for my father, real sublimated and real covered up in me. I think I found his image to be supportive even though I was never close to my father at all.

I was his little daughter. Basically, because I was a girl, to him I was weak. I have a lot of empathy for him. I love him a whole lot but it's more like I love him because there's so much to understand; he's so much like a child. He's basically a real good person, but he's pretty unaware of himself.

He calls me up all the time, and we have a real wonderful trust. But every time I accomplish anything now on my own, whether in music or in photography, he gets deeply offended.

There are many of us who could not see that our fathers were not returning the out-of-proportion affection we lavished on them. (Of course, there were fathers who did, despite their training in the male role, manage to be affectionate with us, to relate to us with some warmth and human commitment.) Those of us who were truly "daddy's girl" have continued to prefer our fathers into adulthood, or have only begun to change with feminist consciousness.

My father always seemed superior to my mother. By the time I was an adolescent, and had begun to be severely critical of my mother, the difference between them was couched in intellectual and political terms. I thought my mother was empty-headed and boring; my father was well-read and always abreast of current happenings in the world. Even my mother's years as a competent and powerful PTA executive seemed to me trivial; I called her and the other workers "PTA Ladies." My father appeared to be always in command of his emotions. My mother and I were beneath him in this respect, and control over personal feelings was given high priority in my family. I remember my father saying to me, as I sprawled on my bed, sobbing uncontrollably, often after a screaming fight with my mother, "When you can control yourself, we can talk about this . . . ." He would sit there on the edge of my bed, waiting for me to stop "being emotional." (I cannot remember how or when my brothers gave up their tears and shudders; I was at least expected to have them, being a girl.) My father seemed reasonable, my mother irrational. My father was always soft-spoken; my mother gave way to hysterics. My father seemed to me handsome, my mother ordinary-looking. Unpopular decisions made by both of them, or perhaps solely by him, but of course delivered and administered by my mother, were always blamed on her. To this day, his quiet demeanor and reticence to engage on an emotional level often allow him to escape notice in family discussions, and excuse him from criticism where my mother is an easy target, since her behavior and psychology fit so well the popular negative stereotype of middle-aged women whose children are grown and gone.[10] Moreover, because she does engage, fights back, challenges my argument, she is far more visible than he.

When I began to see my mother through my new consciousness, I had to view my father as her husband, not "daddy." I have resisted that understanding through five years and more of struggling with my mother around feminist issues. I didn't want to demote my father; I thought I could separate him out of the problem. Once more, I tried to excuse him. In becoming conscious of the way he operates within my family, I can see that this American businessman is as much a patriarch as his father, the political philosopher, and his grandfather, the peasant rabbi. The style, to be sure, has changed. The family attitude has always been that he operates in a democratic fashion, reflecting his intelligence and decency. All of us, my two brothers, my mother and I, acknowledged his power and position in the same subtle way he wielded it—no blatant show of authority was necessary. In my adolescence, I would brag about him, and put down my mother, by saying, "My mother yells all the time, but my father never has to raise his voice. All he has to do is give that look, and I know I've done something really bad."

Even as I write, I have to force myself to say anything that even implies criticism of my father. I keep wanting to soften it. I think of my mother as having to face the truth just as I do—but I seem to feel that he won't be able to accept it as we can. He has internalized and lived out male supremacy for over sixty years. He is like other men; he is not excused. In order to relate to him, and to relate to my mother, his wife, I have to accept and work through that understanding.

Many of the other "daddy's girls" in the study have had similar experiences. Not only did 39 percent of the interview daughters state that they preferred their fathers, and demonstrate that preference as they spoke, but another 9 percent who said either that they preferred their mothers or that they preferred neither parent, *also* preferred their fathers, as their interview texts revealed. Most of us are women who identified with our fathers, were known within the family to be like our fathers, looked like them, and followed their interests and habits. Where this is not the case, it is those "masculine" aspects of our fathers that have attracted us to them. We prefer reading newspapers to romance magazines, want to do carpentry or mechanical work, like to consider ourselves independent. Positive aspects of these choices derive not only from the activities themselves, in which we may well have genuine and serious interest, but also from their high (male) status, their connection to male power. We do not choose to associate ourselves with our mothers, with the "feminine" sphere of interests and activities, even if we feel an affinity for, or a fascination with, such work, because it has such low status. Sometimes it is even enough just to hang out with our fathers, to pal around with them when we are girls, to avoid the stigma of the female role.

I did prefer him to my mother because he seemed more intellectual. He had the time to read books because he didn't take care of us. I remember he always got the Wall Street Journal and was interested in the stock market. And I would ask him questions, like why do men wear ties, and he would give these long answers. I looked at him as someone who had the same intellectual bent as I did.

I was most like my father in the family, and whatever my father did or wanted, I was part of it. It wasn't favoritism, but it was just that I was the most like him, and the only one who wanted to be with him—he was a very hard person to deal with.

In many ways I was like my father, and he liked that, even my bad habits. For instance, when I would get mad at somebody I simply would not talk to them. That's what my father did too. My father and I would get up the earliest of the family and eat a huge breakfast together, and he liked that too.

Some of the fathers actively encouraged their daughters to identify with them, competing with the mothers to do so. Others didn't encourage it openly, but continued to foster the close tie in covert ways. One interesting small group made the choice to favor a daughter over a son. That is, the daughter was promoted, out of proper social order, to be her father's favorite, when there was a son who should have taken that role. Often this promotion was against the wishes of the mother, and certainly must have been to the disappointment and shame of the son.

My father was really interested in me when I was little, but my mother killed that. She felt he should be with his son, but he wanted to take me everywhere with him. My brother was a sickly child, and the only times my mother would let me go with my father were when my brother was sick. Then my father could say, "Well, Ernie's sick." He would sneak me out at night sometimes. I felt guilty because I would be out having a good time with my dad when my brother was sick. I would be hoping he'd get sick so I could go with my dad.

My father has real strong and definite expectations of what he wants from me in terms of academic and financial achievement. He always compares me to his sister, who has the same name; he'll say she was real smart and this and that. He expects me to perform better than the other children, including his son, which has been very hard for my brother. My brother has real hard times meeting family expectations— so my father put a lot of his expectations on me. When we were growing up, my father saw how hard it was for my brother, who didn't learn all the tricks in school, so he put it all on me.

I am my father's son. Last time I was there for dinner I criticized my father and my brother was just horrified. He said you don't say things like that to your father, etc. And we got into this big argument. My father intervened, and said that the criticism was correct and justified; "She's not just supposed to sit there and be polite if she has something to say—of course you would be polite." My brother's a pansy like that. My brother is not terribly masculine. He's very soft-spoken but may get into fits of rage. He's not the achiever. He's not my father's son. I am not daddy's little girl, though that's what he calls me. I am his son and I know I am his son.

Long past feudalism, primogeniture is still with us. The social value of a son, for a father, is far higher than that of a daughter, or even a wife. In this group, the daughters allude to the inadequacy of their brothers, their lack of overt "masculinity." Moreover, in this group also are found several father-daughter relationships which include expressed sexuality. This sexual attraction of the daughter makes the father's choice of daughter over son, and his competition with the mother for her affection, much easier to understand.

Many daughters in the study acknowledged the sexual relationship between daughters and fathers. Only a few women spoke in overtly sexual terms about their fathers, but dozens more alluded to the incestuous aspects of the relation. Fathers and daughters are faced with a problem which has no satisfactory solution built into contemporary society, even with traditional roles crumbling as they are. When daughters pass through puberty, they become women; they are no longer the small girls whom fathers may casually fondle. Fathers are only given the one set of behavior with which to relate to daughters, and this cannot be applied to adult women. It may undergo a change if the daughter marries, and especially if she becomes a mother, because then she is "safe." She is no longer a free agent, an unattached young woman in the father's life.

Men are socialized to regard women sexually. Married men are not supposed to have friends who are young women with whom they do not have sexual intercourse. It is more socially acceptable to have a mistress, or a series of sexual liaisons with women "young enough to be his daughter," than for a man to have a serious intimate friendship with his own daughter. Fathers, therefore, often do not know how to deal with their daughters as people, as adults, as women. As we might expect in a culture which values women in terms of their physical attributes, fathers prefer that their daughters be "pretty," and take pride in their daughters' appearance. They may become uncomfortable, however, when we are sexually attractive to them. There is constant contradicton between the fact that men learn to regard all women as sexual objects and property, and the taboo which denies men the sexual use of their daughters, though daughters are twice over their property.

Most of our fathers submerge whatever real feelings they have for us—including sexual responses—under a continuation of the paternal role left from our childhood. Both parents, in fact, find themselves living out roles which have no real function in an equal relationship between adults, when their daughters move from adolescence to adulthood. We daughters, no longer little girls, are at a loss to relate to our fathers. We no longer require, if we ever did, their protection and support; their expressions of affection often become an embarrassment or a burden.

It is in the years of childhood that the contemporary incest taboo carries its most value—to prevent the sexual abuse and exploitation of daughters by their fathers. And, here, where the weight of the taboo is required, it fails. Those fathers who break the incest taboo, who rape their daughters and/or sustain a relationship which includes overt sex, may feel guilt or remorse, but generally have an active rationale to support their behavior. These men, in psychological testing, do not appear "psychotic or intellectually defective." In fact, "these fathers claim the sexual initiation of their daughters as a patriarchal right."[11] Though they and those fathers whose rapes are undiscovered may also feel shame and guilt, the "right" of the father remains their rationale—they have the right to do what they want with their daughters. Interviews in which women did not describe their fathers in sexual terms often had sexual undertones. For instance, in describing their discipline or punishment at the hands of their fathers, women would reveal that the harshest words, the most stringent rules of behavior, or the most violent beatings were all centered on sexual themes. At least half a dozen women spoke of their fathers ripping the clothes off of their bodies in rages that were set off by the daughter's real or imagined (by the father) sexual experiences.

At a meeting of my women's group, we talked about incest-rape; we included fathers, brothers, uncles, grandfathers; and we realized very soon that there wasn't a woman among us who hadn't experienced, when we were young girls, some overtly sexual manipulation by a male relative. Most of us had "forgotten" these incidents; often they did not make up part of the conscious picture we all carried of the men in each case. One woman described how her father repeatedly told her that she must open her mouth when she kissed him; he always tried to put his tongue in her mouth during their "good-night" kisses. The same woman had said nothing about this when I interviewed her for this book. How many other daughters left such things unsaid when I asked them to describe their relations with their fathers?[12]

Some transcripts gave implicit evidence of the sexual quality in the father-daughter relation:

When I was growing up I wanted to please him a lot. I always found my father very attractive, very handsome. He was a very strong, moral figure. I was afraid of him; his was the stroke that really counted. I always thought that daddy was handsome and charming.

We were very close when I was real little. When I started showing signs of becoming a woman he got kind of scared, and he didn't want it. We moved apart from each other in that time. I felt like I had done something to my father by getting married; I always wanted to be like a little girl with him. When I was getting married he cried a lot and asked why I was doing this to him. He said he'd do anything, but please not to get married.

Up until the time I got married he didn't have much to say about things pertaining to sex, but now he's coming right out of the box, no holds barred. He leaves me shocked all the time now.

In another group of descriptions, the behavior involved was more explicit, described in this fashion:

When he felt warm toward me he would grab me, pinch me, and hug me, and then that was it. I never talked to him privately, never went anyplace with him.

Our relationship was what you might call lovey-dovey; there was a lot of daddy's little girl thing, hugging and kissing.

When I was around 10, I had this very sexual feeling with my father. It was New Year's Eve and I was allowed to stay up late. My father was quite loaded, and kissed me at midnight, and boy, was I elated. I felt, "I'm the one," but at the same time I was scared to death. I was scared to ever tell my mother. I felt that my father had recognized something in me and acted on it, and it made me crazy thinking about it. My mother had very uptight views on sex. (laugh)

He would formally spank me. He would take my pants down and go wham, wham, and it was more humiliating than painful. The only time he was really violent was when I was 10 or 11; he pulled my dress right off my body. It was pretty traumatic; that was over my having sex play with some of the kids in the neighborhood.

It was a quasi-incestuous relationship between me and my father; it made me very uncomfortable. I didn't want my father slobbering over me. I didn't want him to touch me. My father tried to be affectionate a lot, but I knew that it was sexual. Every Sunday morning he would come in. (My mother swears she didn't know this would happen.) He would come in and give me this inquisition about what I had done the night before and talk about how I would end up walking the streets. I was a virgin when I got married at 19, so you can imagine how little I did then. By the time he was through with me I felt that no one cell in my body was connected to any other cell.

The smallest group were those who frankly described incest in their families:

Our relationship was sick and it got less sick. It was a lot of him telling me, "You're my little girl," and it was sexual, and a lot of it was him buying me clothes. My parents were divorced, and I would wear my funkiest clothes when I would see him; he wouldn't want to take me out in those clothes, so he would buy me a new outfit every time. He was very jealous of all my boyfriends, but what was interesting was that he tried to force me out of the intellect of "just" being a girl. He always told me I was smart and I could do whatever I wanted to do. He taught me how to fix my car, how to do carpentry. Then it finally came to the point where, because of the sex, it became hateful. I had started when I was ten, and when I got older, I finally came to the point where I said, "I'm not going near you anymore." Then I didn't see him for a long time. And when we finally came to see each other again, it was made clear to him that that part was ended. The emotional support and teaching he gave me was of great value, and I've been able to separate the sex from that in my head. Also, I see him only maybe once every year for a few days, so I can keep it clear.

I think the way my mother looked at my father was that he could not satisfy her physically, but she accepted that. And he came to me for physical satisfaction. This went on when I was real young, not just my father but my uncle, would come to my bed and get on top of me in the night. My sexual feelings were aroused very early. When I was an adolescent and my father came to me I finally figured out what all of this stuff was that he was doing. I had been aroused to the point where I liked the feeling, but now I started to hate my father. And my mother was right there in the house. Could she have slept through all of that? I don't know. My mother must have been so damn afraid that she didn't know what to do with the situation. And my father was dependent, even physically, on my mother. I remember him being so shaky that he couldn't shave himself, and she was in the bathroom and shrieking at him. I was just a kid and I felt so sorry for him. Here he's scraping and making everying bloody, and she said to me, "Go in there. I can't handle it." So I went, feeling sorry for him, and the same time feeling all this hate. Once my brother told my mother something that made her have to deal with it—at the dinner table. And she said to me, "Does your father touch you? Does he?" I knew that if I said yes my father would be kicked out of the house. I sensed that. And I knew that my mother wanted me to say no. So I said no. She didn't want to make that decision. After my father died, and now that we are living far from each other, maybe we can start being mother and daughter again.

Among those daughters whose interview transcripts do reveal the sexuality between father and daughter, the majority of the daughters continue to feel affection for their fathers. In the two most explicit incest cases, wherein women were

138

repeatedly forced into sexual intercourse, the fathers are also seen by the daughters as sympathetic figures. One is disabled, the other an alcoholic. Both men treated their daughters quite well in other respects, and had satisfying and affectionate relations with them during the same time period as the rapes.* Herman and Hirschman also found this to be true in their study of incest victims; women who are so abused by their fathers may also receive real nurturing and caring from their fathers.

Including these last two women, those daughters whose relationship with their fathers included sexuality were, more often than not, among those women who felt real affection for their fathers and preferred them or identified with them. These were also frequently, though not always, women who competed with their mothers for the father/husband's attention or approval. It is notable that daughters sexually involved with their fathers, who competed with their mothers *for the father*, are a small minority, despite the prevailing assumption that a Freudian-defined, sexually-based desire for the father is often at the root of mother/daughter problems. Moreover, we are incorrect to assume that such competition, when it does exist, is initiated by the upstart daughter, moving in on her mother's man. There are mothers in the study who began to discourage their daughters' relations with the father/husband when the girl was not yet five years old, who perhaps even fostered competition unwittingly in that discouragement, their purpose being more closely related to parental competition than to mother-daughter sexual rivalry. Certainly, there are fathers who manipulate the competition themselves.

There was that feminine rivalry between my mother and me for the attention of the men in the family. I could get anything out of my father. He always stuck up for me against my

*Both of these men were among those who preferred their daughters to their sons, and raised their daughters in "masculine" ways of thinking and performing.

mother, no matter what. We had good rapport, my father and I, because we could talk together about things in the outside world; she was not interested in politics. Her mind wouldn't stay on it long enough; she wasn't very well educated.

When he wants to comfort me, he never does it in front of my mother. It's always on the side, so she doesn't know.

My father put me in a position where I was almost as important to him as my mother. Now that's a very bad position to be in. If he wanted an opinion sometimes he would ask me instead of my mother. So he set up competition between my mother and me.

When he would horse around with me, she would always break it up. It was like she didn't want us to have such a good time. She would come and say, "Don't do that with her; you'll break something; you'll make her wild." So she would step between us.

I remember him trying a few times to be with me when I was young, and my mother would interfere. He would take me out to breakfast. When he would take me to kiddyland, she would always come along. It could never be just him and me.

In direct opposition to the competing pairs of mothers and daughters are those who collaborate consistently to outwit, outmaneuver, or simply leave out, the father. These fathers were frequently present in the home, and functioning "correctly" in the nuclear family, but were considered to be of no consequence by both their wives and daughters. In some cases, the mother and daughter both felt and verbalized that they had a special relationship, from which the father, and perhaps other children, were excluded. In other situations, the daughter, in rejecting her father, is affirming not only what her mother perceives as her father's insignificance, but her mother's superiority as well. Some daughters are well aware of the chances their mothers take for them, in spending "too much" time, affection or money on the daughter, or in approving behavior the father would disapprove. Not so often as this, but often enough to note, daughters knew that their mothers were risking their own security to defend the daughter against the father, verbally or physically, in violent confrontations.

I was too much the footstamper, and "I want my way," and my mother would back me up on it. It was not only an emotional or disciplinary alignment between my mother and me. It was economic. He usually thought, "Well, she knows what's best for the kids"—so he'd let her spend the money she said she needed for us.

There were things she only talked about with me, like the relationships she'd had with men before my father married her. Or the marriage she had before him. To this day, he doesn't know that I'm illegitimate.

Once when my father was very ill, and I was bitterly resentful, I said to him, "You haven't done anything. Ma does everything." He smacked me good, and I crept under the bed and never said anything else. He did do some good things; I don't mean to intimate that he was a bad father, but I had a real passion for my mother.

My mother always stood by me in just about everything I want to do. The one thing she'll throw in at the end is, "I don't know what I'm going to do when your father hears about this." That's her little problem.

We were beaten very brutally, very violently, with belt buckles. He really has a violent temper and he would get us up against the wall or in a corner and he just wouldn't stop. My mother tried to pull my father away. She's a tiny woman and he's a big man, but with all the screaming and crying, she didn't just stand by.

Among those of us who've not formed a bond of this type with our mothers—the majority of daughters, to be sure— there is still some anger smoldering under the constant acceptance and allowance, the "excusing" of our fathers. The coming of feminist consciousness, or the influence of the women's movement may account for the acceptance and recognition of the anger expressed by daughters in these interviews, but not for the feeling itself. Most of it is old-fashioned righteous indignation, based upon ethics and morals, upon our hurt feelings, our realization that our fathers are not the models of perfection we'd been led to believe. Much of the anger we feel, the criticism we make, is based upon our recognition of our mothers' oppression. Far more daughters than the social stereotypes would suggest are women who see their fathers' treatment of their mothers as unacceptable. This step is one we all must take so that we may regard our mothers as equals, and understand that our fathers are wielders of power that we and our mothers have never shared.

In the last two months of my life I have finally been angry with my father, and the anger has to do with what he didn't teach me in terms of business; not because I wasn't bright, but because I wasn't male. In the last few months I have been furious with him, and I started to relate that to some of the things that "didn't happen" with mother—probably due to the same attitude in him. Mother was a very intelligent woman. She was bright and probably had a good business head on her. Each time I go over there I suddenly feel angry at my father, and I never felt angry at him.

The worst part about my father is this: When my mother and I would scream at each other, when she would manipulate me, or hurt me, I remember my father sitting there and not saying, "What the fuck are you saying?" My mother was doing all this and my father was sitting there reading the paper or something. He doesn't know; he doesn't care. That makes me so mad because I feel that my father is more with it than my mother. My mother's crazy; that's her excuse; she's such a crazy shit that she doesn't even know she's crazy. But my father knows, and he knew, and he didn't interfere. I was more mad at my father. It almost seems that my mother's not responsible for some of the stuff she does.

My mother never talked about her sexual relationship with my father and my father never stopped talking about it. He said things when I was 16 or 17 years old, even 10 or 12, that shocked me then, and it shocks me now. I don't think it serves children well to tell them what a rotten lay their mother is. He used to say a lot of things like that, and she never said a word, never. Now she says he was not a good lover, and that she was disappointed. He was so mean to her sometimes, and she wouldn't want him close to her; she would punish him sexually, which is the only weapon a woman has.

They were very Victorian. She knew where her bread was buttered. One night she stayed out with an American woman, who got her to go to a PTA meeting. She came home late and he made such a fuss that she never failed to have supper on the table after that. She had to cater to him all the time because she didn't know how to make a living on her own. We had to have a linen table cloth on the table for breakfast, and even then, as little as I was, I couldn't see why she would have to do that. We children invariably spilled on the cloth and then she would have to walk four flights down to wash that cloth.

I still love my father a lot but lately I've fallen in my mother's camp, so to speak. My father is really fucked up and has lots of problems, but she's completely sacrificed her identity to him and her survival, and she's the one who's gotten the cancer because of it.

Sometimes the anger we feel at our fathers cannot be separated from anger at our mothers.* We might be outraged at the fact that our parents subscribe to the "united front" theory of child-raising, which requires that, much of the time, at least one of them is lying as they represent their position. If the father lies, we are angry at him. If the power of the father

---

*Some daughters could not seem to ever separate their fathers from their mothers. When I would ask a question using "her" or "she" these daughters would respond with answers about "they" and "them."

makes the mother lie, we are angry at both of them. When our mothers act as go-betweens, taking reports to our fathers and bringing responses back to us, we are angry at both for their respective parts in the play.

Some of us feel that our mothers have abandoned us for our fathers. We are angry at our fathers' power to command the fidelity we want; we are furious at our mothers for choosing our fathers instead of us. One woman described what she called "the deal" her mother made, which was as follows: The father wanted a divorce; the mother balked. The father then offered the "security" of continued marriage if his wife would "be more of a wife and less of a mother." Her daughter dates this abandonment, "being dropped like a hot potato," from her early adolescence. Previous to that time, this daughter had been the focus of her mother's activity and energy, to the father's anger and resentment, to the second daughter's envy and loss.

Other daughters' transcripts contain fragments of similar situations—tiny abandonments—which indicate that most daughters see, if not understand, that many mothers serve their husbands' interests before their children's, and it goes without saying, before their own. Their choosing to serve *themselves* first is perceived by many daughters as abandonment. Despite our disagreement with such mothers' goals and desires, it behooves us to recognize that, on one level, in "abandoning" us, they are acting in their self-interest, by bending to the father's will. Our mothers are usually women dependent on men, economically, emotionally, or both; they often allow their husbands or lovers to abuse their children and themselves, take their money, and use prime food, space and equipment in the home. Seeing ourselves as abandoned, we come to understand that our secrets are told to our fathers when we mean them for our mothers alone. We want attention from our mothers, and find that all the energy left after housework is given to their husbands; in this sense, time spent with us is a chore—"childcare." We realize that not only are men more important than women, but, specifically, that our mothers' husbands are more important than their

144

daughters, and that's the way it's supposed to be. I do not advocate that, by definition, a daughter (or a son) be more important than a spouse or lover. After all, I was raised in a middle class Jewish household wherein both parents subordinated their needs and desires to all of their children, and I see that mistake clearly. It is the institutionalization of the choice that I protest, and its patriarchal source. This abandonment comes out of the father's power, his control of the situation, not simply out of the mother's choice; she has no freedom to make the choice.

She'll jump up in the morning to cook him breakfast, and later to see that he's got a good dinner; but when he's not home, we get tuna fish.

I couldn't talk to my father for a long time. But my mother and I were kind of close all along, until there were a couple of incidents in college that drew us apart. I had told my mother some things in confidence, and she told my father instead of having the strength to say no. Ever since then I have felt I cannot tell her everything that I could have told her before.

My brother and I were severely beaten by my mother's second husband. It was so bad that we literally screamed for the police, my brother and I. He used to hit us with high heels, hangers, belts, all sorts of stuff. It wasn't until just three months ago that I mentioned it to my mother, in rage, finally dealing with it after all these years—I confronted her and said, "How the hell did you let this happen?"

"Abandonment" which occurs when the mother is in middle age is a desperate choice—out of our mothers' deepest fears of aging, sickness and loneliness. Women choose to remain in empty marriages, negating the potential of the last third of their lives, out of these fears. Rather than "abandoning" their daughters, who are now adults, these mothers slip away, like Eurydice—we might try to bring them along with us, we might offer an alternative to the father-husband, but they are buried in their dependency; they cannot move or change.

Fathers occasionally interrupt the flow of a mother/daughter relationship. They intercede in arguments, lecturing one or the other party (usually the daughter), in cases of disagreement. Though their motive, born of patriarchal right and paternal duty, is to preserve harmony in the household, the effect of this intervention is to come between the mother and daughter, offering one or both alternative respite and refuge, pushing them to avoid further confrontation and subsequent resolution. Such separation and alienation among women serve the cause of patriarchal capitalism; the nuclear household is its bulwark. The motive of the father, conscious or not, is to reassert his power.

My father believed in all these things, like supermother. He was the enforcer, like, "Your mother is always right; your mother is always kind; your mother is always good; you must always respect your mother." He reinforced that role for her.

I remember sitting down and having a family discussion which turned into a crying and screaming fit between my mother and me, and my father just said, "I don't see why you two can't get along."

My own father assumed this role when my mother and I were at odds. We had the common misfortune to be moving through the life crises* of adolescence and menopause at the same time, and thus, for two or three years, we quarreled frequently, bitterly and to exhaustion, riding the waves of hormonal and emotional upheaval. My father, possessed of no knowledge of the menstrual cycle—and not so different from my mother and me in that respect—armed only with the phrase, "Your mother is going through a very difficult time," would try to calm us, would guilt us into self-control. He would separate us as a referee must when the fighters are

---

*These crises are culturally caused; they are not "natural"; all women do not undergo crisis periods at these times. (See Silverman, "The Life Crisis as a Clue to Social Function," in *Toward an Anthropology of Women*, ed. R. Reiter.)

clutching each other, drenched in sweat or tears, continuing to flail weakly about. We instinctively knew each other's vulnerability, as if we smelled the blood, hers ebbing, mine flowing—the blood demanded recognition, even in that bloodless suburban kitchen.

Between these two menstrual women stepped my father, little realizing that he broke an ancient taboo as he did so.[13] The rational man, whose authority reminded us that we were behaving badly, he made us ashamed of the grief and violence between us, and caused us to subside into false truce—which denied the pain and thus forbade us to seek ease from it. We could not rage on; we must be nice to each other. There was no menstrual hut on the outskirts of our village, to which we might go to pass our time of bleeding, no place where our cycles were regarded as the proper order of things, where we could have acknowledged the strength of our blood. I know that one of the sources of my pain during these years of crisis was the sense that I had lost her—as if, in becoming a woman, I could no longer be her daughter—no more her child, to be comforted by her body. I see now that those years marked the beginning of real shame in my own body, and the beginning of my conscious preference for my father.

Our mothers' bodies are the model for our own; in losing the model, we lose the sense of the mirror, the support of the sameness of female bodies. My father would not allow my mother to be naked in front of me if he were present in the room. If I were in the room while she was getting dressed, and he came in, I had to leave. Of course, *he* never said this to me. The message was delivered by my mother, who said, "Your father doesn't like it when. . . ." His own shame, and perhaps the sense that her body, her sensual self, belonged only to him, decreed this. When I was older, I would sleep with my mother, at her request, when my father was out of town. She would want to snuggle, to hold me in the curve of her body, for warmth and comfort. But by then the shame and embarrassment were well rooted in me; I felt "funny" doing it, even felt that she was childish to want me to sleep with her—though my deeper feeling was secret pleasure—both at her desire and at the sensual experience.

What might the last twenty years have been for my mother and me if the culture—which designated my father as our overseer—had allowed us to tell each other what was happening in our bodies? The alienation we struggle through now began in those years; male culture, in the person of my unsuspecting father, denied our blood rites and broke us apart. Those were the days when I would lock my bedroom door and whisper to my mirror, "I hate her; I hate that bitch." Love, or the acceptance of its presence between us, had become as taboo as our blood. The blood bond *is* the love bond; without the recognition of *how* we are bound to our mothers, we are easily seduced by power and authority, the "superiority" of our fathers.

6
Leaving:
The Pain of Separation

The young girl in the house of her mother
is like seed in fertile ground.

—MONIQUE WITTIG

I have been sleeping through a long cold
in the hollow branch of my mother
it is time now to splash through
the thawed ice

—MIRIAM PALMER

Mother, I am something more
than your girl

—HELEN CHASIN

My mother remembers the agony of her womb
And long years that seemed to promise more than this.
She says, "You do not love me,
You do not want me,
You will go away."

—LOUISE BOGAN

Patriarchal motherhood demands that we leave our mothers, and that they let us go. Institutionalized sexism and the prevailing negative view of mothers facilitate the break—we need not feel regret at such an escape; indeed, we *ought* not. The guilt we all feel is thus a result of the contradiction between the social form and the actual relationship. Confused and problematic though our daughterhood may be, we are bonded very heavily to our mothers—and, despite the psychoanalytic view of such a bond, it is based in our essential

149

womanselves. What we need is not to break the tie, but to make it healthy—to wrest it from its patriarchal context, to allow for its full impact on us, strengthening the line of woman. Rather than burying the proof of our tie to our mothers, because of our embarrassment at identifying with that role, let us examine it. Let us try to understand what it means to have lived our mothers' lives, to have raised us, to have to separate from ourselves.

In patriarchal tradition, daughters leave their mothers when they are carried off by men.[1] Leaving our mothers is leaving the world of woman, moving into the realm of man— an acceptance of man's dominion. Though Persephone is our model, we are not all abducted and raped, held captive and tricked into eating the seed of Hades. Rather, most of us are seduced. "Seduction is a kind of education. When you are educated—educed—you are led *out*. When you are seduced, you are led *aside*. A girl's first seduction is where/when the separation from her mother begins."[2]

Our "education" is such seduction, through both our schooling and cultural socialization; it prepares us to leave woman for man—to, in fact, distrust and despise ourselves as women—so that we seek our growth, our satisfaction, even our joy, in men. We have seen the means by which both daughters and mothers learn their proper roles, the methods and results of our mothers' teachings, the loss of our mothers' bodies and touch, and the role our fathers play in the separation of daughters from mothers. This inexorable process spares no daughter, so that for all of us, even those who never leave their mothers' homes, the separation is inevitable.

Natural separation of daughter from mother, which allows the daughter to be whole, unto herself, and the mother to continue her life without depletion, has been distorted through the degradation of women. In the mythic past, when daughters were faces of Woman, different aspects of the Great Mother, like phases of the moon, the natural growth of the daughter led out of her mother; she flowed from her mother's womb. And she could return to her mother again and again in *being* her mother, in creating herself. Each time she returned, she was strengthened, so that she might go out again, go farther than before, create of herself as her mother had done— be like her mother, but belong to herself. This is the cyclic nature of woman.

But the movement away from our mothers that we make today, and the anxiety we exhibit when that basic *sameness* of mother and daughter is acknowledged, are not born of this natural separation. Mothers and daughters today do not accept the cycle, the understanding that we are one woman even as we are separate women. Instead, the split is a creation of woman-hating. It is born of the disgust and revulsion we learn to feel at the dark wet caves of our vaginas. When we leave our mothers, we are escaping from all that we have learned to despise in woman, embodied in the one woman who is most like us, who personifies the dread of our future as women. Unlike Persephone, we are eager to leave; we have *already* lost our mothers by the time we go.

Among the daughters I interviewed, 75 percent were glad and eager to leave when they moved out of their mothers' homes. In this society, children, especially female children, are regarded as dependents, incomplete citizens even into their early twenties.[3] Leaving home, leaving mother, is the symbolic entry to one's majority, a sign of autonomy and adult competence. Many of us leave our mothers when we marry; some of us go off to school and never come back; others leave to make their way in the world—an adventure usually reserved for younger sons. Very few of us stay with our mothers.

Less than 10 percent of the women I interviewed had remained in their mothers' homes or taken their mothers with them when they left. Six women were living with their mothers at the time of the interview, but these were all under 25, and none of them anticipated staying. Their positions varied, from one who said, "I'm not in any hurry to get out of the house and to be on my own. It would be nice, but there's no big rush," to another who basically only used her mother's house as a depot, and really lived at her lover's apartment. Those few women who had lived with their mothers through most of their lives told me that even when their mothers were old or ill they still did housework and childcare, raising grandchildren and cooking meals. These daughters had great sympathy for their mothers' situations, serious interest in their mothers' feelings and ideas, and respect and affection for them—sometimes more in the mothers' advanced age than earlier on.

For the rest of us, daughters who've left our mothers, the leave-takings have generally been crises. Fifty percent of our mothers are reluctant to have us go; they feel devastated and betrayed at our departure. Approximately 14 percent of us don't want to leave, and another 11 percent are so disturbed as to deny the emotional content of the situation. As I sifted through the words of all the interview daughters, I discovered more and more evidence of ambivalence about leaving. Even those women who were "desperate" and considered their leaving an escape were conflicted. Despite an urge to go, prompted in the most extreme situations by fear, hatred and guilt, we still have trouble leaving.

I felt I was escaping from prison. It was very, very difficult to do. I know I needed to do it. I always looked forward to the day when I would be leaving. I cried and prayed for it for so many years. It got worse the last year I was there. Everyone was crazy in that house and I knew I couldn't put my life together there. She didn't want me to go. She tried to bribe me. She'd say, "You're moving so you can have friends, and you can have friends here." She would give me money if I stayed, and tried to scare me about what the outside world was like. I left home saying, "I love you a lot but I can't stay here. Maybe someday I'll be able to, but not now." I remember saying that to her and I think she understood.

I think I was 17 when I left home. (laugh) I hated to be there. I hated to be there any longer and I just wanted to leave, so I left. It's hard to say, but we hated each other. I don't think I knew that then; I don't know if I hated her as much as I hated the whole situation. It was very emotional. If she were to think about it, she would have wanted me to go. Maybe under other circumstances, where it wasn't so ugly—it might have been different between us.

I was leaving because I was moving in with John and it was a very tense situation. She did a lot of screaming. I felt like I was leaving her to the walls—very guilty—and she was real nasty and tacky about it, but I did it anyway. I'm glad I did.

Those of us who are not fleeing home, but are moving into a new phase which is acceptable to our families and society at large, should, it seems, have less trouble. For instance, going off to college, for middle class young women, is not only accepted, but expected. This split is for everyone's good; the daughter will be advanced both intellectually and socially, and the mother will be freed of her burden of responsibility. But, since the mother's major purpose in life has been to educate her daughter, and to care for her, not only does the advent of highly formalized schooling put the mother out of a job, it also denigrates the learning the daughter has done at home. Now the daughter is going to learn what's really important, going off to a world of intellectual endeavor which the mother, in many cases, has either never entered, or has given up for her maternity.

When I left home for the state university, I was nervous and scared, but I was thrilled to be "on my own." I dimly realized that I was still tied to my parents financially, and that the university, as an institution, was acting in place of my family. But on the first day that I was there, I went for a walk by myself. I wore the new plaid wool bermuda shorts and matching sweater my mother had supplied me with, but I did not wear a girdle. I had worn a panty girdle all through high school, one with long elastic legs to "firm" my thighs, and I hated it. My mother had told me that it "wasn't nice" to go without one, and had always implied that I "needed" it. I remember the physical pleasure of that walk, and the delight in my realization that I wasn't "fat." I remember thinking that my mother would disapprove of my walking about so freely. But previous to this freedom walk, as I had sat on my bed in the small room, my roommate not yet arrived, and watched through the window as my mother and father drove away, I had cried. I thought, "What am I doing here? I don't know anyone here; I'm all alone. What will become of me?"

Years later, when I told my mother about both of those feelings, she took pleasure in hearing that I had cried, as proof of her importance in my life, as evidence that my leaving her had been a loss to me—even as she resented the girdle story, and wanted to disavow its connection to herself. Our mothers' loss is more poignant than ours when we leave, for often we leave them *behind;* we go beyond the lives they have lived. Though this is the purpose of all they have taught us, it still causes pain. They've prepared us to move ahead of them, to live "a better life" than they have. They've planted the seeds of their own rejection all along, in lauding that world beyond their grasp as housewives and mothers.

Those women who do not go off to college, working class and poor daughters, or those middle class women who leave their mothers when formal education is completed, are faced with a real break. This is no trial run, under the watchful eyes of deans and dormitory counselors. When these daughters leave, they go into the world; they are setting out to seek their fortunes. Of course, most of us find our fortunes in marrying the most successful or potentially successful man we can find. But many of us do experience independent adult life before we marry; and some of us, a growing number, live out our years as independent single women, once we leave our mothers.

This leave-taking is the most difficult of all, and it is no accident that the greatest pain and desperation experienced in the interview group was among these women. When they left their mothers they understood, though perhaps not in conscious political terms, that no one else was going to support them, economically or emotionally; there is no collective responsibility for providing shelter, food, or love in patriarchal capitalism. The provision that has been made for women in this culture is that they are to attach themselves to a man, who will provide for their needs. Women who do not marry or live with a man are outside of the social system, even today when that system is falling apart.

Our mothers, as the main source of our socialization, have taught us how to find and marry a man to take care of those needs. In so doing, they have taught us how to leave them, to deny this most basic love of our lives, to supplant them with strangers. This explains our mother's reluctance to let us go, and our grief at going, even though we are eager to be independent, and they have accepted the dual nature of their role. We all understand, daughters and mothers, that we are not supposed to come back together; we know the social and psychological impropriety of loving each other, and the embarrassment that awaits us if we acknowledge that we desire to touch; we realize that leaving is supposed to be final. Close relationships between mothers and daughters are to be left in the 19th century,[4] when this love was accepted and considered natural for adult women, left in our childhood, when we were unashamedly symbiotic.* We both accept the rule that says we must part, but we cannot suppress the feelings evoked by that parting.

I came home that first Christmas, 1965. I flew home because it was unheard of not to be home for Christmas—the whole family would fall apart—and she took me to the airport to go back. She took my bag out of the trunk and said, "You'd better get going," or something like that, and I said, "Mom, I wish I could stay." We both started to cry, and I knew that I had to go. She knew it too. To cry like that was totally unlike her. I knew she had many things she wished she could have said. It was very painful.

Well, she was real mad that I was leaving, but she didn't try to stop me, as I had hoped she would—of course I had hoped she would come in the car and drag me home. It was necessary for me to leave; it was torture to live with my stepfather.

When I left, she was very upset and I was very upset, but I thought, "This has got to stop"; we could not be companions

*Again, I want to point out that this situation is not yet universal. In Italy and France, for instance, mothers and daughters still walk about arm in arm, kiss and hug each other, see each other frequently.

for the rest of our lives. Ever since I moved out we have not been close, and that is how I want it; it was getting claustrophobic for me.

Even though my brother's still at home, it's hard for me to leave her. My next oldest sister said the same thing. It's hard to think of her there all alone—to leave her there, cute little lady. I've got to make my own life. I just can't worry about what her problems are, the needs that she has.

Most of us continue to believe we have not really separated from our mothers, we are not yet adult women, until we are married. This belief is based in the assumption that women must marry, that a mother/daughter pair ought not to live together once the daughter is grown—"You can't have two women in the same kitchen"*—and that marriage, ideally, provides the daughter with her own husband, children and household to manage, thereby making her (finally) her mother's equal. The irony is that we leave our mothers' dominion for our husbands', picking up the same role that oppressed our mothers and made us want to leave them—and we regard this move as a liberation.

I felt absolutely desperate. I had to get out. She was not pleased when I moved out, because she wanted to keep me under her power, under her domination.

One of the reasons I wanted to get married was that marriage afforded me a chance to get out. Not too many of my female friends left home. They lived at home until they got married. It was a way out.

I left her house for good when I was 20. That's when I got married. I was so glad to go. She was sad to see me go; she said, "Don't get married," and she made things as miserable as she could.

*And until very recently, women were not supposed to move out until they were wed—despite Apt. 3-G's tenure in the comics.

I think she went into shock, really. I was also extremely nervous, but I can tell you it was something new. I was a little shocked myself, at 38, but thank God I had a chance to be myself for a change.

You have to understand I worked my whole life to get out of my mother's home. (laugh)

I escaped through marriage into another frying pan. She was delighted that I got married. Just so I didn't go to Paris, which I had been fantasizing about, just so I didn't do anything to lose me from the fold. She ws delighted because I didn't really leave; there was no reason for her to be distressed. I was very excited about becoming a grown-up. Actually, of course, that didn't happen.

Further complicating this leave-taking by marriage is our desire to please our mothers. Every woman I interviewed, even if she was bitter, frustrated or angry at her mother, wanted her mother's approval. Those women who never *see* their mothers, who speak guardedly to them on the occasions when social interchange is required—even these desire mother's love, and want to give daughterly devotion in return. And so, in the decision to marry, many of us are attempting to please our mothers—to give them what they've always told us they want, and want for us, of course. Taking a husband satisfies two social requirements—we have separated from our mothers, and we have satisfied their expectations and hopes. Now that we have given them what they want, they will love us unreservedly—now they will be the mothers of our dreams. (Maybe they'll stop saying, "You look so much prettier with your hair brushed *away* from your face.")

For our mothers, too, the daughter's escape through matrimony is double-barreled. They have primed us for this—whatever emotional contradictions may exist for them—and yet, as we fulfill the dream, we leave them. Our mothers weep Demeter's tears even as they push us out and away from them. They may be ashamed of such feelings, and regard them as possessive or clinging—but despite what

gynecologists and therapists make of this maternal grief, it
stems from real loss—not only the loss sustained by women
who are kept from full growth and must live through their
children, but the ancient depression of the Goddess. In the
wake of the daughter's departure, "the void is filled only by
the possibility of making something out of yourself."[5] How
many of our mothers have the strength or the opportunity to
create themselves anew, depleted as they are by the time we
leave? "It is a barren time for the mother when she can no
longer delight in her own creation."[6]

*My mother has this real hard thing about children separating
from her. At one point after I left, she would not speak to me.
She was very upset about my being away from home. She
wanted me to come home. "Why can't you do what you're
doing in Albuquerque?" I would write these long letters
about my need to be separate, to be a person apart from the
family, and it's real hard for her to understand.*

*It's been two years since I left, and she still asks me to come
back. My mother's been to my house twice. She can't understand why I am living with somebody else, and not living with
her. She wasn't angry; just hurt.*

*I left my mother's home when I was 18, immediately after I
graduated from high school. She was hysterical; she was upset
and hurt; she put a lot of guilt on me.*

*I went to see her the week after I moved out, and she said
things like, "Oh, God, you're wrenching my heart out," and I
wanted to say, "I'll come back; I'll come back," but I knew I
couldn't do it.*

*I went away to school at 16. I was ready; she wasn't quite
ready. The first couple of weeks, here she came down the road
with dinner and my mail every day; she even brought the dog
to visit; but she got used to it after a while.*

Some of our mothers, a minority, supported our leaving.
They did so in spite of their own needs, accepting the separa-

tion as both natural and healthy. They overcame their desire to keep us with them in order to further our desire to go. Some of these had to oppose their husbands, who couldn't accept the loss of their daughters, or the idea that their daughters were adults.

Mother realized that there was a great deal of dependence on my part, so she encouraged me to go to North Carolina, where an aunt of mine was living. I'm not so sure that I could have broken away at that stage of my life, and just said, "Look, I'm going to go," but my mother, in her wisdom, sensed that that was what I wanted. She encouraged me to leave my job, and with her blessing and encouragement, I did. I liked it so well there that I never returned. I think she might have been disappointed, if the truth were known, that I did not come back.

I felt terrific about leaving; she was crushed. Emotionally it was very difficult for her. As a mother, I'm beginning to understand that. She said to me that she knew it was something I had to do. She said it was good for me and I was ready to be on my own. It was the hardest thing she ever said. I believe that she believed it, but it was real hard for her to say.

I was 19 when I finally left. My father didn't want me to leave and she said, "Do it." He kept me home for a whole year after high school. She said, "Don't worry about it; just do it. He'll give you the money." Finally I just packed up. It was her support that let me do it; I needed that support against him. She encouraged me, while he kept saying, "You're not going, you're not going."

Complications arise when our mothers apparently don't care if we leave. Whether we've been hung up on the going away or not, this lack of response is hard to take. The fact of no emotional display does not mean that there *is* no emotion, but daughters are often hurt by what seems to be callous acceptance of their moving out. Especially in those cases where we've felt for a long time that our mothers didn't care about us, this aloof goodbye is proof of our mothers' coldness.

Unlike the daughters who have to struggle to avoid guilt over their mothers' display of loss, these daughters wanted some indication that they mattered to their mothers, though they generally deny that they have such desires.

I don't think either of us had great sorrow. If my mother felt any regret, she must have had a rule against saying it, because I don't remember her saying anything.

She would always say, "Oh, honey, I'll miss you," and I had the feeling she might have been a little tearful about it, but I never gave it two thoughts. She didn't interfere or mother me, no protest, or send a lot of letters and demand a lot after I left.

I was so happy to leave Springfield, Ohio—but as far as my mother was concerned, it was no big deal. I never went back. As a matter of fact, I came straight here. She never said what her feelings were about my doing that. It was kind of understood—she would put us through college and we were to make our own way after that. Oh, not that we couldn't come home. . . .

I didn't feel she particularly missed me. You see, I never felt that she cared for me. There certainly were no feelings that I sensed. I always felt glad to be living at boarding school. I was glad to be away from my mother. I was glad to see her every once in a while, but I said to myself and to other people that I was happy to be in the boarding school.

My mother tells me now that if she hadn't had my younger brother at home, she would have gone crazy when I left, but at the time she didn't say anything, and I never thought about it—that's just the way things were.

Worse than saying nothing at all, worse than breaking down in hysterical grief, worse than trying to keep us at home, is being relieved to see us go—delighted to be rid of us. Suspecting that our mothers do not care for us is painful; feeling certain that they'd rather we be gone creates a kind of bitterness and resentment that may be harder to deal with than any of the other responses daughters described. These daughters have tried to resign themselves to being essentially mother-less, and by that mother's choice.

She didn't seem broken up over it. I think she was kind of glad to get rid of me. She had two younger children at home. It was fine. We didn't get along all that well.

I always thought my mother was glad when we all left. She would never admit that.

How did she feel when I left? She redecorated my room as a den. (laugh)

It became apparent I could not live at home. So I found a girlfriend in the same situation, and we moved into an apart-ment together. My mother had been anxious for me to go. She wanted me out. She was finding it hard to deal with anything at that time.

Once again, the irony of the situation is that these mothers—having either rejected the maternal role out of their own needs, consciously or not, or having been driven to such a state that one daughter must say, "She was finding it hard to deal with anything"—these mothers experience no satisfaction in spurning their daughters. They make no gain; the loss is as detrimental to them as it is to their daughters, who are turned out of their birthright—their mothers' love.

Many of us seek to return to our mothers—not only those daughters who left reluctantly—but even those who fled, eagerly rushing into "freedom." Much of the inclination to return is caused by the realization that there is, in fact, no warmth and comfort provided by our society, no support for fears or weaknesses. Once out of school, there is no "auto-matic" source of friends, women with whom we may share our feelings. And those of us who leave to marry (marriage being the only sanctioned offer of solace available) frequently find ourselves disillusioned within the first few years, es-pecially if we have children.

162

Since most of us recognize that we cannot actually go back to the maternal safety and dependence we need, given the shock of being an adult woman in this culture, we hold ourselves in check. We visit our mothers, call them on the phone, believing that we can't go home again, and often realizing that we'd not get what we needed if we did. Some of us arrange special agreements with our husbands—as part of the marriage contract—which allow for visits home at specific intervals.

When I got married I told my husband there was one thing I wanted to do. I said I wanted to go back to see my mother at least once a year, and he said that was all right. I was very homesick when I first left.

I really learned to appreciate my mother when I moved away. And I don't care what my husband says—I told him, when it comes to mom, that's it; I must do what I must do (I mean, I don't abuse it); I will leave and go to her. If she needed me, you can be sure I'd go, I'd do anything, financial assistance, anything. I wish she would ask more often.

But there are a few daughters whose needs become so great that they transgress; they break the rules and go back to mother. In the folklore of my family is the story of my father's elder sister. Of course, her story was not told to me until she had divorced her husband; it is classic. After a few years of marriage to a man her mother had disapproved of to begin with, who turned out to be, as grandma had predicted, unacceptable, my aunt took herself and her children and went home to mother—who told her to go back to her husband. She did, and remained married to him for nearly 30 years, waiting for her children to grow up so she could leave.

An even more poignant example of the same desperate attempt to return to mother, and the assumption that mother will accept and protect us, is found in *A Proper Marriage*. Martha's husband has attacked her, attempted to rape her several times, and has threatened her with a gun. Both his mother and hers are aware of the struggle the young couple is going through. Ultimately, Martha runs from the house one night, very late, under attack from Douglas. She goes to her mother. "I'll stay with her till morning, she thought, and then come and get my things." Her husband follows her, pulling at her; "her arms were almost being wrenched out of their sockets. It had never entered her head that her mother would not let her in. Now she saw it was obvious she would not." To her daughter's pleading, "Mother, I want to come in. . . . Mother, I must come in, let me in. . . . He's hurting me. . . . Mother, you aren't going to let him bully me?", Mrs. Quest replies, "Well, you deserve it. . . . He's quite right. . . . Go back to him. . . . it serves you right."[7]

Earlier, her mother had agonizedly told her that "it was a woman's role to sacrifice herself, as she had done, for the sake of her children. . . . And what will people say?"[8] In these last two phrases she strikes at the heart of the matter—the strength of our mothers' socialization as women, and our own. They tell us to go back, and we go. If our mothers abide by these rules, and know that their own security depends upon their obedience, we must see that they cannot take us back.

With a few exceptions, it is primarily white middle class mothers, whose stake in the society-at-large is greater and perhaps closer to the core of their lives, who reject those daughters who come weeping home. They uphold the rules with a vengeance. Working class and poor mothers may have a greater sense of their own disenfranchisement, and be able to relate more readily to their daughters' situations. Ironically, it is these mothers who are least able, physically and financially, to support their daughters if they come back—their resources are so limited. This limitation keeps willing mothers from accepting daughters who want to come home.

Whether we desire to return to our mothers or not, most of us assume she'd be there if we did. But that is sometimes an unwarranted assumption. There were mothers in my study who were mad, who were alcoholics and suicides; they were those who could not bend to the role without breaking. Others gave their daughters over to foster homes, because they

164

were simply unable, economically, to keep a home for their children, so vicious is this system. Two women who gave up their daughters so that the girls might be raised in "better" conditions (more money, a father and a "normal" family situation) are Jane Cannary Hickok, known as Calamity Jane—scout, gambler, driver of the infamous Deadwood stage; and Charlotte Perkins Gilman—author, lecturer and feminist.* They both have left us a record of their pain at leaving their daughters. Gilman, in her autobiography, writes:

> My mother was dead. My friend on whom I had so counted, was gone. . . . there was new work opening for me in San Francisco, but in a place unsuitable for a child. It was arranged that she should go to her father for a while. . . . Since her second mother was fully as good as the first, better in some ways perhaps; since the father longed for his child and had a right to some of her society; and since the child had a right to know and love her father—this seemed the right thing to do. No one suffered from it but myself. This, however, was entirely overlooked in the furious condemnation which followed. I had "given up my child". . . . I lived without her, temporarily, but why did they think I liked it? She was all I had. . . . she climbed gaily aboard (the Overland train). . . . She had long shining golden hair. We smiled and waved and threw kisses to each other. The train went out, farther and farther till I couldn't see her any more. . . . That was thirty years ago. I have to stop typing and cry as I tell about it. There were years, years, when I could never see a mother and child together without crying. . . . I used to make friends with any child I could so as to hold it in my arms for a little. . . .[9]

Calamity Jane kept a journal, an album of letters, which she left to her daughter's adopted father, with the instruction that he should give it to Janey when her mother was dead:

*Gilman gave her daughter to her ex-husband and his second wife, who kept the girl for several years. Hickok gave her child to a wealthy Eastern couple who adopted her. She never knew, in her mother's lifetime, that Calamity Jane was her mother.

Your father James Butler Hickok left me after you were born & to spite him I let the O'Neils adopt you. . . . (When I visited you) I held you close Janey & it seemed for one moment I was back again with you in those terrible heartbreaking days in Yellow Stone Valley facing life without your own Father a future black & tragic for you darling. . . . I hope some day you can come to this Country then you will know how I had too exist. (When I visit you) Perhaps then you will think of me sometimes not as your mother but as some lonely woman who once loved & lost a little girl like you. I shall take you on my lap & tell you all about that little girl. Of course you won't know its you. . . . Giving you up nearly killed me Janey . . . . O Janey the years too soon have robbed me—yes the years have robbed me of you. I wanted nothing else but you all these years. Perhaps some day after you have lost everything you ever loved & are an old woman yourself—then perhaps you will know how I feel. . . . [10]

Some of our mothers leave us even as they stay by our sides. Many daughters feel that the mothers they know, the women they see daily as they grow, are not the women their mothers were. That is, as we come to know them, we see that something has changed, gone away; more than just the changes that move naturally over the body and spirit of a woman with the years, we sense that something has been lost; the mother we live with is less attractive, less alive. This woman we can never know may be the one we most need to know. Many interview daughters said that they had seen photographs of their mothers as young women, and that the woman in the pictures hardly resembled the woman they called mother.

As this was repeated to me several times, I recalled photos of my own mother, taken before she married my father. In these pictures she is often accompanied by other young women; all of them are stylishly dressed; some are flirtatious, some are arrogant, a few are frankly sexy. With their cigarettes and shoulder pads, their fur coats and open-toe platform shoes, they are Rosalind Russell and Celeste Holm, Eve Arden and Katharine Hepburn. I need to remember that my mother was this vital young woman before she was a laundress and a cook.

We can see in these snapshots that our mothers left another life to come to the place where we meet them; we can get a sense of that other life in these pictures. The element we all see, in these photographs, that most daughters mention, is the hopefulness, the quality of looking forward, in our mothers' faces.[11] They allow for the possibility of a future, these faces; they have not yet understood what it means to be locked in, to see the closed door as a personal symbol.

Another "leaving" we need to examine and understand is the death of our mothers. We have already seen the responses of daughters whose mothers abandoned them, physically or spiritually, who chose a brother, sister or husband upon whom to bestow their love, or who were not able to sustain themselves within the confines of the mother role. All of us, though, are "abandoned" by our mothers when they die.

Some of us anticipate that death long before it comes, or mourn it long after it's passed. Because we are inextricably bound up with our mothers, their deaths diminish us. Perhaps more important, we often feel that our relations with our mothers are incomplete and unsatisfactory, so that their deaths create even greater frustration than we felt while they lived. If we have never been able to receive from our mothers the truth of their hearts—and if we have never told them our own deepest feelings, their deaths are tragedies for us. Probably it is that understanding which makes us mourn them as we do, and fear their deaths while they live.

I first understood the urgency of women's feelings about their mothers' deaths in a conversation with two friends—both of whom are in their 50's. As they questioned me about my ideas for this book, and I answered with stories about my mother and me, struggling for truth between us, they both said, "How lucky you are; your mother is here; she is alive. When we came to know ourselves, to understand some, at least, of what we had wanted from our mothers, of what they had done with us; when we came to a space in which we could have taken this on, our mothers were dead."

My mother never really leaned on me or depended on me

the way I wished she would. She resented having to depend on me. The crowning example was that she went away to die. She didn't even die near me, or allow me to be present when she died. She went off to Colorado for a visit, and died there, at the home of her husband's daughter. She never turned to me in anything important; I was not included. And she's still haunting me; I'm still trying to win her approval, even though she's dead.

In relation to my mother, I was never an adult until she died, and when she died I was left like a child without a mother. I feel a very strong tie to my mother even now. At 62 I would like to have a mother. I could cry.

I wish I had understood what my mother was going through—I have insights now I couldn't have had then. If I had been aware, I might have been able to make a difference; she might not have had to kill herself.

She started getting sick, sick where she was going to the hospital. I was visiting her, but I felt real guilty because I wasn't spending enough time with her—at that time I had just met Richard. I was spending absolutely all of my time with him. I feel guilty that I hadn't seen the signs of her being real sick, in pain. If I had noticed her at the time I would have seen that something was wrong. According to the hospital—she was in and out—they didn't know what she had. Finally she had a stroke, and I knew; but by that time it was really too late.

There are so many things I would tell my mother; there's so much I would ask her. If only I had understood, had been able to see, why we had the arguments we did, what kept us apart. We had no chance to really know each other.

Every year around the time of her death I think about her a lot, and I'd like to talk about those feelings. For a variety of reasons, I don't want to do it with my friends. This is an important chance for me to deal with myself and the issue of my mother, and her death.

Some few women have had the opportunity to experience their mothers' deaths in satisfying ways. Both Simone deBeauvoir and Colette have written of their mothers' deaths in terms of the impact each felt in her own life—saying words they never allowed themselves to say to their mothers' living faces.[12] Lisa Alther's heroine, Virginia Babcock, gains adult stature when her mother says to her, from her deathbed, "You must do as you think best,"[13] allowing for the independence and womanhood of her daughter. In this study, I encountered a woman, in her early fifties, who had achieved a kind of peace in her mother's death, though she, too, expressed wistful regret at the lack of her mother at this time when she is coming closer to her own real self.

I wanted my mother to die and she wanted to die. I think she wanted to die for a long time. I took a trip that year and prayed she would be gone by the time I came back. Not nice, right? I felt the last time they "saved" her they shouldn't have done it. I did such a crazy thing. I went to someone and asked for a prescription that would kill her. I told him what the situation was. He gave me something. I put all these pills in a coke bottle, and gave it to her. She drank it all, and she slept splendidly, but never died. I did this thing. I am such a coward; how could I have been that brave? My final gift to my mother was an attempt to release her from life, and it didn't work. And even then, on her deathbed, she was for me, whether she could understand me or not, she was for me, and she wanted to protect me. It was so strange. She would still want to know how I was. She would touch my face and look into my eyes—which looked shitty of course, bloodshot and teary. I was so overwhelmed. She was the only person in my life who was saying, "How are you?" even if it was non-verbal. As sick as she was—always. You know, mothers are worth having.

It is not only those of us whose mothers *are* dead who agonize over the impact of that death; we anticipate our mothers' deaths as well.

I used to feel very separated from her but now—I just feel this closeness and I don't know why. I don't know where it started. Around my last year in high school I developed a great fear of my mother dying. I still have that fear today, three years later; I really fear her dying. I imagine all the diseases she could have, and I often think, "How could I take it? What would I do, would I die too, without her strength could I keep living?" I think about that at least once daily. I know it's going to happen one day.

I had to work consciously on the thought that she is going to die, and how I will react to that. And because her death is intermingled with my own, I've had to work on that, and think how am I going to respond. I can see from talking to her that her own preoccupation is with the fact that she is going to die. I'm able to see what it's going to be like for myself, plus the fact that I'm losing a very valuable person.

Judith Kegan Gardiner suggests that in this culture the death of the mother may be necessary for the daughter to achieve her own identity. Through her examination of five twentieth century novels and one short story, she demonstrates the partriarchally produced contradiction between guilt and rage: "our fictions gratify matricidal rage by plots that murder the heroines' mothers slowly and painfully while they pacify our guilt because the deaths are all from 'natural' causes."[14] If we are strangled by our relations with our mothers, it may well be that we'd rather they die than continue to thwart our living.

Another group of daughters presented an interesting sort of matricide in their interviews. These were women whose mothers *might as well be dead,* for all the intercourse between mother and daughter that exists. When I was a girl, I learned about the orthodox Jewish custom of saying prayers for the dead over children who were "disowned"—they had married gentiles or performed another equally unacceptable act—these daughters and sons were as if dead. Worse than dead, for they were not to be remembered. In the same way, Maxine

Hong Kingston tells of her father's sister, who was forgotten, "as if she had never been born,"[15] because of her transgressions. Some daughters live as if their mothers were dead. They never see them, never speak to them, never mention them to their friends.

This response, engendered by a pain that is literally unspeakable, is caused by the strain inherent in the institutional definitions of mother and daughter. The daughters have given up; they refuse to deal with their mothers any longer. They are different from the daughters who allow their mothers a superficial social relationship with no genuine feeling—other than tension—between them. Rather, these are women who separate from their mothers, like those women who maintain a separatist politic about men: why put the energy into such a struggle? Why continue to wound ourselves, drain ourselves, when no satisfaction—no hint of valuable or desirable return—is forthcoming? Even when these daughters are sympathetic, feel pity for their mothers rather than scorn, they have cut themselves off, they have removed mother from their active sphere; she no longer lives in their lives.

I haven't seen my mother in 12 years. She couldn't change; she didn't want to. She had to dominate me, she fought with me constantly. I was 28 years old, and she was still telling me when to come in at night, accusing me of having an abortion when I stayed out late and drank peppermint schnaps—she said my breath smelled of ether. I couldn't take it any more; no one could.

I've agreed a few times to see her, or talk to her over the last seven years. Each time she seems more pathetic, but we never get anywhere. She winds up saying terrible things, and she never understands; she never changes. I don't know how that can be, it would seem that everyone would change, but she doesn't. I don't want to ever see her again.

Every now and then I see my mother or talk to her. She is a very destructive influence in my life and the lives of my children. She never brings good, only ill. If she would die it would solve my problem completely.

My mother is like a dead woman. She's given up entirely. Her life is over.

The hopelessness of killing our mothers this way is akin to the impossibility of rejecting them as models. Despite our real desire to end it, to turn mother out of our minds, we cannot. Once again, it is clear that though the society promotes disaffection between mother and daughter, it provides no mode for ending this painful struggle. As there is no culturally defined development of the dependent girl-daughter into an independent adult woman in relation to her mother (or father), neither is there a cultural mechanism which resolves this dilemma—even for those of us who sever the bonds "completely." No such "completion" is possible.

Ironically, this may be the single positive aspect of patriarchal capitalism's oppression of women. By necessity, we have maintained, in grief and hostility, our intimacy. In that intimacy we may conceive the new love and honesty we need. As Demeter and Persephone must be restored to each other, so must we all, daughters of the Mother, come to acknowledge, with joy and satisfaction, that "every mother contains her daughter in herself, and every daughter her mother. . . ."[16]

7
Daughters Become Mothers
—More Often Than Not

You ask me about my
future, and I tell you
about my children.
                                        —SUSAN GRIFFIN

even past her death, I cannot fully
have language with my mother, not as daughter
and mother through all the maze and silences
of all the turnings.
Until my own child grows and asks, and until
I discover what appalled my mother long before. . . .
                                        —MURIEL RUKEYSER

I say to
myself
my daughter
will escape.
                                        —SUSAN GRIFFIN

The traditional concept of maternal instinct is no longer acceptable—if ever it was. We are too far removed from our animal selves to consider that making babies is beyond social control. Women have lost the instinctive need for heterosexual copulation just as we've lost the estrus cycle. Despite our oppressed state, which results in the lack of free choice, any one of us might, and some of us do, live a healthy life without being fertilized or raising children. Women have children, at this point in time, in this place on the globe, because we are socialized to do so. "Women's mothering is seen as a natural fact, and natural facts . . . are not in need of explanation. The assumption, however, is peculiar, given the extent to which human behavior is not instinctually determined, and given [the] social scientists' insistence upon the social constructedness of social reality."[1]

It is true, I discovered in my own motherhood, that our bodies haven't lost the ability to lock into old patterns. Though women are alienated from our bodies in all other spheres of our lives, maternity is the one place we are allowed, if only partially, to move through some natural sensual responses. When I became pregnant, I was made aware of my body in ways that even the society around me considered positive. Unlike the usual body-consciousness of women, that constant anxiety resulting from objectification and its resultant physical discomfort, the body sensations accompanying a deliberate and healthy pregnancy felt good. I could openly lavish attention on my body, and everyone, including my mother, approved.

I consciously experienced my son's gestation, birth and nursing more as a primate female than I had any other bodily event, including menarche. Not only was I consistently attuned to his movements in my uterus and the development of my breasts, but the growing distortion of my body was of consuming interest, as was its return to a non-pregnant/nursing state in the months to come. On the morning that my labor was to begin, I awoke with a strange taste in my mouth. The taste was menstrual blood. No, I had never tasted menstrual blood before, but I recognized it. So I knew my labor would begin that day; indeed, the plug of mucous blocking my cervix loosened and came away when I got out of bed. In another time, that taste might have been an urgent signal to find a cave, a thicket, a safe place to give birth.

At the hospital, when my son was taken away from me and put into a small room with other screaming newborns, I had to wait nearly five hours before I saw him again. He had emerged from my vagina already suckling, but by the time I held him to my swollen breast, he had lost the reflex. In the first few days, as we worked out our nursing routine and escaped from the hospital, I felt no affection for him, though I found him fascinating. His body seemed incredibly small; his inarticulate helplessness was terrifying. But by the time he had taken in all my colostrum, and the milk had begun to flow, my hormones held sway. Before he was a month old, I held him easily in the timeless posture of nursing madonna; as we rocked together, I was rapt as I gazed into his face—and he into mine. As the milk flowed, so did "love." Now came maternal instinct—triggered by a chemical reaction. Lactation bonded us.

That I had not loved him in utero, nor when I first perceived him as an actual person, was absolutely true. After all, as I joked when he was three weeks old, who ever knew a person who weighed ten pounds? Could this baby in fact *be* a person? If so, what I had always assumed I knew about people had to be drastically revised—and it was. One of the revisions was an understanding that "maternal instinct" appeared after the child did, and depended initially upon the intimacy of nursing plus those economic and social factors that gave us the luxury of weeks and months together in warm, well-fed comfort.

In exchanging stories with other women, those who are mothers and those who are not, we often speak of the seductiveness of babies. Those hot, soft little bodies, those tiny fingers winding round your thumb—is there a woman who doesn't feel drawn to pick them up, to automatically assume the position: one arm round the back and under the bottom, the other hand supporting the head, patting rhythmically as her body begins to sway? Yes. There is such a woman. In fact, there are thousands. Moreover, men feel none of this seductive lure we attribute to babies. So it must not be in the babies, that pulling force. Just as there are little girls who play with trucks and swords, there are women who might easily diaper the wrong end, and with no inclination to correct their mistake.

These women often feel "odd" and guilty about that difference, feel that perhaps they aren't feminine, haven't developed their "womanly" qualities. The fact is that almost all women, and certainly almost all men as well, assume that the proper woman has these maternal inclinations. When we hate our children, want to consummate our most infanticidal desires, or when we realize we don't want to give birth, to raise children, or continue to live with the ones we have—we fear that we are "unnatural." (Those of us who have damped this fear still understand the swift and vicious social penalty for acting on our impulses.) The fear is accentuated by our own continuing acceptance of the idea that women make and raise people because we want to, or need to—that women somehow must mother. We understand that we are helpless in the grip of an instinctual urge too powerful to resist.

In fact, just as we learn almost everything else through the model of our mothers and the reinforcement of social pressure, we become mothers because our mothers did. It is clear that despite our denial or reluctance, our mothers have been our role models as much—or more—in this as in anything else. Whatever differences there may be among all the millions of our mothers, they share maternity. Greater even than the overwhelming example of their marriage, their motherhood stands before us. We do not always see this particularly clearly, of course, and generally feel that either our "decision" to have children is actually a decision, or that the children we have are there because it is a "fact of life," i.e., women have children; we are women; therefore, we will have children. Almost none of us who are mothers (certainly not I) understood initially that our "choice" to make a person was no choice at all. Since our instincts long ago failed us, and cultural evolution has brought us to a place where almost no elements in our lives are natural, we must be educated to re-produce.* What woman would truly *choose* the bondage of patriarchal motherhood? The only way any woman could be induced to deliberately bear and raise children to live in this society, to subject herself and her babies to the pain and grief, duplicity and repression required, is the way in which we've all been raised—through a constant flow of sex role

---

*The lack of safe, effective contraception and abortion are factors which, though I cannot discuss them here, cannot go unmentioned.

stereotyping, promoted through rewards of security and praise, balanced against heavy penalties for women who do not succumb.*

Obviously, this inducement succeeds. On our mothers' bodies we learn our lessons. Most women do make children; nearly two-thirds of the daughters in my statistical study were mothers. Of the remaining third, less than half said they did not want to have children; approximately one-fifth hadn't decided yet. All but four of these non-mothers are aged 29 or younger. This is not to say I am assuming they will all bear children; I include their age out of an understanding of the pressure they will sustain, and the resulting sense that before they are thirty-five, some of them will become mothers.

Many women say that they think their reasons for having children are "selfish." They believe that having children will gratify and satisfy them, and they feel guilty for desiring that pleasure. Within the context of our socialization, wherein motherhood is seen as womanly fulfillment, there can be no purpose to childbearing that is *not* "selfish." The making of a child is not for the child. The child, nonexistent and much less than fully understood even in its potential, can have no voice in the decision to conceive itself. Rarely do prospective mothers consider what it means actually to make a person. Women often speak of "wanting a baby." The person being created is only going to be a baby for two years—even in a conservative estimate. She will, however, be dependent on her mother, in this society, for fifteen to twenty years or longer. One does not hear women saying, "I'd like to have someone physically and emotionally dependent on me for most of her needs for fifteen years." But that reality is hidden behind the socialization that makes us want "babies."

There are two politically conscious reasons for having chil-

*Animals in zoos often refuse to reproduce under conditions they know are unacceptable for raising young. Were they socialized as we are, readers of the urban dailies might be spared photographs and stories about "unnatural" mother lions and tigers and bears who simply kill their babies, rather than raise them in captivity.

dren; neither one, to my mind, overriding or replacing the urge to mother we learn from our mothers. Feminists want to have daughters, little Amazons, free women. We seek the revolution in our daughters, forgetting that many of our mothers sought their escape in us, and that we hated them for it, forgetting that our daughters need models, and that what we must do is make the revolution in ourselves. Third world women want to replace the babies that genocidal imperialism has murdered—or kept from being born.[2] They want to make freedom fighters—red, gold, black and brown skinned children, small phoenixes to rise from the ashes of their people's struggle. These positions both are filled with contradictions and conflict, born at the intersection of old and new consciousness.[3] But for any woman, it is a painstaking process to come to know her real desires, and to analyze the source of those desires.

This process, the "coming to know" is usually absent from our coming to conception and pregnancy. Ignorance and shame about our bodies, combined with the acceptance of maternity as destiny, render us mothers before we can come to any understanding of ourselves. In interviewing women for this study, I asked those with and without children if they had wanted to become mothers and, whatever their response, I asked why. Only a minority gave unqualified affirmative responses, though more than two-thirds said they wanted to have children. Less than one-fourth said they did not want to have children, though many, many responses, even among those already mothers, demonstrated ambivalence.

When I thought I might be pregnant, I wouldn't even admit it to myself. I had morning sickness; I had every sign in the world, and I said, "What could it be?" (laugh) I didn't even call the doctor. I had my husband call the gynecologist. He calls the guy and says, "My wife's having all these symptoms; what do you think?" Of course, he says, "Sounds like she's pregnant."

I want to be a mother. I didn't for a real long time, because I was terrified of the idea, because I thought, "How can you raise kids and not fuck them up?" I was terrified of me being responsible for these people, children. These days I feel I could do it, and I could be O.K. It's just not going to be right now, maybe ten years from now. For a real long time I didn't even like kids.

I would have to be in a situation where I was in love with someone. Because of our society. The ideal seems to be to get married and have kids. If it weren't for that I probably wouldn't even consider it. Probably not.

I can see how easy it would be—even now when things are supposed to be different—to have children. How easy it would be for me to get into it, and do that exclusively, even though I may bitch about it. It might be hard for me but I can see myself doing it. And I'm fighting against that. I thought until a couple of years ago of not having any kids because of what my grandmother did to my mother and what she did to me and the others, but I know it's inevitable; I'll do it. I think I'll regret it after I have it. It will be too much strain on me. I don't want to do it. I can't escape from it. The biggest factor is my husband. If we stay together it's going to happen.

It seems like I've been raising kids all my life. I know I did it with my brothers and sisters, and I think I'm real good at that, and I like it. It scares me to want to make a person.

I never "wanted" to be a mother; I never had it as a need. Only when I inadvertently became pregnant did I decide to have a child. I think that it's a set-up from beginning to end—the whole mother/child thing, and specifically the mother/daughter thing—I have to oppress any child I'm responsible for, in order for them to survive, and it's true as you go down the line economically and racially. There is only one source of power, which is personified by white men, and in the family by one man. On the one hand you're defending this child—especially a woman-child—against this whole system, and on the other hand, you're at odds with her. You've got two oppressed people—head on—in a situation where the source of power is available to neither. There are no exceptions as far as I know.

I was always very positive about motherhood. I like to be a mother because you can be a teacher, you can be a psychologist, all rolled up into one if you're a mother. That's what I thought at first. Then I knew it had to be connected to marriage, and that freaks me out. I didn't want to lose my independence. That was a big thing before I got married and had my kids.

I'm afraid. I want to be but, yes, I'm afraid. I want to be but I'm afraid and I'll put it off. I would never go seek it now. An accident could happen but I'm not out after it. Also, connect that with the fact that I'm real selfish and real independent. I would have a child tomorrow if I were rich enough. I don't want my privacy or my life style invaded. And I have this feeling I would have boys and there would be the sexual energy there and that would be hard for me to deal with. I would rather have a little girl. That's real dumb too because we'd probably be in competition. I don't think I really will have children.

I do not plan to be a mother right now. I have got to build myself a sort of a nest. You know, one has to fit in somewhere, and I want to be somewhere. If I had a nest I think I might want to have kids. Yes, I actually have imagined myself as a mother. I've been sort of worried about—my mother used to hit me when I was little, and I would be afraid I might do the same thing because I have a temper. Now I could not cope at all. I don't want to have children.

This overwhelming ambivalence is not surprising in the face of the contradictions apparent to us in our mothers' maternity. Though only 59 percent of our mothers spoke of motherhood,* they demonstrated with their lives (as did those mothers who never spoke) the constraint, the burden, the de-

*See Chapter 2.

pletion resulting from the institution of motherhood—in the same life which may well have displayed maternal tenderness, passion and dignity.

Some daughters, choosing not to become mothers, make that difficult minority decision because of what they've observed in their mothers' lives, or in a conscious attempt to break the influence of their mothers' teachings.

No, I don't want to have children—and yes, I have thought about it. At first I wanted twelve kids. (laugh) Then I talked to my older sister—thank god for her; if I didn't talk to her in these years I might have been insane. I was still under my mother's myth of being a mother making you a full woman, making you happy and all of this. I saw, the other day while I was babysitting, a woman walking down the street. She had a bunch of kids trailing after her; she was holding on to some of them; one kid nearly got run over. I thought, "That's not for me." I thought, "I'll never have kids."

I was anti-children for a long time. I wanted nothing to do with them. I was so disgusted to have all these little people running around to have to take care of them. I knew I wasn't going to have children for a while, after all those brothers I raised.

As I grew to be a woman I didn't want to have children and I was afraid of childbirth. I just never felt close to any kids, and I didn't see myself as watching out for somebody and always thinking about them, taking care of them.

Even though I know I'm not like my mother, I was always afraid. I would never want to do to children what was done to me. Thank god women are coming out in the open now and saying, "You're not going to do it to me."

I'm in a peculiar generation—right in the middle. The younger ones growing up now have all these examples in front of them; my mother never had that. But my group, we're the ones who are taking the brunt, because though now there are possibilities, there's a lot of fighting, too. I don't know what I would do with a child. My god, I don't even know what to do with myself. Maybe I'll never know.

Interestingly, as with those women who wanted children, who felt motherhood would bring fulfillment, several women who didn't want to be mothers also felt that they were being selfish—though most accepted this with little or no guilt. Some, in fact, took their "selfishness" as a point of pride.

I think I'm too selfish a person to have kids, for sure at this time in my life. Because if I'm going to be a musician, I want to be a very good musician—and that takes a lot of time. I also have all these interests that have nothing to do with children.

Whenever I think of children I think of not having them. (laugh) I've felt that for many years; I would rather not have children. I've worked extremely hard all my life, and I'm just beginning to enjoy it. I feel very selfish about all my time, everything that's mine, and I don't want to share it.

Many women who prefer to have no children demonstrate that serious consideration was given their choice—they are conscious of the weight of their decision, and aware of its emotional impact in their lives.

I know what it's like to be a mother. I've lived with mothers and children and accepted childcare responsibilities and all that goes along with them. I know what it is to have a child and take care of a child and what that would mean to my life, and what would happen to me because of that. I don't want that to happen.

I don't want the sole responsibility—which would be mine, of course, if I had a child. Sometimes I think it might be fun to have a little person. I see other women with their kids and it looks fascinating to watch them go through their changes. It's exciting. But I think that as they get older, I wouldn't be so excited any more. There's no way I would want a twelve-year-old child. I just know that would turn out to be something I

*would hate. I don't want to live with someone or be respon-
sible for them if I hate it.*

*I didn't want to go through the physical pain of giving birth. I
didn't want to distort my body with a baby. I didn't want any
of that; I just thought it would be a pain in the ass from beginning to end.*

*No. For sure. Absolutely not. I am a mother; I have a dog—
that's all the child that I can handle.*

Despite this conflict, we assume woman's place as we grow
into the women our mothers are. And, daughters and mothers
alike in adulthood, we seek the love and support the mother/
daughter relation promises. Whether we share love and ideas
with our mothers or merely tolerate the relationship as an
unfortunate social problem, all daughters understand that
having children appears the ultimate attachment we can
make to our mothers. Even if we do not become mothers, we
understand this.

In my earliest efforts to confront the truth between my
mother and me, I asked her this: "Why do you love me,
mother? You say that you love me. Yet, we don't see each other
very often, we have no work or friends in common, and our
politics, our philosophies, are very different. What is it you
love?" She said to me—understand that I did this as we sat at
the busy counter of a suburban coffee shop eating lunch—
undermining, as usual, the very closeness I sought to engen-
der, in my eagerness not to waste one moment of our time
alone—she said to me, "I love you because you are my daughter. What do you mean?" I told her that wasn't good enough,
that it didn't mean anything, that it was just a role—"daughter"—and I wanted to know her feelings about *me*.

So she thought for a time and then said, "I love you for
giving me Daniel." (Daniel is my son, six years old at the time
of this writing.) Forget that I attacked her, raised my voice in
public and embarrassed her, said to her, "My God, mother, a
cow can do as much! Making a baby is nothing to base love
on! And what do you mean, 'giving him to you?' I don't own

him, and if I did, I wouldn't give him to you!" Forget all that and realize that my mother, when I asked her why she loved me, told me that my having made a child, construed by her as being *for her,* was at the core of her affection for me.

Between these admonitions to forget, I have remembered something. I remember that when I decided to make a baby, I had to restrain myself from telling my mother that I wasn't using contraception any more; when I knew I was pregnant, I did not wait one minute to call my parents, and when their response was unalloyed pleasure, I cried. And when that baby was born, I knew, I quite consciously understood, that I had garnered unlimited approval; total acceptance was finally mine. I did *not* then say to my mother, or to myself—"A cow can do as much!"

How did my mother respond to the births of all my children? She was delighted! There is nothing that would bring a look of ecstasy to my mother's face more than a baby.

The only thing I've ever done that she's liked was to have my children. The only positive thing I can remember her saying, about six months ago, in fact, she said, "They're nice kids." I said, "Why do you think I have nice kids?" and she said, "You know, you've done some things that are ok."

Conscious or not, with or without an immediate positive response from our mothers, we fulfill one of the basic requirements of the role of "good daughter" when we become mothers. Having babies brings us, albeit temporarily, to unity with our mothers. Our mothers may even be able to give us the approval we've continued to seek, because we have affirmed their value in our motherhood.

For when daughters become mothers, their own mothers are validated. The daughters *are* like them—in a way no one may deny, that serves to mark the sameness daughters have feared since their adolescence. There it is—you see, we are alike; you shall do as I have done, be as I have been—mothers may say in the face of their daughters' maternity. When daughters become mothers, their stature increases in the eyes of their mothers (in the majority of cases); "adulthood' is attained. Our mothers may never see us as full equals, but most of them do acknowledge this new position.

Those adolescent women who bear babies and keep them, who say that they have "no curfews" now, that they may "date" whomever they please, that their babies are the signs of their maturity—these young women are a perfect symbol of the confusion of biological capacity with wisdom and life experience. Though the fact of becoming mothers does, inevitably, bring the opportunity to be close to our mothers, it does not create the ability—in either woman—to cease negating both the truth of our similarity and the need for honest revelation of life experience.

When the baby was born she came down and took care of us for two weeks after we were home from the hospital. That was great. She actually cooked without burning anything. She had a good time. Then a year later she and my father came together and she was totally different. She was depressed, incompetent, withdrawn, and just a total mess. I didn't enjoy her at all.

When she found out that I was pregnant she wanted to help me, and she took care of me a lot. Now, when she looks back on it, in fact, she tells me not to have another baby because she can't go through all that again. I had a lot of complaints and I was always getting up in the middle of the night asking her what to do. She did enjoy it. She would come over and clean my house.

I had some difficulty breastfeeding and I called her and she told me how to do it, so there was this re-establishment of the relationship made by my motherhood, which felt good because there couldn't be one on a political basis. That was when she started communicating with me a lot; when my second child was born at home, she came and assisted and stayed for a week—it was a real positive experience.

When the children came, my mother took a more active interest in me as a person, especially when my first daughter

186

*was born. She came and stayed with me for a couple of weeks.
That was pretty good, as she didn't criticize me a lot or tell me
everything I was doing was all wrong. She told me what she
knew; we shared the problems; she was there to help me.*

*My mother was very pleased that I was having children. There
was a lot of fuss made over it, but it was a pleasurable fuss,
joyful. Did it bring us closer together? Nothing brought me
and my mother closer together. My mother did her shtick and
I did mine. When I had my kids it gave her something to talk
about, something to do. She was happy to babysit, and all of
that—that was her thing.*

Daughters who choose not to become mothers, holding out
against the force of years of female socialization, may well
inspire their mothers' disappointment, anger and secret envy.
But neither do daughters who produce grandchildren escape
the mother/daughter struggle. Our own maternity does not
necessarily further the development of a satisfying mother/
daughter bond. And those women who seek to become
mothers and cannot, who move through fertility clinics, oper-
ating rooms and adoption agencies, sustain grave injury and
insult to their bodies and minds in their desire for children.
These women are not rewarded with the satisfaction of even
fleeting maternal acceptance; they cannot affirm their
mothers' model.
Do not infer that it is *solely* to please our mothers that we
make babies; as with all else pertaining to women's social
roles, teaching and reinforcement are constant throughout
the society, and maternity provides a refuge (of sorts) from the
demands of one's own dreams—the forgetting process is
heightened in us by the demands of motherhood. But it is important to see that many interview women recognized just
before or soon after their children's births that an important
element in our so-called choice to become mothers was the
need/desire for our own mothers' approval and acceptance. It
is shocking and painful, to daughters who hoped maternity
would bring the tenderness and comradeship we'd longed for
since our childhood, to find that serious and longlasting im-

provement in the relationship does not automatically ensue; in fact, there are new grounds to quarrel over for those pairs so disposed, and, for all of us daughter-mothers, there is the realization that now, we too play a dual role.

I wanted her to come and stay when Zoe was born. She came to Los Angeles; I remember feeling that I really wanted my mother to be there. But she wasn't comfortable being there. Then, when Zoe was seven months old I got hepatitis, and was real sick. One of the big things my mother always has made clear is that her mother would not come and take care of my sister and me; she just wouldn't do it. So I called my mother and asked her to come. I didn't have to; I could have hired someone. She came—but it was horrible. She complained the whole time; I really saw her in a different light.

When Sallie was born, I thought the normal thing was that you had your mother come for a few weeks, so I had my mother come for a few weeks and it was the worst thing I ever did in my whole life. For one thing, when I am around my mother I instantly become a daughter—as opposed to a competent human being. It was the wrong time to have that conflict laid on me. I was a new mother and I was this daughter, both at once. Also, my mother just never took charge—which was what I expected her to do—and I was real freaked out. I would ask her, "What do you think about this," and she would say, "What do you think?" It really pissed me off, because I wanted her to say, "Probably normal—don't worry about it." Also, she was not into the fact that I had a lot of negative feelings about this kid. She would say things like, "I certainly never hated you." My mother also made comparisons between Sallie and me as a baby—to my kid's loss. I wasn't real pleased with that either. The thing is that while she didn't tell me what to do, she didn't actively encourage me to be independent either. When she'd say "What do you think" I'd say, "I don't know anything abut this! If I knew, I wouldn't ask you!" (laugh)

When I became pregnant, she said, "I hope it's a boy; boys are so much easier." Of course, I was hoping it would be a girl, but it was a boy. After he was born, she was somewhat helpful, in helping me take care of him, but the help didn't make me feel self-confident. When I had my daughter of course, she really disapproved, and she never did like Alice as well as Richard, because she really did like boys better. She always favored Richard; he was the apple of her eye.

In the face of these expectations from daughters, there are many possibilities for disappointment. Some mothers, for instance, even among those who feel satisfaction in their daughters' maternity, are unable to touch their infant grandchildren. As it is with the "grandmamma" in *Tell Me a Riddle*, so it has been with many women who have raised their families and then begun to struggle, often inarticulately, to stay free. She reports that when they put the grandchild in her lap, the grandmother was barely able to restrain herself from begging that they please don't ask that of her. She felt overwhelmed with the mothering responses; the constant caring, which pushed aside all her own feelings and needs. This grandmother, her body filled with cancer pain, seeks the journey of self discovery. But her husband and children, with no sense of her n eeds or her desperation, push at her, to feed what Olsen describes as an addiction—sinking into a need: the need of being needed. She sees her grown daughter trapped in her old pattern; the seductive sounds of babies and children singing; and, for counterpoint, the screams of a fatigued mother. It is the baby she struggles against; she is not repulsed as they believe her to be; *that* is her fear. As daughters with babies, we often cannot see our mothers' conflict or appreciate those fragments of truth which surface between us.

For some reason my mother became absolutely cold-ridden as soon as she had to confront my child. She couldn't cross the room; she would sneeze; she would blow her nose; she couldn't pick up the kid—and the same thing happened with her second grandchild, my younger sister's. She couldn't come near the child. She said to me, when I asked her about it later on, "How did I know how I would feel as a grandmother? I didn't know. I didn't know if I would like my grandchild." Of course my first reaction was, "How dare you?"

She came over when I brought Andrew home, and I said, "Aren't you going to hold him?" She said, "He's too little; I can't hold him." I said, "Mother, you've raised two kids!" She said, "I don't want to touch him. I don't want to touch him until he's older." I nearly fell over; I thought she was nuts!

Another source of pain, despite the alliance of maternity, is that our mothers do not change their character when they take on the new role—"grandma." They remain the same women we have struggled with for years. Just as the coming of our motherhood doubles the role requirements for us, so grand-mothering multiplies the expectations our mothers must meet. As daughters we do not relinquish the fantasy of grand-motherliness—whatever style: Is she to be the well-groomed elderly lady, the downhome granny, sweet and tranquil, wise and stern, a cookie-baker and quilt-maker?

Since my mother is far away, and is living a wretched exis-tence anyway—uses drugs, uppers, downers, whatever she can to get her through—my daughter doesn't have a grand-mother, she doesn't understand the wonder of a grandmother, someone who doesn't question you and everything is wonderful.

I really look forward to it if my daughter should choose to have children. That would be the neatest relationship to have with a kid. I would take them to Marshall Field to see Santa Claus and all those special things, do all the fun things with them and then you take them back to the parents. It sounds like a cop-out, but I think it's great to be a grandmother. Of course, my mother doesn't do any of that with Mara.

My mother relates to my kids pretty much as she does with me: she looks to them in anger and in disappointment and in hurt for them not meeting her needs and making her happy.

She consistently refers to them as her grandbabies. They are almost ten and fourteen, but my mother would like to keep her grandchildren as babies. And yet, she came very close to killing those relationships, precious as they are to her, because in her drunkenness she made awful overtures, and wanted to hug and fondle them all the time. I told them that their grandma was an alcoholic; as with death, I didn't think it was something I should play games with. They needed to know.

Holly has been trapped into feeling caught in the middle between her grandmother and me. Originally, she needed everything to be happy like a storybook family between my mother and me, and she felt somehow responsible because it wasn't. My mother furthered this. It has all come to a head lately. Holly came to me and said, "Mother, Grandma keeps calling me and saying this and this and that to me, and she's making me feel bad, and on and on and on." So I told Holly, "Look, I won't do that with her. I can't go back and get what I didn't get as a kid. You can't go back and get from me and grandma what you didn't get, and you can't give grandma what we never got, either. Don't let yourself get trapped." If we can get what we want now, even if that means we have to leave grandma out, that's what we need to think about. We see her when we want to, and we include her when we want to, but we don't play those games, and most of all we don't let her get all of us.

Ironic as it may seem, that majority of us who strive to be different from our mothers find our own motherhood the greatest opportunity to work out the distinction we seek.

Perhaps the first time I made a step that was totally different than mother's was when my daughter asked me if I was having an affair, and I said yes. It was a tremendous departure, that level of honesty.

My mother never wanted kids in the house—they made a mess—and she never went out of her way to befriend other people who had kids my age. I have found a whole lot of women I really like as people through my kid, but the purpose was to find friends for my kid. There is no question about that. That's why I sent her to nursery school.

I didn't raise my kids in the self-sacrificing way my mother did. Sometimes I think I went too far the other way, from some of the things they tell me that I didn't have the faintest idea about. I was reared so strictly where everything was a sin, even roller skates were a sin. So I wanted my kids to live, and practically turned them loose. "Live, there's the world, the big beautiful world, go live." And they have.

Some of us can acknowledge that, whatever our own problems with our mothers might be, our children have managed to sustain mutually agreeable relations with their grandmothers. For some daughters, this may be a source of great jealousy and resentment; we don't want our children to love the woman who has given us such grief, or we can't let our children have any of the love we want for ourselves. Often, what is happening in the latter case is that the love our mothers had always wanted to give us unconditionally, but never were able to demonstrate (for the thousand reasons we've examined in previous chapters), the physical affection, the indulgence and praise, approval and affection beyond our chastened dreams—all are transferred to our children. The fact is that these children, chubby and clever as they are, cannot possibly have engendered in our mothers the love showered upon them. After all, they are new, and in most cases, they are barely acquainted with their grandmothers. Where does it come from, then, this true mother-lode? It must be ours. Deferred and deflected, it's passed us by, and we must watch it poured out on these undeserving little newcomers. Even those daughters who have no conscious sense of this changeover, this release, make note of the strength and depth of their mothers' affection for grandchildren.

She lived with us when my second child was born, and that was the happiest year of her life. She was just crazy about that child. That was Rochelle, a beautiful child, and she just lived for that baby.

She raised my children, too, in a way. I left them when they were 14 and 16. I just threw up my hands and said, "You'll have to lead your own lives." So she took over. She didn't move in with them, but she brought them food and nurtured them.

My mother always wanted to be a grandmother. She's loving it; she's warm and affectionate with my daughter. She doesn't have to do any of the shit work. She doesn't have to be the heavy; she doesn't have to discipline. That's what she likes. They just do fun things; she doesn't have to teach her morals and all of those things.

When I separated from my first husband, I lived at home with my mother, and I had a small son. My mother was very attached to the boy, and she was a tremendous help to me. She did the diapers and everything; it was like we were both her children, really. She was a big influence on my son; his wife credits my mother with his good attitude about women.

When I gave birth to Jacob, I could only have one visitor in the hospital because I wasn't married. So my mother was my visitor. While I was in there, she cleaned my apartment, bought a few baby things. When I told her, "Yes, I'm keeping the baby," she went wild, and went shopping all over. When we came home she came every day to visit and help. She really loves Jacob.

But whatever the relations between our mothers and our children, our own mothering, in style and technique, remains based, quite firmly, in the models our mothers have presented. Even those of us who appear to have gone in the opposite direction—who curb our children's emotional expression because we feel that we suffered from being given "free rein," or who devote time and energy to our children's activities because we felt deprived when our mothers were not scout leaders—we make these compensatory adjustments superficially, without recognition of the fact that motherhood is far more complex than this one-issue vision would suggest. As we are predominantly patterned after our mothers, most of us raise our children by reproducing the emotional dynamic we experienced as our mothers' daughters.

Frequently, we reflect our mothers' internalized experience of sex-role stereotyping. Among those daughters who said they (had) wanted to become mothers, 20 percent expressed no preference for the sex of the child(ren). They said things like:

I only hoped they would be whole, physically and mentally.

This statement reflects the usual stance women feel they must take, because any expressed preference may bring disappointment, and that disappointment is extremely difficult to deal with—especially in the absence of a tradition of honesty. (Preference among already living children is also generally denied by mothers, though of course the biases are usually obvious, and children always understand their own status.)

Pressure to produce male children is common enough, and is said to rarely be equalled by desire for female children— such is the assumption society makes, at any rate. In this study, I found that many more women prefer to have female children, or children of both sexes, than desire male children, though most understand that making males will garner more praise and status. Many women express relief when they fulfill this requirement early, or first, so that they can relax, or stop having children altogether.

I frankly didn't give a damn, but my husband was the only son of an only son, and there was a lot of pressure to have a son. Even though it is the man who determines the sex of the child, it is the woman who has to hear the snide remarks when she doesn't produce what is expected or required. His family put a lot of pressure on me.

I knew a woman who produced five daughters, each two years apart, before she could insist upon halting her husband's quest for a son. She had, I recall, unending patience, as well as a "wifely" sense of humor—a quality absent in most fictional versions of the same phenonmenon, like Golde in *Fiddler on the Roof*—though she sustained the same kind of criticism and frustration as her more burlesqued sister.* (There were thirteen daughters in this study who knew their mothers had preferred to have sons; all expresssed at least some resentment, even when they understood that their mothers were trying to satisfy husbands, in-laws, societal requirements, etc.†)

Among those women who did wish for daughters, who could, without ambivalence, state that they did prefer to have female children, there were several variations among their motives. Most common were those women who related their sexual identity and life experience, both positive and negative, to their wish for a daughter.

I wanted a girl when I had Mandy. My mother wanted girls, and I somehow thought it would be nice to have a little girl. My husband probably would have preferred to have a boy.

You know the old ladies who feel your stomach and tell you what sex your baby will be? They all told me I was going to have a boy. I was really huge. When I went into labor, I was very scared; I wished I had never become pregnant, and I

*I've always wondered what the five daughters felt, knowing they were, progressively, less and less desired; has the last one ever felt herself to be a disappointment?

†A very small minority, represented by only two or three women, spoke of the satisfaction of being a mother in terms which have no connection to the sex of the child, or to the social role of mother. These women were concerned with the spiritual aspects of maternity: "I see myself as a creator, and I wanted to see the creature I had created. It was so exciting when I saw her. I went through pain to make her. She was premature, and I would say, 'Oh—she cannot die.' She was a miracle. It's a miracle to give life."

began thinking about my mother, and how I wished she could comfort me then. I thought of how close we were, and that's what I would want for my child—for us to be real close. I knew I couldn't be that close to a boy, be buddies and friends and do everything together. I wished "Please let me have a girl; please let me have a girl." When I saw her I was so happy; I feel real close to her now; I would like to have six daughters.

I want a daughter. I want to be the mother that I never had. To the daughter I never was. That's what I want. I want a sister.

I wanted girls. It was sort of a gut thing. I was saying to people with the first one that I wanted a girl, but it was a boy. Well, that was fine, but then I had Frederick and it was a boy again, and I was disappointed, but of course, I finally accepted him. There was some stuff that went on when he was a baby—for a long time I did not accept the fact that he was a boy. I wanted girls for that connection; the connection with my mother is that we are women, and my connection with a daughter would be the same thing.

I grew up one of five girls—girls as a rule are very easy to raise, very unrebellious. My mother was such a good model; most of us did not break rules. We were all very good children when we were growing up.

I wanted girls. Of course I knew I would get girls because a husband with gout only produces girls. Girls stick around the house longer than boys. It's not that I want to hang onto them, but after six years old, boys are with the world, and girls are still at home. Working, as I always had, six years goes by in a hurry, and you don't get much excitement out of your children. And with boys, once they get married, it's all over.

Whenever I think of having a kid of my own, like when I watch Sesame Street and wish I were watching it with a three-year-old, it's always female. Every once in a while I catch myself and say, "If you got a kid, it could be male, after all." It just seems like it would be so easy with a girl. Part of that is that I would want it so badly to be different with me than it was with my mother—so I think about it in terms of a daughter. *My mom had a better relationship with my brothers than she had with me. She loved them. She was OK for them.*

I would like to be a mother of daughters. That's probably the result of my mother's attitude—she likes girls a lot, better than boys, and she just enjoyed having me around.

I want a girl. I like girls. I'm a girl. I would understand more what it's like to be a her rather than a him. Also, I don't have any faith in the prospect of having a child with a man and having it last forever, and I would be much more comfortable raising a girl by myself than I would be raising a boy by myself. I also feel I have a lot to share with a girl.

Others quite clearly had specifically feminist or feminist-influenced attitudes about their preference for female children. These were often similar to the reasons above, but applied a political consciousness to the strong feelings they shared with that first group.

Both my husband and I were happy to have a girl. I was glad. I'm even gladder now, because I wonder how I would treat a boy. Being in the situation I'm in, divorced and struggling to make it as a woman in a man's world, there's probably less hostile bullshit that I'm doing subconsciously to her than I would to a son. It's a lucky break to have a daughter. She identifies with me, and I find that very good. I know women who sometimes seem to hate their daughters and it makes my blood run cold. They say things to them like, "You're going to be the mommy when you grow up"; I can't bear it.

By the time my second child came, I had been in a lot of women's activities, plus I had grown up with a lot of girls, and I felt like I wanted a girl. When he came out, I said, "It's not a boy." I saw that he was a boy and I said that. I lived in fear that I would try to make him into a girl. I don't want to have any more children, but I would like to adopt a girl.

I wanted to have a daughter first and I did. I think the reasons I would have given then were nonsense, like a daughter is gentle to the family, she's helpful and all this stuff. Now I think I wanted a daughter first because I know more about me than I do about men. That was more real than the other things.

I wanted a girl. Why? To grow a woman, you know.

I say it all the time—I only want a girl and I hope it's a girl, because otherwise I just don't know what I'm going to do. I don't want to raise a man. It would be a joy to raise a female. It seems to be like I've had men too much in my life.

I think about having a daughter and having the relationship with her that I didn't have with my mother, doing all the things with her that my mother didn't do with me, telling her all the things my mother didn't tell me. I don't know if I want another child just to do all that, but I think about it a lot. I still wish I could have had that, and I can't even have it now with my mother. I feel a great loss. I know I can give a lot to my son, and I hope we'll have a good relationship, but it's not the same. It's just not the same. I look at him now sometimes and I see him as a man, and I hope I'll do right by him. I hope he'll be the kind of man who will be decent with women but it worries me even now.

Yet another group, rather different from these latter two, wanted to have female children because they didn't want to raise sons. It was less that they desired to make daughters than that they rejected the notion of mothering boys, that put them in this category.

I always wanted girls. I think I dislike men. I could write a book on what those bastards pulled on me.

I wanted to have a girl because I felt I couldn't cope with raising a boy; I felt I didn't know a lot about boys.

Probably I preferred to have girls, because I was scared of not knowing how to deal with a boy. I never had any dealings with male children, male peers really, or male authority figures.

Well, I never had any brothers and had not been around young boys, and wouldn't know much about them. Also, my father had died, and I never established a good relationship with my stepfather. I wondered whether I could do that with a son.

I mainly wanted girls because I wasn't sure I could relate to a boy; it's just that simple. I was convinced that if we had a boy it would be a kid who would want to be in the Little League and all of that, and I would die if my kid were a jock. As it turned out, my second daughter is as much like a boy as she is like a girl in terms of activity, sports, etc. But I just felt I could relate better to a girl, and interestingly, so did my husband.

When I was pregnant with Gabriel I always thought I was going to have a girl. Then one day it occurred to me that it might be a boy—and my first thought was, "I don't want it if it's a boy. I'm not going to have a boy." And then I thought, "It might be a boy; it might be a boy," and I began to reconcile myself to having a boy. I have always found it hard to have baby boys. I found it such a pleasure to have a baby girl; it was a pleasure. When my next son was born, after my daughter, I had a real keen feeling of disappointment that he was a boy. Of course when my next son was born I was kind of numb. I didn't really want him anyway, so I didn't feel anything when he was born.

Most of the women in this group make the assumption that differences between the sexes are all natural; the distinctions are not seen as results of sex role stereotyping, as an outcome of the socialization process. Baby boys are seen as men in miniature, with feelings and sensibilities at odds with their mothers' by definition. As the mother of a son, I recognize the frustration and pain of knowing that my child is at once of my body and alien to it; I live with the anxious understanding that my boy's life is not in my hands, that all I want for him must be wrested from the patriarchy that claims him. Though I made and fed him out of my flesh, I am now "other" than he. He has been given to know that we are engaged in a struggle, and that that struggle is over what I am, and what he will be, when he comes to his full power. I am raising a middle class white man; it is best that we both understand what that means.

Perhaps those daughters who don't want to raise male children have understood on some very deep level that we are creating and nurturing the agents of our own oppression; once we make them, their education as men in this society will pull them from our arms, set them above us, make them the source of our degradation. To keep that from happening we must enter into conscious struggle with our sons, to actively, in our motherhood, change the "traditional" definitions of male and female behavior. Daring to defy the socio-psychological canons that call us emasculating or seductive mothers, we must raise our sons to feel their needs, to truthfully express them. They will be sensitized; they will develop the capacity to nurture, and they will understand that to live thus is to embody and be surrounded by contradictions. They cannot help but learn—despite our teachings—that males are, and are expected to be, "less physical, less cherishing, more intermittent in their presence, more remote, more judgmental, more for-themselves, than the women who are around"[5] them. And they will see the rewards for that behavior in social acceptance, material goods, and power.

We cannot, in our commitment to this change in ourselves and our sons, underestimate the power of our own socialization—as in the fears that will surface when our little boys begin to live in the new ways our struggles open for them. Mothers of little girls can say with breezy facility to their three- and four-year-olds, "Sure, you can wear pants as well as skirts. Why not?" But the reverse becomes a nightmare in our attempts to explain to small boys why long gowns are only acceptable for priests, short skirts for dead Egyptians. They might wear the costumes of both sexes, but they must be warned about the humiliating, frightening and violent reception that awaits them if they do. As their mothers, we juggle to attain a balance between supporting the strength of their spirits and undermining the power of male supremacy.

The grief inherent in this situation is fearful, and may be basic to the rejection of male children even by women of no conscious political commitment.

There were also women who had originally wanted girls, who began by saying that their preference was for daughters, but who turned to ambivalence—sometimes even as they spoke to me.

I would like a girl because I'm a girl. I don't think I'd know how to deal with boys. Bill would like a boy because he doesn't know what the fuck to do with a girl. Actually, if we were to have a child and it turned out to be a boy, I'd take that as no great disappointment. It really doesn't matter.

Up to the time I was pregnant I swore I wanted a girl and said I wouldn't know what to do with a boy. I knew I wanted to raise a girl. That's one of the first things everyone *asked me when I went home to Albany, and all of a sudden I just don't care any more. I can't think about that any more, and I'm going to deal with whatever it is. I don't have any choice. If I had three girls I would be just as upset as if I had three boys. I want to experience both sexes.*

As this last woman makes clear, the pressure can become terrific, and the outcome is totally beyond our control—so ambivalence becomes the safest position.

Some women who wanted daughters changed their views in deference to the baby's father's wishes, or couldn't know their own wishes in the presence of the man's desire for a son. Again, though they recognized that they had no power in the situation, or perhaps because of that realization, they desired what their men desired, or came to the sense that producing a son is paramount.

Actually I wanted a daughter, and did have the three girls in a row. If I had had a boy after the first one I wouldn't have been upset. In fact, after the first, I wanted a boy, because Manny wanted a boy. No, he didn't say that to me, but I just felt it. I had wanted girls because I just knew that a mother/daughter relationship could be real nice.

It's funny, but the whole time I was carrying him I thought he was a girl. I couldn't imagine me having a son. I was raised with women, and I didn't think I could raise a son. Part of it was that I felt pressure on me to have a son, and I felt if I kept saying it was a girl, then if it was a girl no one would be surprised, and if it's a boy, OK. And I said that I wanted a girl. When he came out and the doctor said it was a boy, I was shocked, and I remember feeling relief, and some pride that I had a son. I didn't think I could do it. I wasn't in touch with those feelings then but I know now that that's what it was. And Harold never said he wanted a son, but yet I knew he did.

Among those interview daughters who wanted sons (approximately one-fourth), there were many who knew from the beginning of their considerations of motherhood that they wanted boys. Certain as they were, these women reflected both the influence of their men and our sexist society, which values males over females.

I would have to say I wanted a boy. It was just the general shaping of what we think; you're supposed to have a boy first and then a girl.

I wanted a son. Now why I wanted a son I can't tell you, except I think I was influenced a lot by what I thought would be more valuable, or how I would get more praise. I'm sure I wanted a son.

I guess I thought deep down that I would like to deal with a little boy. Sam's father, deep down he wanted a little boy. When I'd talk about the child while I was pregnant, he would always respond very strongly to the idea of a little boy. He's very glad to have a little son because he's very traditional and liked the rough-housing and the sense that they could be strong, but with little girls you have to be very gentle. I think it scared him to consider a little girl.

The first time I wanted a boy and I got a girl. I had assumed that fathers would like to have sons, which was all wrong, because he didn't. He was delighted to have a girl, because there hadn't been any in his family. But you know it was the first one, and then the second time I really wanted to get it over with, and fortunately it was a boy. I had thought it would be nice to have boys because I thought boys like their mothers and it turns out it's not quite that way. I really like my daughter a lot.

I wanted a boy; my husband wanted a boy. I wanted to have someone in his image.

When I had the two boys, when Vince and I were married, it was very important to him to have boys. This proved his virility, his masculinity—big, big achievement. So he wanted boys. I was delighted to have boys. I think I had been slightly interested in having boys just to have boys; it has made me understand a lot of things I didn't before; you know I grew up with no boys and few men around.

A few women felt that there was "something special" about having a male child. These women intimated that there was an indefinable purpose, or need, to be fulfilled by having a male child, and generally did not think of sons as babies or "little boys," but identified them with/as men.

I can remember when my second daughter was born; in the delivery room I felt a twinge of disappointment. I had one girl and somehow thought the second one was supposed to be a boy. All I can remember is this feeling that it would be fun as a woman to give to a male. I just thought that would be an interesting thing to do. My husband never gave me any feeling that he wanted a boy.

I guess that I really did have a preference for a boy; I thought I was going to have one. Maybe part of it is that I had a brother instead of a sister. It seems to me that most of the close relationships I have had, that have been really meaningful to me, have been with men.

*At the time that I had my son, I don't know if it was my age or
the length of time I had been married, or if I hadn't had that
many years of relationships with men—I just felt I could be
closer to a boy child. It's something strange. I can't say what it
was.*

Some daughters expressed their desire for sons in terms of
their lack of self-esteem. As girls, and into adulthood in some
cases, these women had no positive experience of their female-
ness. Though this is hardly uncommon in contemporary
urban culture, only a minority of women were conscious of
the problem *and* applied it to their maternity.

*I wanted boys. I thought I was a lot of trouble when I was
growing up, and when I had my kids I hadn't yet begun to
figure myself out at all. The reason I thought I was so much
trouble was that you had to protect girls, and even if boys did
the same thing as girls did and got into trouble, you didn't
have to protect them. So I thought it would be much easier to
have boys. And I have them. Now I wish I had a girl.*

*Yeah, I wanted a boy. At that point in time I didn't like my-
self. I related more to men. I liked men more. I didn't know
much about women at all. My mother was not a typical
woman. What I thought of as the typical woman—at that
time—I didn't like.*

*I tried not to have a preference but I did. I wanted a boy be-
cause I thought I wouldn't know how to raise a girl. I had two
brothers that I was real close to. Girls I didn't know because I
didn't think I had done too hot as a woman. Now I think I'm
great.*

*Both of my kids were adopted, and I chose to have two boys.
After we had gotten them both I realized that I didn't want the
competition—the kind my mother and I had had. I didn't feel
that I was healthy enough to make sure it didn't happen. I
didn't want it to happen to a daughter I would grow to love,
and, quite frankly, I didn't want it to happen to me. Now, if I
were suddenly pregnant and had a girl, I feel that I could deal*

with it better than before. I feel better about myself, obviously, than I did then, but I feel much better as a mother of boys.

A small group of daughters wanted sons because they had identified with boys as they grew up, maybe even wanted to be boys or men. Their children then could live in the reality they were denied as females.

I wanted sons. With the second one it would have been ok to have a daughter, but I'm just as pleased having a son. I have always wanted to be a boy. I don't think there was anything conscious about this at the time. I thought I could be a better mother to boys than to girls at that time. Now I would love to have girls if I were to have children, but I don't want them.

When I think about being a mother, I would want to have both sexes, but I also want to make sure that I have a boy, and that makes me real nervous. When other people say that I get mad. I guess I like a lot of the stereotypes of what boys are. But if I have a child, I'll raise it real differently. I guess I like thinking of the child as being aggressive, and I would be real nervous about a little girl. She would get a lot of stereotyping from other people if not from me, and I wouldn't want that.

I wanted my first child to be a boy, because of the syndrome of the older brother, the older child, the stronger first child being male. I thought also that boys would be easier, I identified with little boys growing up. I always wanted to be a little boy, and I did all the things that boys did. That had a lot to do with it.

One final rationale among those women who preferred to have sons, which was verbalized by only a few women, but which raises an important issue, is the notion that it's "easier" to raise boys becaused they won't be so "messed up." The assumption is that little boys may be left to partriarchal socialization, that it is positive for them, but little girls present the necessity for painful struggle. Such thinking would imply a desire to have *two* sexes raised to be emotionally unrespon-

sive, spiritually undeveloped, and obsessed with power,
rather than to foster development of two sexes who may both
realize their full potential as emotional, intellectual, and
spiritual beings.

In interviewing women who were mothers of daughters, I
found a repitition of many of the same themes expressed when
we had talked about their mothers: the difficulty of
adolescence, the problems attendant upon truth-telling,
competition within the family, and the ongoing struggle to be
close—to share love—while fighting through the welter of
mutually unrealized demands and unmet expectations. Most
interesting is that there is relatively little negative comment
by daughters about their daughters. About small girls or
grown women, descriptions of the relationship are mostly
positive. Though criticism grows as the daughter grows,
sometimes with a series of crises or sustained conflict marking
the daughter's adolescence, most of the women I interviewed
describe their relations with their daughters in a far more
accepting and self-critical vein than they do their relations
with their mothers, and appear more willing to work through
their conflicts with daughters than with mothers. This must
be based at least partly in the fact that in relation to mothers,
they perceive themselves as powerless, or at least consistently
frustrated, in terms of effecting change, and see their
daughters as "possibilities"; after all, these are the women
they have raised, who were dependent on *them.*

*My own experience as the mother of a daughter is good. It was
a delight to raise a girl. The reason I had trouble with my
mother is that she was such a hostile person, such an unloving
and angry person, so bored and unhappy in her own life. I
could never understand why people who didn't have those
kinds of mothers should have trouble, have problems. Really,
I'm not aware why mothers and daughters shouldn't get
along beautifully. I feel they should. Only if they had my
mother they can't. (laugh)*

*I have always delighted in my daughter. I groove on her. I love
her. She came to visit me, and I thought, "My beautiful little*

apricot is here." Moreover, and I don't deny that she can be shitty at times, I have a great debt to my daughter. She was so incredibly good with my mother. I'll never forget it. She would go and stay with her in that big empty apartment. She would take her shopping. She was 13, 14, 15 at this time. My mother could not speak at this point, but Karen always knew what she was saying. She went to visit her the last days in the hospital; she was the last person to see her alive.

I have a great deal of respect for my daughters. I like them as people. I don't feel too motherly though, and that's the horrible part. There is that age differential, so I don't feel like a regular friend, yet I do. I mean I am their mother, but I just like them as people. They are completely different from each other and me. Dolly is a slob; she's like I am in that. Carrie is very well organized, efficient, and golly, I really admire that one. She intimidates me a bit. (laugh) She does; she's so goddamn efficient. She even writes notes for me.

Hers is a different generation. My daughter is a lot further than I am. She can go up against me. She has—and after me being her hell-raising mother all of those years. God, I must have intimidated her terribly, going down to city hall and spitting on the mayor and all. Who knows what that did to the kid's mind. On the other hand, for all the years before that, she saw me tied down all my life. She even said, "Ma, you and grandma never got to have any fun"; and she says, "I'm not going to tie myself down to anything."

I'm very proud of them, and I really like them. Even if they were not my daughters I would like them. I enjoy being with every one of them. I think they're good people. I'm not saying that because I was their mother. I'm actually envious of the lives they lead. They're all doing more or less what they want to do; I like the way they handle their lives.

This is not to say that there is no ambivalence expressed by daughters who mother daughters, no contradictions within the relationship. Indeed, from several women, I heard the same complaints and criticisms that appear to have been leveled by their mothers at their grandmothers. It is simply that, in speaking out of the *mother* role, as they were when questioned about their daughters, most women were less likely to blame, far less likely to resent, and almost never inclined to ridicule or demonstrate contempt, as they were when speaking of their mothers.

We are more willing to take responsibility for our half of the relationship in our role as mother than we are in our role as daughter. When discussing the negative aspects of her relationship with her mother, it is very rare for a daughter to assume any responsibility at all. We are unable to forgive our mothers; we cannot blame ourselves as daughters. At the same time, we cannot blame our children; we never absolve ourselves.

No matter what their age, when daughters described raising small girls, they invariably smiled and recounted feelings of gratification. Even when they spoke of problems, most of them expressed pleasure at the thought of their daughter's childhood.

My daughter is different than my mother—how much prettier, more interesting, full of life she is! We used to call her chocolate pie, for she was this little elfin thing, with big brown eyes.

I'm delighted with her. She and I have very different personalities, and I'm fascinated with the way her mind works. It's so different from mine, and I encourage that. (laugh) I enjoy raising her. I enjoy thinking of what I can do to help her out. I try not to make her into a girl—I keep telling her that girls can do what boys can do; if boys can do it, girls can do it. I like her sense of humor; I love to hang out with her.

I think we have a really good relationship. She tells me her thoughts, and we share. I like having her. It's warm; we hug each other and there's a lot of affection. I call her my lady bug, and when she was little I was her honey bunny and stuff like that. I can still feel that heart twinge I had when they told me I had a girl. I still feel, "Wow."

Well, let's see. Donna never, ever sassed back or gave me any arguments. She didn't always agree and she let me know she didn't, but she went along. Sandy, on the other hand, would, as we say, open up a mouth, and she would cry, but in the end she would usually give in, with a lot of tears and all. Terry was the sickly one, but she was the most stubborn. I'm not so sure I handled her right, because I really used to hit her. I remember once she came and asked me could she do something, and I said no. She kept coming and coming and I kept saying she couldn't and finally I just hit her and she cried. Then she went out of the room, and came back again *and said, "I don't know why I can't do it." Apparently I hadn't given her a logical explanation, just said she couldn't, you see. She didn't think that was right. She was very exasperating and wouldn't take no for an answer. Even when I hit her she came back again. Donna very seldom cried. Sandy cried all the time. Terry never cried at all—unless I hit her hard; she was stoic. To me they were all much easier to raise than their brother.*

When women described their daughters' adolescence, even in cases of extremely serious problems, dealing with sexuality or physical violence, even in the face of their daughters' contempt or disregard, these mothers still expressed a positive sense of both their own daughters and the mother/daughter relationship.

I consider the adolescent period of my daughter's life difficult, and I have noticed that this is characteristic of a lot of mothers. I did not have this problem with my son. It was very heavy for me, that she had such contempt for me. Since my own mother always identified with everyone except me, I try very hard to identify with Belinda and give her support against whatever it is that is giving her trouble.

The hardest time between mother and daughter is the teen-age period. I even had to take a little physical action with Rochelle. Sonia was more understanding; you could talk to her.

But Rochelle was as bull-headed as I am.

When my daughter was about seventeen she was going out with this guy who was beating her up, and she accepted it; as much as I told her, "How could you think of a thing like that? You were never raised that way, where a man could be violent and beat up a woman." She said that was because I was never with working class men and that's what they do. All that meant to me was that when they're that age they're so anxious to get a guy they'll do anything. But then she began to change. She became quite a feminist herself in a way, though she has to work out a lot of practical problems. For example: she refuses to get married.

I was a little flipped out the first time she told me she had gone to get birth control. I was proud of her. She was fifteen and had gone out to take care of herself. I was a little disenchanted that no one asked me, but, oh well.

I found out my daughter's going to a motel with some boy; she's fifteen and he's sixteen. I said to them, "Listen, it's normal. If you want to do it, go in your bedroom and shut the door, and the cops won't get you." Then later I thought, what's he going to think? Is he going to think that I don't care for my daughter? So I talked to him again and I said, "Listen, I care very much for my daughter, so if you do anything to her I'll just knock your ass." I said, "Look sex is just as natural as eating; I don't want her in jail for it." He started crying. He said, "I never heard of a mother saying such a thing; I think it's beautiful." You see kids understand more than you give them credit for.

Some daughters demonstrate a feminist perspective or inclination when they describe the kind of teachings they give their daughters. They have come to consciousness through experience, and turn to their daughters with the new wisdom. Whether they are speaking to small girls or grown women, the truth and urgency of their words are obvious—despite the ubiquitous contradictions.

I'm working very hard not to repeat the same pattern we used when I was growing up, that we manipulate daddy. My husband's aware of that, and that I work on it. Sometimes it's so difficult—it's so hard not to do the same thing your mother did.

Once, at the in-laws, Cindy came into the dining room where all the adults were sitting; she had a piece of cloth arranged like a veil on her head. My sister-in-law said, "Oh, you're playing bride." I said, "Bride? I don't think you want to think about bride at least until you have your education. How can you think about that? Play teacher, student, anything!" My sister-in-law said, "You're so harsh! She's just playing." I said, "That isn't playing; that's practice!" They really thought I was a neurotic nut. Well, that was a few years ago. Now instead of talking about wedding gowns and princesses, my daughter talks about going to Cambridge. She wanted to study the violin, so I arranged for her to study with a woman conductor. Every once in a while I feel this fantasy creeping in that she'll have a marriage and children—some day. I would like to have grandchildren.

I have tried to raise her to think for herself, to be self-reliant, not to feel that she had to follow in anybody's footsteps or be put into a mold. She should become her own person and always try to do what is right. The main point was to become independent, and I know she is.

One of the things I've always told her is, "Jinny, the reason I want you to be able to do something—have a trade, a skill, an occupation—is that it's very hard for a woman to be independent unless she's financially independent." All these years—it's never been a bone of contention between me and my husband—but after the children got grown up and my role disappeared, it was terrible for me. I had no idea that I had no money. That's why I wanted to join Wages for Housewives. You know a woman's work in the house is considered nothing, absolutely nothing, as hard as they may work. If something doesn't have a monetary value, it doesn't count, you see, so where does that put women? It puts us all the way down. It was terrible for me. I thought, how am I going to go to work? First of all, my schools are all forgotten, and then I would have to compete with a lot of young people, and who would want me? It was a terrible thing.

Nearly one-fifth of the daughters in this study had daughters aged fifteen and over. These women almost universally appreciated their daughters, both in relation to themselves as mothers, and as autonomus women. They spoke freely of their problems, and made some complaints, but retained a wistfulness and poignancy even through the occasionally expressed resentment. They shared deep and sincere concern for their daughters' lives, and keen understanding of the emotional dynamic of the mother/daughter relation. This is in marked contrast to the way in which they, and the other daughters in the study, viewed their relations with their mothers. There is far more understanding or attempt at understanding, of their daughters as people, as separate women, than there is of their mothers.

When mothers and daughters have problems, it's because they don't communicate, and don't have that secure feeling between them. I know when I found out Donna was on the pill before she was married, I was upset. I had been so naive myself at that age, you see. And then I realized that all the girls had apartments and it was very convenient. Nobody said anything about it. It's the same thing now, with Terry. For a long time neither Harry nor I would let each other know we knew what the situation was. Now, every once in a while, Harry will say, "I've got a daughter who's living in sin." These things are very difficult for people of my generation to adjust to. I won't say we'll come to accept it, because there's still this feeling from way back; you still feel that it's not right, because our whole life it was drummed into us. I can say I envy women today and I don't think that marriage is the ultimate. . . . but I still feel that I could not have lived any differently.

I feel that I'm closer to my daughter than to any other human being, and I always have been. We're so close whether we live together or not. She moved out when she was sixteen. She would tell me almost anything. She has told me things that I know for sure most girls don't tell their mothers. The only reservations I have are when I see things that she's doing more clearly than she does, but she's young, after all. Sometimes I hold back a little bit on the criticism, because I don't want to hurt her.

I care for her; I'm glad she's my daughter. I don't mean it's all sweetness and light, though I want sweetness and light sometimes. I've felt hurt that she didn't want to be my mother and support me. I still want her to.

Right now I wouldn't say that I have heart-to-heart talks with my daughters too much. I feel disappointed that my relationship with my daughters doesn't seem very close at times. I worry about that, and I think it must be because relations with my mother weren't very close. Maybe I'm doing the same thing without realizing it.

Living with Rochelle is like living with my mother. For forty years I lived with my mother, and now I have a daughter who does the same things she did. She doesn't even know; she does things she never saw my mother do. My mother had a way of changing her life by changing her furniture—and she's always put a chair kitty-cornered, in the corner, never lining them up straight, but always at an angle. Rochelle would do the same thing. She would push my house around without asking, and all the chairs would be kitty-cornered. And if Rochelle wants anything, she appropriates it; my mother would do the same thing. If she wanted to use your jewelry, she would, but don't use hers. Just like my mother.

I don't see as much of her as I would like to. Our relationship is good, except that I was so much closer to my mother than she is to me. It troubles me, and at times I do say rather snotty things. My relationship with her is very important. She had won a scholarship at Oberlin, so of course she went. Well, the worst thing I ever did was—I was invited there to speak—I went because I wanted to see her and to get the money. Oh, my god, I regretted it. I only made a stupid speech. I didn't give a shit about the speech. But ever after that, she was known as my daughter—I truly still feel very bad about it.

I really love Glenda and we really get along fine. I'm not sure what hostilities might still be there, but I do know that she does like me, respects what I do, finds me a good person. We enjoy spending time together. She just recently came here and spent a week. We seldom write. Occasionally she'll phone, so there's no hangup that she has to call mother every Sunday or anything. She's 32.

I really don't have any of the difficulties that you hear about with my daughter. I won't say I never have. There were times, especially when she was growing up. From age 11 to 14, she was very difficult. Sassy. But after she got over that we had a very good relationship. Not that I don't criticize her and not that she doesn't get angry when I do. She doesn't accept criticism easily. Yet I am not afraid of her, and I intend to say what I think. Oh yes, she criticizes me. I am not as sassy to her as she is to me. She likes to dish it out but she can't take it. That doesn't frighten me. I guess I'm getting what I put out. I was sassy to my mother many times. I know that.

Right now Dorry and I aren't so close and it bothers me. She comes over when she needs something. So I don't like her attitude and I told her. For once I didn't lose my temper. I said, "Dorry, I'm very concerned about you. Why don't you go into therapy and find out what's wrong with you. Your hostility towards me is terrible." On the other hand, she gets furious and says to me, "Grandma couldn't have been as good as you say she was." I don't understand that attitude, unless, with her hostility toward me, she feels guilty that I don't have any hostile feelings toward my mother. I think my mother was a weak woman, but what the hell? If you've got ten kids, and you have to get rid of your husband because he's abusive to the children, and especially back then—what could a woman do? It's different now; we don't have to go through that. I married at fourteen a man with a two-and-a-half-year-old child, had a

214

baby right away—no daughter of mine would do that. I would have broken her back for her. I always kept an eagle eye out for Dorry; I thought I had to tie her up in her room; I wouldn't let her date until she was sixteen. So then she got married at nineteen—much too young—to a fellow I didn't like and I wouldn't even go to the wedding. I couldn't bear the thought that she was quitting college seven months before she would graduate. Actually, I tried to live my own life over through her. Maybe I expected too much from her.

My daughter was a very difficult child to raise. It was much easier with my son. In her teens, it was the sixties; she was in on everything, the drugs and all. It was a very trying period. Although we were very close, we were also very hostile. I was disappointed with her—see how it repeats itself—as my mother was with me. Now, sometimes I think we're too close. We need to be more separate. She's twenty-five now, with an eight-month-old baby, and far away, but here's the pattern: She always wants my approval. She says, "Mother, don't you think I'm right?" She wants my approval for everything she does, so, in different circumstances it's just what I did with my mother. I tell her she should not expect me to agree with everything she does. It's not fair. Then I would have to dissolve myself as an individual, and say, "I am living you."

We have, by and large, abandoned our mothers to the burden patriarchy has laid across their bodies, disavowing our connection to them, rejecting the possibility of a communion many of us seek in our own children and each other. Not only do we perceive our mothers through the sexist vision that degrades all women, blaming and slandering mothers in particular, but we are kept from experiencing power or fulfillment through our mothers in a patriarchal culture. As daughters, we want to evoke our Demetrian mothers: "Each daughter . . . must [long] for a mother whose love for her and whose power were so great as to undo rape and bring her back from death."[6]

We must seek out our mothers. We must again revere the old wise women, and learn from them. We cannot discard the women who made us, as if all they ever did was to prepare us for slavery. Much of what we choose to keep, as we attempt to discard the negative trappings of "woman," is what our mothers gave us—a warm sensitivity to people's needs and desires, the capacity for caring and nurturing, intuition, ties to the earth and the moon, the strength of our blood cycle. All these have come to us from the mothers—despite their pain and bitterness, or their disavowal of pain and bitterness.

Given that none of our mothers can be the Goddess for us— nor we for them, given that we may now see the gap between the male-defined construct "motherhood" and the female reality of bearing and raising children in this society, we need to view both motherhood and daughterhood in a new way. We cannot make the required changes simply by trying not to be what our mothers have been. We must create a new form; we must seize ourselves; we must wrench ourselves out of the track laid down for us. Change cannot take place without that wrench—the tearing out of old forms, and the commitment to go where there are not yet forms to follow. Women have always been pattern makers,[7] creators of forms. In that tra- dition, let us redefine the roles of daughter and mother. Let us mother each other; let us accept the responsibility that fol- lows upon our demands for acceptance, affection, approval, admiration. Let us acknowledge as our enemy that violent re- pressive social matrix which now sets the pattern for mother/ daughter pairs.

Moreover, we must live as if our dreams had been realized: We cannot simply prepare other, younger daughters for strength, pride, courage and beauty. It is worse than useless to tell young women and girls that we have done and been wrong, that we have chosen ill, that we hope they'll be more "lucky." If we want girls to grow into free women, brave and strong, we must be those women ourselves.

Appendix

This is the basic form I used in interviewing the women who assisted in my research. Answers to the first ten or eleven questions were written down by me, as we talked. All the rest were recorded on audio tape.

INTERVIEW FORM

1. Name   Address   Phone

2. Age   Ethnic ID   Schooling
   Profession/Major Interests and Activities, Source of income

3. Marital status   Motherhood

4. Ever lived: alone, with lover, with children not your own; Living now with

5. Mother's Name   Address
   Age (now or at death)

6. Mother's ethnic ID   Is it strong?   Religious?
   Ever religious in daughter's life?

7. Adopted or born? Mother's age at daughter's birth?
   Mother married to father? Mother's age at marriage?

8. Number of mother's children   Daughter's
   numerical position   Ages and sex of siblings

9. Son preferred at daughter's birth? At any point? Sought?
   How do you know? Mother care more for brother?
   Because he was male?

10. Daughter nursed? How long? Mother tell you about pregnancy, labor, delivery at your birth? What kind of attitude expressed?

11. Mother and father live together as you grew up?
    Did you live with them? Others in household? Who?

12. Mother do principal raising? Father do any?

13. Mother hit you? Weapons? Beatings? Father hit you?

14. What other kinds of touching passed between you and
    your mother? Now?

15. Mother "sickly" when you were young, or healthy?
    Now?

16. Do you think your mother good-looking? Past, present.
    Mother think so?

17. Mother satisfied with life as you were growing up? Now?
    How do you know?

18. Prefer mother? Prefer father? At what ages?

19. Father's occupation(s)

20. Competition between mother and father for daughter?

21. Competition between mother and daughter, any sort, any
    time? Describe.

22. Father's role vis-à-vis mother/daughter relationship

23. Describe mother/father relationship as parents, as
    married pair; describe father/daughter relationship

24. Mother ever in therapy? You? Together?
    Related to, or prompted by, the mother/daughter
    relationship? Mother institutionalized? You?

25. Mother employed outside of home when you were
    growing up? What kind(s) of jobs(s)? Now? Purpose
    purely money? Mother's attitudes about her work?

26. Mother's activities/interests outside the home when you
    were growing up? Now?

27. Mother talk to daughter about:

Body, its functions and care?
Marriage/Motherhood?
Relationships with men?
How to "get along" in the world?

28. Mother "teach" you? Deliberately? Consciously?
    What did she teach? How?

29. Mother tell you what you wanted to know?

30. Have you considered your mother a "role model?"

31. How old were you when you left your mother's house?
    Circumstances? Emotional response of mother? Yours?

32. History of relationship since you left, or since autonomy
    —if it exists.

33. Current status of relationship—or at mother's death

34. Mother tell you the truth? Have you been truthful to her?

35. Has your mother's raising made you the woman you are
    now? To what extent?

36. Are you the woman your mother raised you to be? To
    what extent?

37. Are you like your mother? How?

38. Do you feel a tie or bond to your mother?
    Describe it.

39. Describe your mother as a woman, not as your mother,
    now or at her death.

40. How would your mother describe you as a woman, not
    her own daughter?

41. Do (did) you want to be a mother? Why? Why not?
    Had (have) you a preference for the sex of the child?
    Explain preference.

*42. Do you mother like your mother?

*43. Describe your mother's relations with your daughter.

*44. Describe your own relations with your own daughter.

*43. Describe your mother's relations with your daughter.

*44. Describe your own relations with your own daughter.

 45. Do you consider the mother/daughter relationship to be
     generally problematic, troubled?

 46. If so, what do you see as the possible causes for the
     problems and troubles?

*Denotes questions not asked of all daughters; only where applicable.

Notes

Chapter 1

1. Virginia Woolf, *A Writer's Diary*. New York: Harcourt Brace Jovanovich, 1954, p. 5.

2. Adrienne Rich, *Of Woman Born*. New York: Norton, 1976, p. 169.

3. Nor Hall, *Mothers and Daughters*. Minneapolis: Rusoff Books, 1976, p. 5.

4. Evelyn Reed, *Woman's Evolution*. New York: Pathfinder Press, 1975, Chapter 1.

5. Ibid., p. 13.

6. Rich, op. cit.

7. Ibid., p. 46.

8. Ibid., p. 53.

9. Ibid., p. 247.

10. Ibid., p. 243.

11. Ibid.

12. Phyllis Chesler, *Women and Madness*. New York: Doubleday, 1972; see also, *Sanity, Madness and the Family*, by R. D. Laing and A. Esterson. New York: Pelican Books, 1970.

13. For further description of this phenomenon, see Pauline Bart's "Depression in Middle-Aged Women," 1970.

14. Poster © Times Change Press, New York.

15. © 1976, Dana Bass; by permission of artist.

Chapter 2

1. Doris Lessing, *Martha Quest*. New York: New American Library, 1964, p. 227.

2. Ibid., p. 243.

3. Doris Lessing, *A Proper Marriage*. New York: New American Library, 1964, p. 25.

4. Ibid., p. 44.

5. Andrea Dworkin, *Woman Hating*. New York: Dutton, 1974, p. 35.

6. Ibid., p. 42.

7. Jo Freeman, "The BITCH Manifesto." In *Notes from the Second Year*. Chicago, 1967.

222

8. Barbara Deckard, *The Women's Movement.* New York: Harper and Row, 1975, Chapter 4.

9. See Anne M. Seiden's *Black Rage in White Women: Problems in Mother-Daughter Relationships in Contemporary America* (1973) for consideration of similar theory.

10. Judy Chicago, *Through the Flower.* New York: Anchor/ Doubleday, 1977, p. 139.

11. Lessing, *Martha Quest,* op. cit., p. 234.

12. See *Woman's Evolution* by Evelyn Reed, *Selene* by Z. Budapest, *The First Sex* by Elizabeth Gould Davis, others.

13. As published in *Womanspirit,* Winter Solstice 1976, Volume 3, #10, p. 21, by permission of the poet.

14. Read Virginia Woolf, *A Room of One's Own.* New York: Harcourt Brace and World, 1963; and Eleanor Flexner, *A Century of Struggle.* New York: Atheneum, 1974, especially chapters II and VIII for woman's struggle to educate herself.

15. Deckard, op. cit., Chapters 5 and 6.

16. Sherwood Anderson, *Winesburg, Ohio.* New York: Viking Press, 1968, p. 25.

17. Chicago, op. cit., p. 151.

Chapter 3

1. Montagu, op. cit., chapter note.

2. Tillie Olsen, *Tell Me A Riddle.* New York: Dell, 1961,p. 2.

3. Rich, op. cit., p. 224.

4. Ibid., p. 243.

5. Charlotte Perkins Gilman, *Autobiography.* New York: Harper Colophon, 1975, p. 23.

6. Suzanne Arms, *Immaculate Deception.* Boston: Houghton Mifflin, 1975, p. 61.

7. Ibid., entire text and napsac report, other studies.

8. Gilman, op. cit., p. 78.

9. For further discussion of this idea, see also Nancy Chodorow's *Reproduction of Mothering,* 1978.

10. Paula Weideger, *Menstruation and Menopause.* New York: Delta, 1977, p. 177.

11. Dworkin, op. cit., pp. 114–15.

12. Ibid.

13. Alta, *MOMMA.* New York: Times Change Press, 1974, p. 75.

14. Margaret Mead, *Sex and Temperament in Three Primitive Societies.* New York: Wm. Morrow, 1963.

15. Montagu, op. cit.

16. Rich, op. cit., p. 256.

17. Ibid., p. 276.

18. Alta, op. cit., p. 54.

19. Gilman, op. cit., p. 34.

Chapter 4

Chapter 5

1. Reed, op. cit., p. 341. For other references to primitive ignorance of paternity, see K. Gough, "The Origin of the Family," in *Toward an Anthropology of Women*, op. cit.; also, M. Harris, *The Rise of Anthropological Theory: A History of the Theories of Culture*, New York, Crowell, 1968, and M. Stone, *When God Was A Woman*, New York, Harcourt Brace Jovanovich, 1976, others (Hartland, Malinowski; others).

2. Reed, op. cit., pp. 343–45.

3. Dworkin, op. cit., p. 44–45.

4. Ibid., p. 45.

5. Quentin Bell, *Biography of Virginia Woolf*. New York: Harcourt Brace Jovanovich, 1972, p. 62.

6. Ibid., p. 64.

7. Virginia Woolf, *A Writer's Diary*.New York: Harcourt Brace Jovanovich, 1954, p. 135.

8. See Shulamith Firestone, *The Dialectic of Sex*. New York: Bantam Books, 1971; the chapter on love, #6.

9. Chodorow's *Reproduction of Mothering*, 1978, includes discussion of this idea.

10. See Bart, op. cit.

11. Herman and Hirschman study, "Father-Daughter Incest," in *Signs*, vol. 2, #4, p. 735, 1977.

12. See Florence Rush's article, "The Freudian Cover-Up: The Sexual Abuse of Children," *Chrysalis*, number 1, p. 31, for further insights into paternal sexual abuse and Freud's theories thereupon.

13. See Reed, Weideger, etc.

Chapter 6

1. See Chesler and Hall for elaborations on this theme.

2. Hall, op. cit., p. 21.

3. See Shulamith Firestone's *The Dialectic of Sex*, and John Holt's *Escape from Childhood*.

4. Carroll Smith-Rosenberg, "The Female World of Love and Ritual . . .," *Signs*, 1 (Autumn 1975), p. 15.

5. Hall, op. cit., p. 36.

6. Ibid., p. 24.

7. Lessing, *A Proper Marriage*, op. cit., pp. 342–43.

8. Ibid., p. 339.

9. Gilman, op. cit., pp. 162–164.

10. Jane Cannary Hickok, *calamity jane's letters to her daughter*. San Lorenzo: Shameless Hussy Press, 1976.

11. Judith Kegan Gardiner's "A Wake for Mother: The Maternal Death Bed in Women's Fiction," 1977, discusses the same phenomenon in literature.

12. *A Very Easy Death* and *My Mother's House and Sido*, respectively.

13. Lisa Alther, *Kin-Flicks*. New York: Signet, 1975, p. 431.

14. Gardiner, op. cit.

15. Maxine Hong Kingston, *The Woman Warrior*. New York: Vintage, 1977, p. 1.

16. Carl Jung (of all people), "Psychological Aspects of the Kore," in *Essay on a Science of Mythology*, Princeton University Press, 1969, as quoted in Hall's *Mothers and Daughters*, p. 34.

Chapter 7

1. Chodorow, op. cit. (original article).

2. See Bonnie Mass' *Population Target: The Political Economy of Population Control in Latin America*. Toronto: Canadian Women's Educational Press and the Latin American Working Group, 1977.

3. Read Marge Piercy's *Woman on the Edge of Time*. New York: Fawcett/Crest, 1976.

4. Olsen, op. cit., pp. 83–84, 87.

5. Rich, op. cit., p. 199.

6. Ibid., p. 240.

7. The metaphor is suggested by Carole Fisher, speaking about her work in March 1978 at Columbia College, in Chicago.

Bibliography

Alcott, Louisa May, *Little Women*. New York: Grosset & Dunlap, 1947. This book has been a standard for mother/daughter relations of the white, western middle class, and thus the generalized social standard in our society, through most decades of the last century. In it are all the stereotypes we may choose among as daughters, and, of course, the never-attainable sublime "Marmee." (It is always interesting to note that Alcott, like Austen, never did marry, or eschew her lifework, as her writings helped lead so many of the rest of us daughters to do.)

Alta, *MOMMA*. New York: Times Change Press, 1974. A book the author calls "a start on all the untold stories" about ourselves as mothers and daughters—mostly deals with her struggle as a mother of her two daughters and a writer—very close to my life and the life of this work.

Alther, Lisa, *Kinflicks*. New York: Signet, 1975. Novel which has at its core the mother/daughter relation, especially the death of the mother.

Andreski, Iris, ed., *Old Wives' Tales*. New York: Schocken, 1971. A collection of information about the lives of women in Nigeria, as they pass from their own culture into the white European model, examining the concepts of duty and responsibility between Ibibio mothers and daughters.

Angelou, Maya, *I Know Why the Caged Bird Sings*. New York: Random House, 1970. Autobiography of the author's youth; treats heavily the mother/daughter relation.

Arms, Suzanne, *Immaculate Deception*. Boston: Houghton Mifflin, 1975. An examination and expose of American obstetrical practice.

Arnow, Harriette, *The Dollmaker*. New York: Avon, 1971. A novel which treats its main character both as her mother's daughter and as the mother of both daughters and sons.

Austen, Jane, *Pride and Prejudice*. New York: Signet, 1961. Austen, never a mother, writes here of the five Bennett sisters, and their mother and father, a clear study of the mores and social roles created by and creating the mother/daughter relations of her time.

Bart, Pauline B., "Depression in Middle-Aged Women." 1970. Study of women who, in the process of aging, have been removed from

225

226

the only role position they were allowed to hold—wife/mother.

Bass, Ellen and Howe, Florence, eds., *No More Masks*. New York: Doubleday, 1973. An anthology of women's poetry, containing dozens of poems which treat the mother/daughter relation.

deBeauvoir, Simone, *A Very Easy Death*. New York: Warner Paperback Library, 1973. The author's account of her mother's death, their relations at that time, etc.

_____. *Memoirs of a Dutiful Daughter*. New York: Harper Colophon, 1958. The author recounts her youth—only valuable here for the relatively few descriptions of her interactions with her family when she was quite yoiung.

Bell, Quentin, *Virginia Woolf, a Biography*. New York: Harcourt Brace Jovanovich, Inc., 1972. A worthwhile and informative book, though Bell displays not enough respect for his aunt, especially when in conflict with his mother.

Bernikow, Louise, ed., *The World Split Open*. New York: Vintage, 1974. 400 years of English and American poetry by women; many poems treat the mother/daughter relation.

Boston Women's Health Collective, *Our Bodies, Ourselves*. New York: Simon & Schuster, 1976. I read this over, straight through, thinking of it only in terms of my book. I see it as an example of women taking up the responsibility to teach our daughters— those women younger than us—to teach them truly and well, and also a sign of our being able to accept teaching from our mothers— those women older than us—no longer to consider "old wives' tales" as falsehoods, but sources of real wisdom and specific information.

Broner, E. M., *Her Mothers*. New York: Berkeley Publishing Co., affiliate of G. P. Putnam's Sons, 1975. A novel, journal, poem, memoir, rather autobiographical; a wonderful book.

Bronte, Charlotte, *Jane Eyre*. New York: Signet, 1960. The classic novel by one of the motherless Bronte sisters, which shows us a motherless pauper girl who becomes a "mother" (governess) in the home of a wealthy landed gentleman who keeps his mad wife locked in the attic. Jane's relation to all the other women in the novel is that of daughter—except for her sexual rival.

Brown, Rita Mae, *Rubyfruit Jungle*. Plainfield, Vt.: Daughters, Inc. Both the beginning and end of this novel deal with the relationship between the major character and her mother—a fine description of their coming to terms with their past and with the violence of their differences.

Budapest, Z., *Selene, the Most Famous Bull-leaper on Earth*. Baltimore: Diana Press, 1976. Written for young girls, this story presents the culture of the Cretan matriarchy.

Bunch, Charlotte and Myron, Nancy, eds., *Class and Feminism*. Baltimore: Diana Press, 1974. Series of essays which discuss the differences women have thus far refused to deal with in our movement—very helpful to me in analyzing the class distinctions which probably account for much of the variety in my interviews. Also helps me to see and deal with my class bias, especially in terms of understanding the women in my book

Cade, Toni, ed., *The Black Woman*. New York: New American Library, 1970. Collection of essays, stories, poems, articles, etc., which treat the special position of black women in this society.

Chesler, Phyllis, *Women and Madness*. New York: Doubleday, 1972. Helpful in its form, suggestive to me of the ways to use interview research; also this book deals heavily with the contemporary state of woman's psyche, learned patterns of behavior, etc. Chesler also sees women as daughters of the Mother.

Chicago, Judy, *Through the Flower: My Life as a Woman Artist*. New York: Anchor/Doubleday, 1977. Autobiography and treatment of women artists and their work.

Chodorow, Nancy, "The Reproduction of Mothering." 1975. A discussion of how mothers teach their daughters to be mothers.

Colette, *My Mother's House and Sido*. New York: Farrar, Straus & Giroux, 1953. The author's recollections of her mother—one of the best resources for the positive love of a daughter who sees clearly what her mother's beauty and strength have been for both of them.

Davis, Elizabeth Gould, *The First Sex*. Baltimore: Penguin Books, Inc., 1973. Rather experimental anthropology, this book deals with the origin of woman's culture, especially the ancient matriarchy and the roles of our cultural mothers.

Deckard, Barbara, *The Women's Movement*. New York: Harper & Row, 1975. Comprehensive study of women's struggle in the U.S. in this century, especially the last 10–20 years.

Dworkin, Andrea, *Woman Hating*. New York: Dutton, 1974. Most valuable to me for its discussion of women's roles in fairy tales, and footbinding.

Esterson, A. L. and Laing, R. D., *Sanity, Madness and the Family*. New York: Pelican Books, 1970. Case studies of 11 "schizophrenics," all women, with their relations with almost all family members very clearly demonstrated through interview tape transcripts—incredible stuff.

228

Firestone, Shulamith, *The Dialectic of Sex*. New York: Bantam
Books, 1971. An examination of the politics of patriarchy; a radical
feminist analysis.

Freeman, Jo, "The Bitch Manifesto." In *Notes from the Second Year*,
Chicago. An essay that describes the ways women are made impo-
tent, made to give up their power.

Freeman, Mary E. Wilkins, *The Revolt of Mother and Other Stories*.
Old Westbury, New York: Feminist Press, 1975. A collection of
stories, almost all of which include a mother/daughter or sister
pair, and which explore relations among women who live and
work together.

Friday, Nancy, *My Mother, Myself*. New York: Delacorte Press,
1977. An analysis of the mother/daughter relation, heavily based
in contemporary Freudian-influenced psychology, mother-blam-
ing and misogynism.

Gardiner, Judith Kegan, "A Wake for Mother—The Maternal Deathbed Scene in Women's Fiction." 1977. An examination of five
novels in which the mother/daughter relation and the mother's
death figure prominently.

Gilman, Charlotte Perkins, *The Living of Charlotte Perkins Gilman*. New York: Harper/Colophon, 1975. Gilman's autobiography, run through with her feelings about her own mother, who
deliberately, it seems, withheld physical affection from her, and
her daughter, who lived with her only part-time, so she could pursue her work, and make a living wage.

Griffin, Susan, *dear sky*. San Lorenzo: Shameless Hussy Press,
1973. A collection of Griffin's poems, some of which are about her
relationships with her mother and grandmother.

———. *Let Them Be Said*. Oakland: Mama's Press, 1973. A collection of Griffin's poems, many of which are about her daughter,
and her relationship with her daughter.

———. *Voices*. Old Westbury: Feminist Press, 1975. The women
in this play could all be each other's mothers and daughters.

Hall, Nor, *Mothers and Daughters*. Minneapolis: Rusoff Books,
1976. An examination of the source of the mother/daughter split—
in the Eleusinian mysteries of pre-patriarchal Greece.

Hammer, Signe, *Mothers and Daughters/Daughters and Mothers*.
New York: Quadrangle, 1975. An examination of the contemporary mother/daughter relation.

Harding, M. Esther, *Woman's Mysteries*. New York: Harper Colophon, 1976. Harding, a Jungian, has researched the ancient magic
of the queens, goddesses and witches from whom all women are

descended—she describes all the forms of ritual and worship we've discovered of those mothers, and traces the psyche of woman back to that darkness wherein the light of wisdom and power was moonlight.

Hardy, Thomas, *Tess of the D'Urbervilles*. New York: Signet, 1964. A period piece, as they say, but valuable here for a picture of a mother/daughter relation in which the daughter's tragedy displays the duplicity of her mother's lessons.

Herman, Judith and Hirschman, Lisa, "Father-Daughter Incest," in *Signs*, vol. 2, #4, p. 73, 1977. A discussion of results of a study of fifteen victims of incest-rape.

Hickok, Jane Cannary, *Calamity Jane's Letter to her Daughter*. San Lorenzo: Shameless Hussy Press, 1976. A distillation of mother-to-daughter love, self-effacement, denial, and the frustration of making a woman to live in a world where simply *being* a woman is painful.

Holiday, Billie, with Dufty, William, *Lady Sings the Blues*. London: Sphere Books, Ltd., 1973. Autobiography of Billie Holiday, describes her relations with her mother at length.

Holt, John, *Escape from Childhood*. New York: Dutton, 1974. An examination of contemporary childhood, ageism and education in our culture.

Kahn, Kathy, ed., *Hillbilly Women*. New York: Avon, 1972. A collection of interviews with poor working class women in Appalachia.

Kingston, Maxine Hong, *The Woman Warrior*. New York: Vintage Books, 1977. Novel which treats extensively the relations between a Chinese-American girl and her mother in the U.S.

Lang, Andrew, ed., *The Blue Fairy Book*. New York: Dover Press, 1965. Contains many, many of the classic tales of most of our childhoods—from the Grimms to the "Arabian" Nights—therefore including most of the ugliness that has been taught us all about what mothers are and what daughters must be: Cinderella, Snow White, Sleeping Beauty are only the best known of legions of such daughters.

Lessing, Doris, *The Four-Gated City*. London: Panther, 1969.
———. *Martha Quest*. New York: New American Library, 1964.
———. *A Proper Marriage*. New York: New American Library, 1964. These three of Lessing's works all delineate, over many years, the exquisitely balanced, torturous relationship of a mother/daughter pair.
———. *The Golden Notebook*. New York: Ballantine Books, 1962.

Some valuable stuff about motherhood, but primary value here is in the description of a woman struggling to express her ideas in her writing.

————. *Memoirs of a Survivor*. New York: Knopf, 1975. Novel in which the two major charactes are a mature woman and an adolescent girl—not mother and daughter, but living in a mutually dependent relation which experiments with love and responsibility between them.

Mackenzie, Midge, ed., *Shoulder to Shoulder*. New York: Knopf, 1975. A study of the British suffragist movement, especially the women of the Pankhurst family, mother and daughters.

Mapes, Jo, *Glory*. © The composer, Chicago, 1976. A song from the composer to her daughters and "all of us daughters of women" about what we learn from and what we teach each other, as women.

Mathis, Sharon Bell, *Listen for the Fig Tree*. New York: Avon, 1975. Novel in which the mother/daughter relation is the core of the book.

Maury, Inez, *Mi Mamá, la Cartera*. Old Westbury: Feminist Press, 1975. Written for small girls, this bilingual book depicts a mother/daughter pair in a mutually supportive and loving non-traditional life.

McCarthy, Mary, *Memories of a Catholic Girlhood*. New York: Harcourt Brace Jovanovich, 1957. Not very relevant, but for the strong sense of family, the ethnic distinctions in the way social roles are played, and the last chapter, about the author's Jewish grandmother.

Meade, Margaret, *Sex and Temperament in Three Primitive Societies*. New York: Morrow, 1963. Useful here for the discussion of touching.

Milford, Nancy, *Zelda*. New York: Avon, 1971. Biography of Zelda Fitzgerald, whose mother cultivated her carefully, if not successfully, and whose daughter was kept from her in a classic example of father-mother competition over a daughter. Her husband had to lock her in a madhouse to win.

Millett, Kate, *Flying*. New York: Knopf, 1974. Autobiographical novel, two threads of which are important here—Millett's relationship with her mother, and her struggle with the contradictions in her feelings about her work, her politics, and her sexuality.

Montagu, Ashley, *Touching*. New York: Perennial Library, 1971. An extensive study of the role of human skin in our emotional lives and development, and the nature of tactile relationships.

Nicholson, Nigel, and Trautmann, Joanne, eds., *Virginia Woolf's*

Letters, Volumes I, II, and III. New York: Harcourt Brace Jovanovich, 1975–76. (See entry for Woolf, *A Writer's Diary.*)

Olsen, Tillie, *Tell Me a Riddle.* New York: Dell, 1961. Collection of stories; the first story and the last explore mother/daughter relations.

Paley, Grace, *Enormous Changes at the Last Minute.* New York: Laurel, 1974. Collection of short stories, several of which treat motherhood and/or the passing on of experience/information from woman to woman.

Piercy, Marge, *Woman on the Edge of Time.* New York: Knopf, 1976. Novel which includes discussions of the process of mothering, nurturing, raising of human beings, and proposes wonderful alternatives to the present system. Also this novel has as its core the relationship between two women who are not only of different generations, but different centuries, some few hundred years apart.

Plath, Sylvia, *The Bell Jar.* New York: Bantam, 1976. Autobiographical novel which describes part of the process by which mothers and daughters come to grief; the mother's role in socializing the daughter—her consistent sending out of contradictory and confusing messages about what her daughter should do/be.

Reed, Evelyn, *Woman's Evolution.* New York: Pathfinder Press, 1975. An analysis of woman's role in the creation of human culture, especially valuable for discussions of "primitive" people's definitions of mothers and daughters, social structures and roles. Also Reed's analysis of Greek mythology in terms of the conflict between the matriarchy and the growing patriarchy.

Reiter, Rayna, ed., *Toward an Anthropology of Women.* New York: Monthly Review Press, 1975. Collection of studies by women anthropologists, especially interesting for those which treat contemporary cultures in France and Spain, for mother/daughter relationships there.

Rich, Adrienne, *Of Woman Born.* New York: Norton, 1976. An analysis of motherhood "as institution and experience"; the entire work was of use to me, heaviest concentration in the chapters on the distinction between institution and experience, mothers and daughters, and maternal violence.

Rush, Florence, "The Freudian Cover-Up: The Sexual Abuse of Children," in *Chrysalis,* number 1, p. 31. Study of Freud's work on paternal sexual abuse of children, his fear, repression and ultimately malicious dishonesty.

Seiden, Anne, "Black Rage in White Women: Problems in Mother-

Daughter Relationships in Contemporary America." 1973, author's copy. Examination of the thesis that mothers are preparing their daughters for oppression.

Smedley, Agnes, *Daughter of Earth*. Old Westbury: Feminist Press, 1973. Autobiographical novel including another fine portrait of a mother/daughter pair—this one in which the daughter is able to see clearly the reasons for her mother's pain and oppression as a woman, and act on that knowledge to change her own, and her mother's life.

Smith-Rosenberg, Carroll, "The Female World of Love and Ritual . . .," as in *Signs*, 1 (Autumn, 1975). A study of relationships among women friends and relatives in the 19th century United States.

Stone, Merlin, *When God Was A Woman*. New York: Harcourt Brace Jovanovich, Inc., 1976. A study of the Queen of Heaven, She Who Bears Many Names, Mother and Goddess, Ruler of All Things, and Her defeat at the hands of monotheist patriarchs.

Walker, Alice, *In Love and Trouble—Stories of Black Women*. New York: Harcourt Brace Jovanovich, 1967. Collection of stories, many of which include mother/daughter relations, especially "Everyday Use."

Weideger, Paula, *Menstruation and Menopause*. New York: Delta, 1977. Study of the title subjects; *extremely* useful. Major flaw is in her anthropology. She doesn't go far enough beyond Freud.

Wittig, Monique, *Les Guerrilleres*. New York: Viking, 1969. A fantastical telling of the growing consciousness of all women, our refusal to remain oppressed, and our battle for a new world.

Woolf, Virginia, *A Room of One's Own*. New York: Harcourt Brace & World, 1957. Analysis of women as creators of art, women's history, growth and development as writers and some commentary upon mother/daughter relations and the chain of knowledge from woman to woman through time.

_____ . *A Writer's Diary*. New York: Harcourt Brace Jovanovich, 1954; ed. by Leonard Woolf. Extremely valuable in that I needed the support of other women who've tried to do what women aren't supposed to do. If she, a genius of depth, clarity and use of language, repeatedly became "mad" trying to express life in her art, why shouldn't I have problems?

_____ . *Mrs. Dalloway*. New York: Harcourt, Brace & World, 1953. Especially valuable is the relation between Mrs. Dalloway and her daughter, Elizabeth—and the rival for her daughter's affection, Miss Kilman.

_____ . *Three Guineas*. New York: Harcourt, Brace & World, 1966.

Analysis of woman's place, politically, especially in terms of education and advancement.

———— . *To the Lighthouse.* New York: Harcourt, Brace & World, 1955. Most important to me were Woolf's analysis of the mother's role in the family, her relation to male family members, especially the father, the "mother-daughter" relation between Mrs. Ramsay and Lily Briscoe, and the analysis of woman as creator of art.